BASS MADNESS

Bigmouths, Big Money, and Big Dreams at the Bassmaster Classic

KEN SCHULTZ

WILEY

John Wiley & Sons, Inc.

To Sandy, my best supporter

CONTENTS

ACKNOWLEDGMENTS

I am indebted, as always, to my family for their encouragement and support, especially while I have been preoccupied and distracted in the course of researching and writing this book. Special thanks to my wife, Sandy, for her patience and assistance, and especially for making time to record so many hours of Bassmaster Classic programs.

About two-thirds of the way through this project, I was diagnosed with bladder cancer and underwent two minor surgeries and treatment regimens that have resulted in a positive future outlook. I was fortunate to have enough work to do on this book that it kept me focused and able to put unanticipated medical issues to the back of my mind. That may have made it easier for me to ride over this bump in the road than for some of my family members. I am very grateful to Sandy, my mother Virginia, Kristen and David, Alyson, Megan, Virginia and Tim, Ted, Erica, Ruth, Jack and Barbara, Janet and Al, Joe and Jessica, Bill, and Alex, as well as many friends, for their concerns, encouragement, advice, and prayers.

I am also indebted to publisher Kitt Alan at John Wiley & Sons for her interest in continuing to work with me; to editor Stephen Power, who inherited me, conceived and championed this book, and provided valuable editorial advice; and to D. Barnes and Kimberly Monroe-Hill for excellent manuscript preparations. I am likewise indebted to my agent, Gail Ross, who not only facilitated this book but has been helpful with past projects and issues.

It is my fear that some people will be left out of these acknowledgments, so I apologize to anyone whom I may have inadvertently overlooked. In a sense, the conversations and interviews that I've had over decades with people in the sportfishing industry, both on and off the water, contributed to my thoughts and knowledge long before this book was a germ of an idea. So I am indebted to a lot of men and women in the sportfishing and publishing communities.

Many people working for various companies and agencies were helpful to me in the research for this book, and I appreciate their assistance. These include: George McNeilly, Christine Baumann, Jamie Wilkinson, Doug Grassian, Ken Solomon, Kim Jessup, and Cynthia Geary of BASS Communications; Gail Morchower and Glenda Kelley of the International Game Fish Association; Lynne Glover and Bob Imperata of the Greater Pittsburgh Convention and Visitors Bureau; Davitt Woodwell of the Pennsylvania Environmental Council; Chris Aguilar, Abigail Montpelier, and Tim Hemphill of the Kissimmee Convention and Visitors Bureau; Amy Voss of the Orlando Convention and Visitors Bureau; John Saboor of the Central Florida Sports Commission; Theresa Pelton of the Russellville Tourism and Visitors Center; Bob Spaulding of the Houghton Lake Chamber of Commerce; Jack Nichols and Ginger Henley of the Port Aransas Deep Sea Rodeo; Patricia Tinnin of the Port Aransas Chamber of Commerce; Betty Wells of the Texas International Fishing Tournament; and Denise Rubiaco of the Rio Vista Chamber of Commerce.

Many individuals spent time with me discussing various aspects of the Bassmaster Classic, professional bass fishing, marketing and sponsorships, and other topics related to those matters and to this book, or to assist me in finding or corroborating information. I am very grateful to the following for their time, assistance, and insights: Don Allphin, Lou Anderson, Mike Auten, Terry Baksay, Steve Bowman, Joe Brown, Geoff Carlisle, Brent Chapman, Larry Colombo, Mike Conner, Mark Davis, Don Ecker, D'Arcy Egan, Jill Frederickson, Rob Funk, Ricky Green, Glenn Guilbeau, Rick Hauser, Bruce Holt, Deb Johnson, Alton Jones, Michael Jones, Michelle Kilburn, Nick Karas, Stacey King, Gary Klein, Jay Kumar, Sammy Lee, Don Logan, Wayne Lykens, Tom Mackin, Mary Ann Martin, John Mazurkewicz, Alan McGuckin, Jerry McKinnis, Mark McQuown, Mark Menendez, Katie Mitchell, Ishama Monroe, Johnny Morris, Bobby Murray, Dick Nelson, Frank Oelrich, Yasutaka Ogasawara, Lance Peck, Ken Penrod, Steve Price, Ashley Rainer, Trey Reid, Milt Rosko, Steve Roth, Susan Roush, Don Rucks, David Sams, Rick Schair, Ray Scott, Terry Segraves, Cliff Shelby, Dave Smith, Steve Smith, Rob Southwick, Marty Stone, Jon Storm, Dean Summerville, Mark Taylor, Mick Thill, Angie Thompson, Jerry Vaillancourt, Larry Vandiver, Mike Walker, Steve Waters, Larry Whitley, Forrest Wood, and Jay Yelas.

INTRODUCTION

I attended seven Bassmaster Classics from 1976 through 1982 as an invited member of the media. I competed in a national BASS tournament in 1977 and in 1978, in a number of trout and salmon derbies that were held in the 1970s and 1980s on Lake Ontario, in an international bass fishing team tournament in Cuba in 1982, and in a few other informal events over the years.

Although I wrote more than five hundred articles for *Field & Stream* from 1973 through 2004 and for much of that time was the magazine's de facto bass fishing authority, only one article was devoted solely to a fishing tournament. Titled "So, You Want to Be a Bass Pro?" it chronicled my experience as a competitor in a professional bass fishing tournament in 1977 and described the nature of such an event from a participatory level. It was praised by BASS founder and then president, Ray Scott, as being the best article he'd ever seen on the topic, but he probably said that to a hundred other writers over the years.

As an unwritten rule, *Field & Stream* did not cover fishing tournaments. Always fighting the advertising department for space, the magazine's editors justified their position in part because editorial space was limited, there were too many tournaments to write about, the readers primarily wanted to know about how and where to catch fish, and, as one editor in chief expressed many times, "Fishing is not about numbers."

The latter point reflected the fact that the editorial staff in Manhattan and virtually all of the field editors, which then included some of the foremost authorities in the business, were of the philosophy that fishing (and hunting) was a contemplative, not a competitive, activity. I was generally of that opinion, too, although I recognized that fishing tournaments had proven to be a fertile ground for product development in the fishing tackle and boating product industries, as well as a concentrated source of information about techniques employed by highly skilled anglers. Even though professional bass fishing did not interest me as a career choice, I couldn't fault any angler for trying to use this venue to make a living doing something that he or she was passionate about.

The magazine's editors felt bolstered in their view of competitive fishing by the fact that they had received virtually no letters—over several decades—from their then two million monthly subscribers begging for articles about tournaments or professional fishermen. Tournaments, therefore, were a legal but distasteful component of the sportfishing world they could ignore.

Even on a personal level, I could not relate to competitive fishing because competition is not what drew me to sportfishing or fed my passion for catching fish. In my youth I had enough competitive sports experiences to understand and appreciate the value of team and individual sports. So, I "get" the competitive thing in athletic events. I get the personal and team-building lessons that sports can provide. And I get the competitive "spirit" in games, as any member of my family who has ever played a board game with me can attest.

But I never "got it" when it came to pursuing fish, either when I was new to fishing or after decades of fishing in North America and many foreign countries had made me different, by virtue of my experiences and knowledge, from the average avid angler.

And although I've been on many television shows about fishing, I seldom watch them. Watching other people catch fish on television does nothing for me as a fan of sportfishing. Going fishing and catching fish, or being with friends or family who catch fish, interests me a lot more.

But I'm not the average TV viewer, either. I don't watch television reality shows, game shows, celebrity gossip shows, or mindless sitcoms. I have never watched more than an accidental few seconds of a wrestling match, and I don't watch cars speeding around a track for hours.

Although I haven't been to any bass fishing tournament in more than two decades, I know that they have become more popular and more theatrical. They were headed that way in 1982. The "big show" mentality gained steam throughout the 1980s and 1990s as promoters were determined to make a spectator sport out of a participatory activity. Bass fishing as theatrical entertainment may sound good for a one-time Hollywood movie, but it never appealed to me as a steady diet.

So I stayed away.

Much has changed, however, while I was ignoring the specialized world of bass fishing tournaments and not watching them on television, as thousands of other anglers were. And even though I've fished over the years with some of the older bass pros, who for the most part have been very pleasant and enjoyable people, my contact with the current crop of pros in recent years has shown me how much more of a business the game is for these players and how different their approach is today. Much more is at stake, at least for them, than it ever was.

There seems to be a different edge to the world of professional bass fishing, especially since ESPN has become a big player. I wonder whether the television coverage of professional bass fishing—the "sport," as most of the people involved with this activity call it—is overwhelming the two things that originally brought all of this attention in the first place, the bass and the fishing. Has it gotten like the Super Bowl, where the commercials are more of an event than the game on the field is? Has it gotten like professional basketball, which is more about putting on a show than it is about pure hoops? Is it more about catching viewers than catching bass?

In addition, my sense is that increased television coverage of bass fishing tournaments has made instant recognizable stars out of bass fishing pros and developed a subculture of professional bass fishing fans. I've noticed that a few personalities—because they are shouting and cutting up, perhaps—have gotten the attention of generalist media that previously never had the word *fishing* in their lexicon.

I'm puzzled by the bass fishing fan thing, too. I am not puzzled by the passion that anglers have for their sport; I've seen that and written to that for decades. But fans of people who drive fast boats and catch relatively few, and not especially large, fish?

I consider myself a fan of various sports, but only on a generic level, and without deep emotional attachment to the ups and downs of any team or individual. Yes, I am a fan of the New York Yankees, having grown up in the Bronx, played lots of baseball, and attended games at Yankee Stadium every year as a kid. Even when they lose in the playoffs or the World Series, I still sleep fine. If I were in a restaurant and someone said that Derek Jeter was on the street two stores down, I would not get up and go look for him. If I miss a big game, it's not the end of the world. I don't bet on sporting events, and I don't collect autographs, although I was given one by Mickey Mantle and one by Ted Williams. So the idea of people filling arenas to cheer for someone who may or may not plunk a bunch of bass on a scale baffles me. Ditto for race car drivers.

I'm sure there are sports psychologists who can address the needs of people to identify with others through successful sports personalities. And perhaps this phenomenon, although it doesn't resonate with me, properly reflects elements of the world we live in today. I believe that sports reflect the character of society. Often lately—witness steroids in professional baseball and doping in the Olympics—the reflection has not been complimentary. Is this the same now in the world of bass fishing?

Perhaps as I observe the next two Citgo Bassmaster Classics and, tangentially, professional bass fishing and its fans, it will become apparent what draws people to takeoffs and weigh-ins and sitting in front of screens.

Thanks to changes within the hierarchy of the company that owns the Citgo Bassmaster Classic, ESPN, and its marketing plans for the future, the 2005 and 2006 events have been scheduled to be just seven months apart instead of the usual twelve months. The 2005 Classic will be in Pittsburgh, only the second time in thirty-six years that it has been in or close to the Northeast, in midsummer, which is often a difficult period for catching bass. The 2006 event will be in central Florida, only the second time it has been in the Sunshine State, in February, the first time that the Classic has ever been held in the winter. Two vastly different venues.

I'm going to observe both. But to get a feel for where the sport of professional bass fishing is today, I think it is a good idea to first visit the epicenter of bass fishing in the United States. In 1967, the first professional bass fishing tournament was held in Arkansas, so it seems fitting to attend a current event in that state that will have ramifications for the next two Classics.

ONE

Putting On a Show

Anytime you come to one of these big tournaments like the
Classic or the E-50s, you have a lot of credibility with the fans,
and that's what it's really all about, the fans.

—TWENTY-FIVE-TIME BASSMASTER
CLASSIC QUALIFIER ROLAND MARTIN

Saturday, May 21, 2005

5:12 P.M.

A small crowd has gathered along the shoreline near the launching
ramp at Lake Dardanelle State Park in Russellville, Arkansas. Mostly
men in their thirties and forties, some with preteen children in tow,
they are facing the water to watch bass pro Mike Iaconelli. This sometimes hyperexpressive thirty-two-year-old is fishing generally perpen-
dicular to the bank, moving his fire-red Berkley logo–decorated bass
boat to his right in a northerly direction toward the near-empty fishing pier.

It is the final day of the BASS Lake Dardanelle Elite 50 bass tournament, the second of four such events that will lead to qualifying ten
anglers to participate in the 2005 and 2006 Citgo Bassmaster Classics.
Six pros out of a starting field of fifty have made the final Dardanelle
cut. Iaconelli was in last place when the day began seven hours earlier
at this very spot, after the anglers mingled with well-wishers, stood at
attention for a live rendition of the National Anthem, and blasted
away in their boats beneath the helicopter carrying ESPN cameramen.

Now, there's a cameraman on shore and another in a boat a few feet behind Iaconelli, plus four boatloads of fans behind them in the cove, creeping along and watching, not a fishing rod in sight. Dozens of observers leapfrog along the bank to keep pace with the pro as he fishes, being careful to sidestep goose droppings in the grass.

Watching where you walk may not be as much of a problem in the future. The well-endowed Arkansas Department of Parks and Tourism, which gets $25 million a year from its share of a one-eighth of 1 percent state sales tax, is planning a major construction project right where these fans are walking. It includes building a boat dock near the launching ramp and its adjacent, nationally renowned $600,000 tournament weigh-in pavilion, which will be used by fifty-two bass tournaments this year, and constructing a boardwalk along the entire shore to connect the pavilion to the fishing pier. Plans also include the use of an Elmo visual presentation machine, an overhead projector on a cart that can be rolled down the boardwalk to show events and instruction live to children in classrooms.

Bassheads on the water and along the pier watch Mike Iaconelli fish in the closing minutes of the 2005 BASS Elite 50 tournament on Lake Dardanelle in Arkansas. An ESPN cameraman in the far right boat records every moment.

Davy Hite, the winner of the Lake Dardanelle tournament and a past
Bassmaster Classic champion, signs autographs prior to fishing on the
last day of the 2005 Dardanelle event.

"This tournament was won right here last year," says Angie
Thompson, a producer for JM Associates, which produces BASS tournaments for ESPN. She's referring to the Elite 50 event that was held
in April 2004 on this lake. "Randy Howell was fishing along the rock
wall. It's a great spot. Randy's wife and son were here and watched
him win it. It was neat."

The bulk of the fans move toward the pier, which Iaconelli has now
reached, and I head there, too. Essentially an extended wood dock
erected by the Arkansas Game & Fish Commission, the pier's floor-
boards and railings are about to get a gross body weight stress test.

Several dozen onlookers and a pair of TV cameramen quickly line the
pier. They are remarkably quiet and respectful, much like fans around
the green at professional golf tournaments, even to the point of

whispering. Most are intently watching Iaconelli, who appears not to have noticed the unusual grouping. Surely he has, but his demeanor doesn't show it, and so far he hasn't acknowledged the crowd.

To many anglers, this public scrutiny would be unsettling; to others, it could be invigorating. This is the first time that I have ever seen Iaconelli. His black-and-red flame-emblazoned shirt, which screams for attention, seems to indicate that he is probably invigorated.

Maybe the effect on one's state of mind depends on whether there's a good weight of bass in the livewell. If there *is* a good weight, then practically rubbing elbows with the fans while competing could be fun. If there isn't, and with the end of the day just an hour away, the pressure to show the crowd something could be mentally torturous.

5:23 P.M.

Iaconelli's boat is barely forty feet from the pier. His assigned camera boat stays behind and slightly ahead of him, shooting both the angler and the growing crowd on the pier. I move to the end of the pier where a young couple and their daughter are stationed. They carry two folding chairs in sacks to set up later on the lawn in front of the weigh-in stage. The father, in his early thirties, wears a white T-shirt that says Citgo and bears an image collage of the petroleum company's sponsored pros. The woman, thirtyish, wears a green sleeveless top devoid of names or logos, but her daughter, who looks about eight or nine and has a white bow in the back of her hair, wears a white T-shirt with the words *Triton*, *Mercury*, and *Citgo* on the back. It also sports the black-ink signatures of numerous bass pros.

Iaconelli, or Ike, as a statement on the back of his walking-billboard shirt reads, is headed toward the end of the pier. The front right panel of said shirt indicates that he is sponsored by, among others, Dick's Sporting Goods, for whom he was once a store employee in his home state of New Jersey. There is some irony in this, as the nearest Dick's is 254 miles away in Frisco, Texas, while Wal-Mart, which is the leading sponsor of the *other* major bass tournament series, the FLW Tour, has Supercenter stores in Russellville and Dardanelle. And, of course, the headquarters of this retail giant, which probably sells the lion's share of all fishing gear purchased in the United States each year and which opened its first store in Rogers, Arkansas, in 1962, is just 140 road miles to the northwest.

Using spinning tackle, Iaconelli pitches a small worm to the edge of the pier beneath my feet. This is right about the same time that Afleet Alex is rounding the final turn at Pimlico Racetrack in Baltimore. The thoroughbred stumbles on the heels of the swerving front-runner Snappy T, then catches its step and whips the rest of the 2005 Preakness field, including the Kentucky Derby winner Giacomo, before a disbelieving crowd of 115,380 people. Later news accounts use the words *dramatic, amazing, miraculous,* and *courageous* to describe the athletic recovery of the $650,000 prize-winning horse and jockey in what instantly became one of thoroughbred racing's most memorable big-race moments.

But none of the race fans at Pimlico, a private track owned by Magna Entertainment Company, are physically on top of the scene like the bass fishing fans are here at Lake Dardanelle State Park, a state-owned facility on a publicly accessible U.S. Army Corps of Engineers lake. Nearly all of these people are from Arkansas, which has an active racing interest and whose main annual event, the Arkansas Derby, was won earlier in the season by Afleet Alex, yet no one here seems to have a radio tuned to the race.

I look around to observe the people on the pier when Iaconelli hooks a fish.

"He's got one," says someone excitedly.

The crowd murmurs.

Iaconelli's spinning rod is bowed, and he points it quickly from one side to the other. Then he makes a nimble side-to-side shuffle with his feet as if he were jumping over a snake. Actually, he's unsure which way to steer this bass—away from the propeller of the bow-mounted electric motor or away from the propeller of the transom-mounted outboard motor. He sprints to the back deck.

"Giant! Giant!" he shouts, alerting the camera crew. As if they weren't already poised on his every move.

The crowd buzz has intensified, and some people near the shore hustle toward the outer end of the pier for a closer look.

The fish moves to Iaconelli's right, and he races to the bow deck. The camera boat has drifted closer to him.

"Camera boat!" Iaconelli yells. "Camera boat!"

The camera boat operator, sitting in the bow seat with his foot on the electric motor, swings away. Moments later, with rail watchers and ESPN's pier cameramen focusing on Iaconelli, he falls down on the front deck on his right hip, leans over the boat with the rod extended in his left hand behind him, and scoops the fish up in his right hand. The crowd cheers with approval, then gives him an ovation.

As if he was Phil Mickelson and had just made a difficult clutch putt.

As if he was Terrell Owens and had just hauled in a pass in the end zone.

Iaconelli stands up and shows the fish to the crowd, the first time that he's acknowledged their presence. Or maybe it's for the TV cameras on the pier.

Then he turns toward the camera boat and lifts the greenish-black bass high, shaking it. His back arches slightly. "Yeaaaaaaah!" he screams, pumping his fist.

The crowd laughs. "Going Ike" is what fellow pros call this now-trademark yell.

"Way to go!" someone shouts.

A likely 3-pounder, it's no giant and, as it turns out, not even the largest bass caught by the finalists today. But it's enough for Iaconelli to reach into his livewell and pull out a fish that looks about 2 pounds. He's working fast now. Checking the fish. Balancing them on a culling scale. Unceremoniously dumping the smaller one into the water like it was a rock. Changing tags that identify the fish in the well. Getting ready to make another cast.

The pier is abuzz over the catch and the catcher's antics, as well as with the realization that Iaconelli has a limit of five fish, the smallest of which must be at least 2 pounds. Until this moment, the crowd hasn't known how well he's done for the day, but now it's clear. He has at least 12 pounds of bass, probably close to 15, and could—if leader Davy Hite runs out of steam on the backstretch—be in a position to win the $100,000 first-place prize.

Hands-free, Iaconelli stands up on the bow deck, and, with about sixty sets of eyeballs on him, loads of handheld digital cameras being focused, and three TV cameras rolling, he realizes that the show is not quite complete. He quickly squats and does a once-around break-dancing leg sweep—another trademark. The crowd laughs. Some people applaud. They'll see it again later on the Jumbotron and the following Saturday on *BassCenter*, but this is live in-their-faces enter-tainment. Which is virtually unheard of in fishing, a sport not known for being spectator-friendly.

Fans get to watch the bass pros on television and hear them at seminars, but almost never are they able to stand on shore forty feet from one while he works his magic *and* while he's playing for all of the chips on the table—with three ESPN cameras ready to show it to almost a hundred million households, a number touted later by an irrationally exuberant weigh-in emcee who neglects to mention that this is 99.6 million more than the number of people who will actually be watching.

It's not the first time that love-him-or-hate-him Iaconelli has screamed or break-danced, but usually that happens somewhere out on the lake beyond the gazing eyes of fans, where he's mainly per-forming for one camera and a chance to get more of that oh-so-valuable face and name time on the highlight reel.

Knowingly or not, these fans have just witnessed the future of professional bass fishing.

That future is spelled t-h-e-a-t-e-r. As in bass fishing entertain-ment, where players, action, drama, spectators, and cameras converge.

The folks on the pier and on the shore at Dardanelle have the equivalent of a sideline pass in football, seats behind the dugout at a baseball game, a spot along the rope at the eighteenth hole green. And, best of all, they'll be in the highlight video. "Honey, look! That's me on the pier, by the post, next to the guy with the Yamaha hat."

Later at the weigh-in, in front of a crowd of several thousand peo-ple, Iaconelli will say that he wishes there were more places like this, more spots where crowds can gather to watch the action up close and personal.

Jerry McKinnis, a longtime television fishing celebrity and the head of the company producing the ESPN telecast of this event—which will air a week later—hurriedly walks down the pier and motions to the cameraman in the boat behind Iaconelli.

"You getting this?" he asks, making a circular motion with his hand toward the crowd.

The cameraman nods. I'm thinking, *Bet your ass he's getting this. You'd have to be deaf, dumb, and blind to miss the magic here.*

Angie Thompson is now on the pier, too. She and McKinnis might have been watching a live camera feed in the mobile production truck. Or just heard the crowd erupt, like at a golf tournament when someone at a nearby hole has made a great shot or putt.

McKinnis walks past us. "This is great," he says, smiling broadly. "This is a story all by itself."

I know what else he's thinking—the same thing that Iaconelli says later on stage. *Wish we could do this at every tournament.*

5:35 P.M.

Iaconelli catches another apparent 2-pound bass, much like the one he culled, and chucks it back without measuring it against others in his livewell. One of his competitors, Gary Klein, in a red-and-black Mercury-decorated boat, has come into the area and is fishing the other side of the pier, his own TV camera boat in tow. At 5:40, Iaconelli lands another 2-pounder and tosses it back, which tells Klein that his opponent has a decent limit. Each time the crowd applauds.

A forty-something fellow comes over next to me and points toward Klein. "Who's that?" he asks. Then he asks who else is in the final field. I tick off the names.

"What about Mark Davis?"

"Nope."

"Awwh," he says. "He's my hero." Then he looks over at Iaconelli. "He must have some good 'uns if he's throwin' fish like that back. That's two he's tossed back better'n two pounds."

Sitting a hundred yards in front of the pier is a boat with two fellows propping up a six-by-six banner that reads "Never Give Up," a reference to words that Iaconelli shouted to the camera when he caught his final bass, a 3-plus-pounder, to win the 2003 Citgo Bassmaster Classic and $200,000 by 1 pound 12 ounces over Klein. It's a bass fan's attempt to make the highlight reel, à la the football or baseball stadium.

The fans on the pier are just a sampling of the several thousand who will soon gather to watch the weigh-in spectacle, but most of them are fans for sure. Almost all of them are wearing shorts or jeans and T-shirts that somehow express an affinity for fishing—it's the uniform of the rabid fishing enthusiast. Probably 80 percent of them have baseball-style caps on. The rest, like the few women in the crowd, have no cap at all.

Near me is a fellow whose T-shirt front says "Cabela's." The back of another's reads "Alltel Bass Fishing Classic." Another one says "Citgo Fishing." And another wears a T-shirt with a red, white, and blue bass on the front, the stars being placed on the head and the gill plate of the bass. Many of the shirts are stretched over what might politely be called love handles, and some stretch over what can only be called potbellies, contrasting with each of the trim and fit-looking bass pros here.

Aaron Martens, in the orange-and-blue Citgo sponsor boat and with camera boat following, has moved into the cove about sixty yards south of Iaconelli, and at 5:48 lands a smallish bass. Even though he's a good distance away, the crowd notices and applauds, which causes Iaconelli to briefly glance around. Martens puts the fish in his livewell without hesitation.

"He mustn't be doin' too good," surmises someone behind me, the inference being that since he did not cull, he must not have a limit, or he just got his limit-making fish, a none-too-big-one at that.

Another competitor, Dustin Wilks, in the red-and-green Bass Pro Shops sponsor boat, moves into the area with his camera boat following and fishes on the north side of the pier, away from the structure in open water. No spectators go to that side of the pier to watch. They're all on Iaconelli's side.

That makes four of the six competitors fishing within a hundred yards of one another in the waning moments. And four camera boats, each with a TV cameraman aboard, plus two more TV cameras on the pier.

At 5:50, Iaconelli catches another 2-pound bass, quickly unhooks it, and throws it back into the water, not bothering to lean over and give it a more gentle release. No time for niceties. While he straightens out the worm on his hook, he looks up at the crowd and yells, "Where's my caddy?"

The crowd laughs.

Iaconelli is referencing the similarity to a professional golf tournament, but I'm taking it literally, wondering what would a fishing caddy do? Hand him another rod? Check the line for nicks? Straighten the worm out? Put the fish back into the water with a little more care and respect?

"What a comedian," says an amused guy next to me, who is wearing a hat with autographs across the bill and the crown and a T-shirt that has the words "Nothing's perfect" arcing over the caricature of a leaping bass and the words "but fishing is as close as it gets" underneath it.

Behind me, a fellow asks the TV cameraman if he can say hello to his family, as if this were live. As if he were on the bench at a football game saying, "Hi, Mom," at the camera and wagging his index finger. The cameraman says this is being taped; that it would probably never get on the final program. The fellow shrugs. "Well," he says, "I'll just tell 'em to watch."

Then someone's cell phone rings musically, and I notice that many people on the pier are talking on their phones. A kid about ten feet away says to someone, "I'm standin' here . . . watching Iaconelli . . . Ike-un-elle. . . . Yeah, he caught a five-pounder."

5:59 P.M.

Aaron Martens creeps over toward the inside back of the pier, but Iaconelli, bow pointed toward shore, sees him out of the corner of his eye or out of eyes in the back of his head and, still casting intently into the pier, moves down and cuts off Martens's path. He picks up a bait-casting outfit tied to a jig. As Martens turns and heads back toward the middle of the cove, Iaconelli turns and heads back toward the head of the pier, much like a spawning bass protecting its bedroom now that the invader has been rebuffed.

Klein has left for the breakwall on the other side of the cove, and Wilks is out of sight, neither of them having caught a fish here.

Iaconelli looks over his shoulder to see where Martens is and gets in position to cast to the head of the pier, controlling his motor and boat in such an effortless manner that it acts like an extension of his body. Unlike the shirts of most of the other competitors, his heavily patched and logoed shirt is not white or beige but red and black, with a midriff flame pattern, and he's wearing black high-top sneakers, which brought laughs from some people in the previous night's weigh-in crowd when they saw it on the Jumbotron.

There is what could be a smirk on his face, but it's probably just a quirky intense look that has evolved after peering so hard into the water for most of the last 459 minutes. Or, maybe it's his I'm-really-busting-my-ass-and-concentrating look for the cameras. It is, after all, showtime.

6:06 P.M.

The pier crowd is thinning. Gary Klein returns and again fishes the opposite side of the pier from Iaconelli, who slowly marches up and down the same sixty-foot area. After freeing his line from a snag, Iaconelli checks it for fraying and tosses his worm back out, landing it by a post under a young kid who's wearing a Citgo Bassmaster Tournament Trail T-shirt and a hat loaded with the signatures of professional anglers.

Klein has moved so close to the other side of the pier that anyone could jump onto the back deck of his boat. He kneels down so as to pitch under the pier. A tall, bald, burly man leans on the rail looking down at Klein, and when his son calls to him from the other side of the pier, the man turns his head and raises his right forefinger to his pursed lips. Behind him on shore, a whining generator powers McKinnis's mobile studio and video production truck, and in the parking lot, a Russellville fire truck sits with fully extended ladder flying a large American flag over the park's visitor center.

The center, which received more than two hundred thousand people in 2004, contains several aquariums holding a total of eight thousand gallons of water and many of the ninety-five fish species that exist in Dardanelle. Only one of these, the largemouth bass, is of interest to the people assembled outside and on the fishing pier. In fact, there are several 8-pound-or-better bass swimming in the visitor center's main circular aquarium, which is ironic because, oh, how such bass would be coveted right now by Iaconelli, Klein, Martens, and Wilks.

More people are now watching the equally intense and focused Klein, but at 6:18 he backs away and makes a few casts away from the pier out in the open. Iaconelli does likewise, moving away from his side of the structure. A Bass Pro Shops' Sun Tracker pontoon boat with eight passengers pulls into the cove, weaving through assorted spectator and camera boats toward the shore. It will likely deposit its passengers for the weigh-in festivities an hour hence.

At 6:20, the competitors abruptly stop casting. They pull up to their respective camera boats and take off remote microphones, then idle toward the launching ramp where new, bright, matching-colored, sponsor-emblazoned trucks are lined up ahead of boat trailers in the water.

The pier crowd disperses, joining the nearby throng of several thousand that is packed in front of the weigh-in stage and the Jumbo-tron, where loudspeakers have just finished blaring Elton John's "Crocodile Rock," jumping right into the driving New Wave beat of Wang Chung's "Everybody Have Fun Tonight."

Shortly, Davy Hite will be crowned the victor, pocketing $100,000, which pushes him over the $1 million mark in career BASS earnings. Iaconelli finishes second, Martens third. Although there will be two more qualifying tournaments before the July Bassmaster Classic in Pittsburgh, these anglers have helped to secure their position in that event, which promises to be vastly different with respect to the nature of the tournament and the fishery, the amount of fans, and especially the attention of the media.

Despite being in the heartland of bass fishing and being a precursor of how major bass tournaments may be staged in the future, Dardanelle has been a tune-up for the really big show.

TWO

Urban Fishing

Many go fishing all their lives without knowing
that it is not fish they are after.
—HENRY DAVID THOREAU

Tuesday, July 26, 2005

The drive to Pittsburgh from my home in New York lasts more than six hours and takes me through the mountains, past the farms, and along the river valleys in western PA that give rise to the rivulets that beget the creeks that beget the streams that beget the Allegheny and Monongahela rivers and thus the great Ohio River.

I drive past the exits for such good bass fishing spots as Lake Wallenpaupack, the Susquehanna River, and Raystown Lake to go to the Allegheny, Monongahela, and Ohio rivers near Pittsburgh for the so-called Super Bowl of professional bass fishing, the most prominent fishing tournament in the United States . . . North America . . . the Western Hemisphere . . . the world?

Pittsburgh. A bastion of great bass fishing?

Not in any list of hotspots I've seen.

Pittsburgh is an industrial city. A few months earlier, I'd paid particular attention to a report on National Public Radio about how Pittsburgh's sewage woes echo a national problem that the Environmental

Protection Agency (EPA) has been unable to get the city to fix, and which would cost Pittsburgh $3 billion to rectify.

According to correspondent Elizabeth Shogren's April 15 report on *All Things Considered*, Pittsburgh has overburdened sewage plants and crumbling pipes, and its excess sewage is dumped straight into the water. Among the comments made in that report were: "Only one-quarter-inch of rain can overwhelm pipes and trigger a sewage spill. . . . There are hundreds of overflow pipes around Pittsburgh. When overflowing, the health department posts orange flags to warn people. Last summer, orange flags flew nearly every day of the season. . . . Warning flags will continue to fly at favorite fishing spots."

This, and the description of one of the rowing clubs wiping down its crud-caked shells after each outing, did not put a pleasant image in my mind.

Coming into Pittsburgh on Route 28 takes me along portions of the Allegheny River, and I'd like to get there before there's a storm. The weather forecast for late afternoon and early evening is heavy winds, severe rain, possibly hail, and a heat index climbing over 100.

Close to Pittsburgh I can spy only portions of the Allegheny, such is the placement of railroad tracks, industrial buildings, plants, factories, and bridges. Tall downtown buildings stand out in the distance, and I'm having a hard time reconciling this as the site of the most prestigious fishing tournament in the world. Couple that with the fact that the prospects for catching bass, based on pre-event reports, are very poor, and I conclude that the only reason that this competition is being held in Pittsburgh is because Pittsburgh paid more money than anyone else to ESPN, the Worldwide Leader in Sports and the owner of the Citgo Bassmaster Classic, to have it here. But why?

Once checked into the Marriott, across from the Mellon Arena where the Classic weigh-in will be staged, I head down to Point State Park where the ceremonial daily fishing takeoffs will occur and where I'm sure ESPN will be setting up. On Commonwealth Place by the park, a quarter fetches all of 7.5 minutes of parking. The car thermometer is registering 96. I'm guessing the river temperature is in the 80s. I'm still not getting a fishy feeling.

However, there is a welcome banner hanging from the light pole over my car that reads, "1 city. 3 rivers. 47 anglers. Plenty of unsuspecting bass." Nearby, another says, "It's time to separate the hawgs from the dinks."

The thirty-six-acre park is at the juncture of the Allegheny and Monongahela rivers, which forms the Ohio River. Across the Allegheny from here is Carnegie Science Center; Heinz Field, the stadium in which the Steelers play; and PNC Park, the home of the Pirates, who are not in town this week. Across the Monongahela are Duquesne Incline, a historic incline car that climbs to a terrific view atop Mount Washington, and Station Square, a popular dining, entertainment, shopping, and sightseeing attraction. Downstream, the mighty Ohio flows toward Neville Island and eventually winds northwesterly to Ohio. Everywhere you look, there are bridges.

At the tip of the Point is a ten-thousand-gallon pool fed by an underground flow; computer controlled, it spews a geyser that is said to reach 150 feet high and spray six thousand gallons of water per minute. A shirtless man in shorts is sunbathing, faceup, on the wide rim of the pool, and across from him, nearest to the end of the Point, a woman and two children are dangling their legs in the water. On the west rim of the pool, a blond woman in a bikini is lying on her stomach, listening to headphones and surveying the scene; from where I'm

Pittsburgh and Point State Park are bounded on the left by the Allegheny River and on the right by the Monongahela River, which merge to form the Ohio River at this very spot.

standing, she seems almost directly beneath the huge red HEINZ sign across the river on the football stadium. A sign at the Point says that there is no swimming and no wading or fishing in the pool.

This looks like a terrific place to hold an event, a place that will be very camera-friendly in the low light of morning. Noticeably, despite the heat and humidity, there is no smog, no smokey industrial visage, and no stench along the waterfront.

The foundations of a stage are being laid in front of the fountain. A crew from Knoxville, Tennessee, is doing the work. One of them tells me that they erect sets all the time on contract for ESPN; they'll be erecting this stage again next week in Indianapolis.

It's still in the low 90s at 5 P.M. when I board a Gateway Clipper riverboat near the convention center. There's a crowd of people on the boat, and they include many representatives of BASS (the former acronym and current name of Bass Anglers Sportsman Society), some representatives of ESPN, most if not all of the BASS State Federation presidents and their wives, local political and corporate dignitaries, many people from the event's sponsoring companies, and even the president of ABC Sports, George Bodenheimer. A pop band with a singer is entertaining the crowd.

There are also many of the Classic's forty-seven competitors and spouses or friends here. The tournament does not start until Friday, but the anglers' only day of current practice (they had a practice period a month earlier) is tomorrow. Shouldn't they be resting, drinking carrot juice, poring over maps in their hotel rooms, and communing with the fishing gods instead of munching cocktail franks and drinking beer?

A lot of the people seem to know one another. A group of eleven are all wearing the same T-shirts. In some corners there is so much laughing and hugging that I'm wondering whether the Citgo Bassmaster Classic is like an annual party for most of them. It's kind of how I remember the media, some pros, and some sponsors behaving at the Classic in the early 1980s. Very partylike. Except that there are hardly any members of the media on this boat.

The riverboat from the Clipper fleet cruises around the Point, and the blonde is still sunbathing at the pool. Around the corner is a small barge with a bright-white tarpaulinlike top that says "Cabela's" in gold lettering. This is a clever—and probably cheap—bit of in-your-face guerrilla marketing by this giant retail and mail-order marketer of outdoor goods, particularly since one of the big-bucks sponsors of the Classic is its competitor Bass Pro Shops, and a smaller retail competitor, Dick's Sporting Goods, is headquartered here in Pittsburgh.

The riverboat heads up the Monongahela, locally called the Mon. Many visitors are having trouble pronouncing the name of this river, which is said to have meant "river of falling banks" in the Delaware Indian language. When I observe the shoreline, it's obvious that there are few places to get close to the river from the land and a paucity of public access points. Most surprisingly, on what will likely be one of the hottest days of the summer in Pittsburgh, there are very few people boating on the river. A couple of near-shore kayakers, three personal watercraft users, and a ski boat.

Up on the top deck I meet Jim Motznik, a city councilman representing a district with forty thousand people. He does not fish and confesses that he had no idea what the Citgo Bassmaster Classic was when it was first broached, but he's very happy with what's happening and expresses sentiments that will be echoed many times in later days.

"We're projecting a positive image," he says. "Showing that we've cleaned up the rivers. And creating economic development for the future, generating interest around the country."

He walks off to pump some hands. I'm beginning to see a theme. It's not about the fishing.

The riverboat pulls into the dock at Sandcastle Waterpark, a complex of water slides and wave pools built in 1989 on the site of a steel mill railroad yard, and the first modern-day use of abandoned steel mill property for recreation. Perhaps not coincidentally, Sandcastle is owned by Kennywood Entertainment, which also owns America's oldest theme park, Lake Compounce, located in Bristol, Connecticut, where ESPN is headquartered.

Everyone disembarks cheerfully, although trouble is brewing downriver where the sky is getting progressively blacker. About the time that everyone has made it through the buffet line at the Sandbar Restaurant, there's a brisk wind and rumbling in the sky. Heavy clouds are moving toward us.

Out on the river, a ski boat races up and heads into the Sandcastle dock. Several twentyish people quickly disembark and head up to the main courtyard. None too soon, in fact, as torrential rain pours out of the sky for nearly twenty minutes. It should be more than enough to put orange flags on the overflow pipes.

Dale Bowman, the outdoor editor of the *Chicago Sun Times*, and I have sought refuge under the back canopy of the courtyard bar. In the middle of the rain, the driver of the ski boat comes to the bar with one of his friends. Both are in bathing suits, and neither has a shirt on. They are each treated to a free drink and food, as they have essentially crashed a closed party, and they seem bemused by their good fortune.

After getting a drink at the bar, the boat driver turns toward a fellow in front of me and asks what's going on. A party for people who are here for the Citgo Bassmaster Classic, he's told.

What's that?

A professional bass fishing tournament.

He looks surprised, his eyebrows lifting a bit, and in a priceless few words sums up what turns out to be a fairly uniform sentiment for Pittsburghers who do not fish, know little about what's under the surface of their rivers, and have it ingrained in their heads that this is still a smoky steel town.

"There's fish *here*?"

Wednesday, July 27, 2005

If you're talking sports or athletic contests and the words *organizing committee* come up, you naturally think of the Olympics—not a fishing tournament.

Ironically, the Citgo Bassmaster Classic isn't necessarily held where there's a good venue for bass fishing. The organizers hold it at a locality that pays for them to come. And places that pay are usually places that need to boost tourism.

Many Classics have taken place at locations with unimpressive bass fishing, largely because some locality paid BASS (and now ESPN) the most money to host it. Thus, BASS puts out a Request for Proposals and reviews the bids submitted by assorted groups and agencies, most of which have formed a consortium, or organizing committee, to shepherd the project. For many years, if you met BASS's asking price, you got the Classic.

The subject of how, and more important, why, the unlikely city of Pittsburgh is the host for the 2005 Classic brings me to a meeting with Davitt Woodwell, who was watching a Pittsburgh Steelers football game on television one night when a seminal moment occurred.

"The network showed a blimp shot of the Pittsburgh area," he says. "Using a telestrator, John Madden drew a circle around the Point and said, 'The Allegheny goes this way and the Monongahela goes this way, and the Ohio goes this way.' All away from each other! Like there was this big artesian well in the middle pushing the Mon south, the Allegheny north, and the Ohio west! It was totally ridiculous. I turned to my wife and said, 'We've got to do something.' Probably at that point, all Pittsburghers who were watching looked at that and said, 'If John Madden said that, it must be true.'

"We've even had people who have asked, 'Is this fresh or salt water?' 'Is this tidal water?' We were cut off from these rivers for so long, there were no views of the rivers. They were all lined with trees, and we were cut off by the railroads. The mills were all along there, and then they started going away and suddenly these rivers appear. It's been a long time getting back.

"People swim here in the marathon now. We've now got kayak rentals over by PNC Park. There's a lot of kayakers here. The Head of the Ohio Regatta in the fall is the largest one-day competitive rowing regatta in the country. There's been a phenomenal transformation."

An attorney for the Pennsylvania Environmental Council (PEC), a statewide nonprofit group whose mission is environmental advocacy and education, Woodwell is an avid fisherman who loves to catch bass on a fly rod from a kayak, as well as fish for steelhead on Lake Erie. He usually fishes once a year in Florida, as well as at a family cabin in Ontario. A resident of Pittsburgh, the forty-four-year-old Woodwell was a member of the organizing committee that was instrumental in winning the Classic bid for 2005 and coordinating the event.

In the fall of 2001, he went to the Classic in New Orleans in his capacity as a director of the River Life Task Force, a nonprofit organization established by Pittsburgh mayor Tom Murphy to "make Pittsburgh's urban waterfront one of the most spectacular in the world."

The task force devised a plan to get people to reconnect with the environmentally revitalized three rivers in Pittsburgh.

"Growing up in Pittsburgh," Woodwell says, "you were always told two things: be home before dark, and don't go near the rivers. We're trying to change that perception."

Impressed with the New Orleans event, he invited then BASS Tournament director Dewey Kendrick to Pittsburgh the following year and started pitching the idea of hosting the Citgo Bassmaster Classic in Pittsburgh.

"A lot of people around here didn't get it. There were questions about whether there were fish in the rivers. But what we were doing it for was not a fishing tournament, but to have an opportunity to change the image of the city both regionally and nationally, because of the coverage it was getting, because it was growing so big, and because ESPN was buying [BASS and the Classic]. The aspect that it was family oriented, which I think some people are questioning now, also played into it."

Woodwell and others pulled together an organizing committee that included businesses, philanthropies, a job creation agency, the Convention & Visitors Bureau, and politicians, largely because of the opportunity to convince people that Pittsburgh is no longer a smoky industrial city.

"When you come through that tunnel from the airport," he says, "and see the view, you get blown away. Local leaders know this is not a steel town anymore, but a lot of people questioned if we had fish in the rivers, and they probably still do, but what we were doing it for was not the fishing."

The committee justified raising and spending more than $1 million to bring the Classic to Pittsburgh on three themes: economic development, televised image setting, and a means of getting local people to reconnect with their rivers. On the latter point, Woodwell is especially passionate.

"One of the reasons I'm interested in this, as is the PEC, is to get local people to understand that the rivers are ecosystems, that they have a life, that they have come a helluva long way in the last thirty or forty years, and to get them proud of the rivers, to take some responsibility. So when you try to do water quality issues and try to do conservation projects, people will see there's a reason for that. They'll remember that the Classic was here, remember what that did, and what this means. [The Classic] is another step in getting people interested in the rivers.

"ESPN is doing twelve or thirteen hours of programming. If someone catches only a tidbit of it and sees a shot of one of these guys fishing in front of Pittsburgh, that's a mind-altering image for much of the world. If you've got the skyline behind them as they're waiting to weigh-in, and they're doing their last cast somewhere around the Point, the value of that is also economic development—driving people who never would have said, 'I want to do a convention in Pittsburgh,' or, 'I want to do a vacation in Pittsburgh.' That's priceless.

"If these guys find fish and catch fish, it really doesn't matter."

I'm feeling a little relieved that Pittsburghers may come out winners on this deal even if the fishing stinks, which seems likely if only because the Northeast is in the midst of a heat wave. Hot weather is seldom beneficial for daytime bass fishing. And Pittsburgh's rivers almost certainly don't have a large population of big bass, meaning that daily weights may be unimpressively low even if anglers catch lots of fish. Part of me thinks that a tough tournament is a good thing. Why shouldn't the bass pros have to deal with super-tough fishing just like the rank-and-file do?

I'm wondering what local anglers have to say about the fishing, and I'm wondering just what it looks like down on the rivers, so it's time to get a view from the water.

Driving north and parallel to the Allegheny, I retrace my entrance into Pittsburgh on Route 28 for a short distance, using a local map as a guide. The greater Pittsburgh area is topographically one of hills and hollows, ridges and valleys, and precipitous slopes. From many of the local roads, you cannot see the river, and it takes some poking around to find places where you can even get close.

Driving north, I find that the Pennsylvania Fish and Boat Commission (PFBC) has a public access area with a boat launch at Hamarville. It's called Deer Creek Hamarville Access Area, and as I cross the train tracks and pull in, I wonder where the creek is. The ramp is concrete and wide. Downriver, private boat docks are lined up one after the next, with johnboats, speed boats, cruisers, and pontoon boats tied to all of them. There's at least fifty boats as far as I can see.

There's plenty more boats docked upriver, as well as a marked rock bar that runs halfway across the Allegheny, a substantial navigation hazard. The banks are thickly lined to the water's edge with trees, and few houses are close to the water. The lock is out of site upriver around the bend, so I drive up there and find Lock 3 Bait & Tackle on the west side of the road.

Timmy Lager is behind the shop's counter and he's not busy, so after I look around and eyeball the fishing tackle inventory, especially the lures, we talk about the fishing. He doesn't seem too impressed that the Citgo Bassmaster Classic is in town but says that many pros were here during their official practice period a month earlier. He looks through his copies of nonresident licenses issued. Evidently, he doesn't sell a lot of those because he doesn't have to dig deep to find some names: Wirth, Jooste, Scroggins, Clark, Biffle, Baumgardner, Reynolds, Rowland. . . .

Tube jigs and spinnerbaits are good lures here, says Lager. Yesterday in the Allegheny someone caught five bass that weighed a total of 9 pounds. There's plenty of walleyes, and four muskies were caught last week. But it's been very slow.

On the wall is a mounted smallmouth of about 4 pounds, and there's some photos on the wall of recent prize catches, including a 7-pound walleye caught at Lock 3 on June 18, an 11¾-pound walleye caught at the Highland Park Dam on May 29, a 17-pound muskie caught on May 28, and a 3-pound sauger. No bragging bass, though.

I was jotting some notes about the photos when a treasure trove of information walked in.

Lou Anderson is seventy-four, an ex-Marine, retired, and not the least bit bashful. He fishes more in the Allegheny than anyone around, at least three or four mornings a week.

"You're almost always guaranteed to catch eight to ten bass in that time," says Anderson. "Four or five will be legal. Rapalas and spinners are the best lures, but I do well on a popper first thing in the morning."

Then he's off and running, "There's a spot by the railroad bridge with big bass that have sores 'cause they've been hooked so many times. . . . The Mon is full of sauger. . . . There's lots of carp and muskies and channel cats in the upper Allegheny. . . . My biggest smallmouth here is five and a half pounds. . . . Once a week I catch a two and a half- to three-pounder. . . . Two years ago there were big crappies on the docks; last two years, none. . . . There's lots of stuff on the bottom here; one year I lost a thousand jigs."

So, how's the fishing now?

"Worst year I've ever seen. . . . The water's real warm. . . . The guy who owns the bait and tackle shop had a tournament recently with a hundred forty boats in it, and they didn't catch a keeper. . . . I've only caught three largemouth bass all year so far."

Anderson tells me that I should go down to Neville Island and speak to Wayne at Island Firearms. He thinks that the pros should be able to catch enough keepers to produce some limits, and that the winning weight will be in the mid-20-pound class. Somehow the conversation shifts from the pros and the tournament to BASS and its founder, Ray Scott. I did not ask Anderson whether he is, or was, a member of BASS, but out of nowhere he offers a cutting secondhand comment.

"My son-in-law is in the finance field and he says that Scott has pulled some real shrewdies. He saw him in New Orleans. That Ray Scott, he's pulled some shit."

I let this digression go without asking how he or his son-in-law might know anything about what Scott may or may not have "pulled," or without asking exactly what shit he might be referring to, but the comment is amusing because I know there's truth to it with respect to the start of professional bass tournaments, Scott's efforts to hold a Classic outside of the country, and an embarrassing episode in which he imported bass out of Florida for his private lake in Alabama.

A little later Anderson leads me across the road, over the railroad tracks, and behind an old plant to a steep bank where, through the trees, we can see the dam. The lock is on the opposite side of the river, along the east bank, and there are buoys spaced at intervals across the river about fifty feet in front of the dam. The buoys are meant to keep boaters from passing them and also to keep people from fishing between them and the dam. There is a backward pull to the water directly behind the dam, and a boat that gets too close might get pulled in and under and be pinned. Being too close to such dams can be dangerous.

Anderson then has me follow his car to Lock 2 downriver. We cross the Highland Park Bridge and head down the road that I was just on earlier, turn by an asphalt plant and Brilliant Marina, then drive down along the railroad tracks until we're stopped by a locked gate. There's barely enough room to turn around here, but then we walk a couple hundred yards to the lock. The Lock 2 dam looks like the Lock 3 dam, except that the no-passage buoys are farther downriver.

"There's good fishing beyond the buoys," says Anderson. "Guys go in there when they think they can get away with it."

We're facing the west bank, and Anderson points to someplace between the thick trees on the other shore. "See the wall below the dam over there? Look down a short ways and there's a dark spot. That's an outflow pipe. Sometimes there's real good fishing there."

I notice that this spot is well above the buoys, too, in the restricted zone.

Jeepers, I'm thinking, *some of the best bass fishing is right below the dams where it's dangerous and you're not allowed to go, and where pipes bring discharge in from sewer plants and road runoff and who-knows-what-else.* That is not exactly the image that Davitt Woodwell wants ESPN to beam across the continent.

Thursday, July 28, 2005

Neville Island, four miles downriver from the Point on the Ohio River, is no stranger to pollution woes and environmental troubles. About four miles long, Neville is residential on the south end, with barrackslike row housing, and is heavily industrialized on the potholed-north, which is populated by tired old buildings belonging to Frontier Steel, Swedish Steel, Neville Chemical Company, and Express Containers. There's a recycling plant here with thousands of crushed cars in it, a water treatment plant, a large Sunoco chemical plant, and a district office and operations center for the U.S. Army Corps of Engineers.

There's also the Shenango coke works (made from coal, coke is a fuel used in steel making). Five days earlier, the *Pittsburgh Post-Gazette* reported that Shenango had been fined for "gross violations of air pollution standards" by Allegheny County and noted that the company had "a 25-year history of air-pollution control violations." It has been fined more than $2 million since the late 1990s.

About midway on Neville is a regional sports center that was formerly known as "poison park," or the Ohio River Superfund Cleanup Site. On its Web site devoted to Superfund areas in Mid-Atlantic states, the Environmental Protection Agency said that the site was purchased in 2003 by Robert Morris University, which built athletic fields there for its students in 2004 and 2005.

In discussing threats and contaminants at that location, the EPA said, "Currently, the potential exposure for people visiting the site has been limited to ingesting contaminated fish. To avoid it, there are warning signs along the Ohio River and the Back Channel warning against fishing along the banks of Neville Island. Beneath the caps, on-site groundwater is contaminated with benzene, 2,4.6-trichlorophenol and manganese. Soil is contaminated with benzo(a)pyrene, dibenz(a,h)anthracene, and beryllium. Surface water is contaminated with gamma-chlordane, manganese, and mercury. Potential health threats exist from ingesting contaminated groundwater, soil, and contaminated fish, and from inhalation of benzene during showering."

Just north of the sports center, three-quarters of a mile from I-79 and a hundred feet from a 7-Eleven, is a residential building fronted by a "Live Bait" sign. Near the entrance is a coin-operated live bait vending machine in between Coke and Pepsi dispensers. Inside is Island Firearms, a small dimly lit shop packed with fishing and hunting gear that is on the path of northbound anglers and sells a lot of bait and fishing licenses.

At the counter is owner Wayne Lykens. Only three or four bass pros, one from California, were here previously to get fishing licenses, he says. I ask about the bass fishing.

"I've never seen it this bad," Lykens says bluntly. "Three or four years ago you could catch fish constantly, even in the summer. But this year's been terrible.

"Ever since Hurricane Ivan came through and flooded out everything instantly, the whole river system's changed. Places that used to be really hot, there's now nothing there. Catching the really big bass, like we used to in the spring, we didn't have that this year. Even the spring was bad this year. We have had some tremendous fishing here. If they had brought this tournament here three years ago, they would have been catching fish after fish. But I've been here for twenty-two years, and this is the worst summer for fishing I've ever seen. We had a better year after the Ashland oil spill than we had this year."

(On January 2, 1988, an oil storage tank belonging to Ashland Oil had collapsed, spewing 3.9 million gallons of diesel fuel. A 1998 report in the *Pittsburgh Post-Gazette* said that the spill caused "an oily, 4-inch-thick blanket across 23 miles of the Monongahela River and a similar black cover over 40 miles of the Ohio River," and further stated that "The disaster, one of the largest inland oil spills in U.S. history, caused boaters and fishermen to stay away from the Monongahela for years.")

"Most people here go out for a few hours," says Lykens. "There have been times out here when you could catch a fish for almost every piece of bait you had. This is what's nice about the river. People can catch fifteen different species in one spot without moving. We have forty-three species of fish in this river."

"Do your customers eat fish out of these rivers?" I ask.

"I've been eatin' 'em for thirty years," he says. "Walleyes, crappies, and bluegills mainly. The average person won't eat catfish or carp, though. Bottom feeders they don't eat. A lot of my customers are catch-and-release anglers, and they don't keep anything.

"We have certain fishermen who can go out right now, right at this moment, and go up there and catch twenty to thirty fish in the next two, three hours. They know where to go, they know how to use their lures, and they catch the fish. The only problem is, none of these bass people can go to 'em because of their boats."

"Really?"

"Yep. It's within the restricted areas of the dams."

"So the local guys are fishing places that are off limits?"

"Pretty much. It's not that they shouldn't go in there, but when the water's this hot, there's very little oxygen, so all the fish are where the oxygen is. Which is the dams that are churning the water. And that's where they're catching the fish, right in the white water. That's why it's so difficult for these pros to catch fish in this temperature of water. The fish are just not there, or, if they are, they're very lethargic."

"So what do you expect out of this tournament?"

"I think the Mon is where all of the action's gonna come from. It's muddy, it's warmer, and the upper Mon has always been a good bass area. Right now, the Ohio and the Allegheny are just bad for fishing."

"And what kind of weight do you think will win?"

"Between eight and eleven pounds."

"You're kidding. For three days?"

"No, no," he says, laughing. "I'm thinking eight to eleven per day. Unless they get into some really big fish up the Mon. But this time of year, it's really hard to find big fish."

I thank Lykens and head out, thinking that if someone catches 8 pounds a day for three days straight, that will be terrific for Pittsburgh in the middle of the summer in a lousy fishing year. But that would still not be very good in the big scheme of things in the world of bass fishing. Still, I'm impressed that there are lots of local anglers who fish these tough waters. What's wrong with having a tough event for small fish where the contest is a nail-biter? Lots of teeny bass may not look impressive on TV, but this is reality fishing, urban style.

BASS has scheduled a few hours at the Marriott where anglers can be buttonholed by the media. It takes place in the Steelhead Lounge, a location name with twofold irony.

The organizing committee wants to show that Pittsburgh is no longer a dirty, polluted steel town and hopes to disassociate Pittsburgh from the negatives attached to its steel mill roots. Yet from the name of its football team to the U.S. Steel Tower a block away, to the old mills up the nearby rivers, to the production plants down at Neville Island, the connections are profound and lasting. So, in reality, Pittsburghers are steelheads like Wisconsinites are cheeseheads.

And yet, technically, a "steelhead" is a rainbow trout that migrates to sea as a juvenile and returns to fresh water as an adult to spawn. The steelhead is one of the most highly rated sportfish in North America; it grows much larger, on average, than a bass, jumps higher, fights harder, likes cleaner and colder water, and tastes way better.

The chariots of the bass pros are lined up with their tow vehicles in the parking lot of the Mellon Arena, ready for the contest to begin.

There is no Steelheadmaster Classic, and there are no steelhead in Pittsburgh's three rivers. Probably the only steelhead in the Pittsburgh area are on the menus of better restaurants or on ice at the fish counter at Wholey's Market.

Thus, Steelhead Lounge is filled with bassheads this afternoon, as well as with bass pros. All of the latter and some of the former are sporting sponsorwear, the bright logo-crammed shirts, ball caps, and visors that in the case of the pros, they must wear while being photographed, videotaped, and interviewed.

At the podium is George McNeilly, the senior director of Corporate and Consumer Communications for BASS, who is about to announce the results of a John Deere advertising promotion: ESPN's Greatest Angler Debate. This title seems to infer that it takes in anglers from the entire sphere of sportfishing, including all manner of techniques used in all types of waters for all species of freshwater and saltwater fish, and that it was voted upon by people from all segments of the angling world. In reality, the Greatest Angler Debate only includes people who have participated in professional bass fishing tournaments, the majority of which have been owned and run by Bass Anglers Sportsman Society, now BASS-ESPN, and the voting was done by just bassheads.

ESPN has milked this hyperbolic promotion with half-hour programming, commercials, and Web site attention for months. The "debate" is down to television personality and longtime successful pro Roland Martin, who has never won the Bassmaster Classic and did not qualify for it this year, and four-time Classic winner Rick Clunn, who is competing in Pittsburgh and who is known for his studious and near-mystic holistic approach.

"Welcome to fishing's greatest week," says McNeilly, who notes that 70,000 fans have voted in the Debate. Does that mean that there were 70,000 unique bassheads who voted? Or that 70,000 votes were cast by 10,000 people, as in a Third World election?

Clunn wins. His comments are brief and gracious. His remark "I have never been able to perceive our fans' perception of us" seems to imply that he doesn't grasp what makes bassheads so excited about people like him whose job it is to catch bass. Which is notable because he is arguably the most thoughtful member of the bass pro fraternity.

And then Clunn hits upon the hero thing. "We athletes," he says, "get confused with heroes. Heroes are people who save lives."

Amen. But at the very least, athletes are considered *surrogate heroes*, a term confused with role models, especially by youths and overly exuberant media. The fans, especially the kids who watch the athletes, are the ones who decide this.

Clunn is finishing. "For thirty-two years I have followed my dream. . . . I'm just a person who loves to fish, and that's all I ever wanted to do."

Perhaps without realizing it, Clunn has answered the perception question. And also my own mystification about why there are fans of professional bass anglers and professional bass fishing.

The fans love to fish, too. That's a given. Many of them wish like hell that they were in Clunn's shoes, decked out in sponsorwear, making a living by going fishing and catching more bass than the next guy. That's their dream. They identify with Clunn. Their dream was once his dream.

THREE

At the Office

It's hard to even comprehend that one 3-pound bass
will make you $200,000 today and a million dollars
over the course of a year or two.

—1999 BASSMASTER CLASSIC WINNER DAVY HITE

Friday, July 29, 2005

The Citgo Bassmaster Classic begins at 7 A.M. at Point State Park. At six, I leave the hotel and take a taxi to the entrance of the park, then walk toward the fountain and the seawall.

Along the way, a United States Coast Guard representative is handing out a pamphlet and urging people to refer to the contact info in it in case they observe something amiss during the event. One of the fellows walking with me says, "Like a bunch of guys driving too fast?"

"I don't mean that," says the Coast Guard rep. "But if you see anyone shooting at 'em, let us know."

Shooting?

On the last day of the 2003 Classic in New Orleans, Gary Klein, one of the anglers in this event, was driving at high speed down a bayou past a duck camp when a man on a dock in front of the camp pointed a shotgun at him and fired. "I locked eyes with him and kept going," said Klein, who had an ESPN cameraman in the boat with him, but the camera was on the floor while the man was changing the tape. When Klein came back out of the bayou later, he stopped ten feet from the same dock; the cameraman ran tape of the shooter, his camp, and his dog; and Klein filed a police report. The police found a 20-gauge shotgun in the camp loaded with slugs. The man claimed he was shooting at a duck, and the local district attorney dropped the charges.

In the spring of 2004, Stacey King, also one of the anglers at this Classic, was in a BASS tournament on the Alabama River, accompanied by BASS staff photographer Gerald Crawford, when a man fired seven to nine shots at his boat with a .22 caliber rifle. At least one of the shots put a nickel-size hole in King's boat. The man, who was arrested, later claimed that he was shooting at a snake, and the case was dismissed.

Here in Pittsburgh during the earlier practice period, one of the pros was hassled by a marina owner for fishing in the immediate vicinity of his marina. That caused a small stir, requiring local authorities to remind marina owners that the water around their facilities was public and suggesting that they be more hospitable when the Classic was underway.

A crowd has gathered along the seawall, where a low chain-link fence holds people a few feet from the edge and the competitors' boats, which are lined two deep and bow-to-motor against the wall. Large speakers on the promenade behind the Allegheny-facing steps broadcast country music, which is toned down when Keith Alan, the exuberant long-sideburned emcee I observed at the Dardanelle weigh-in, hollers, "This is the World Championship of Professional Bass Fishing," as he walks up and down the seawall, cordless microphone in hand.

He's talking to Zell Rowland when I get to the wall. Rowland is saying in a calm, measured drawl, "I'm in my office now. It's like a day of work today."

The wall and the Allegheny River are a beehive of activity. Several dozen boats, some with large-lettered sponsor wrapping, are clustered nearby, their operators standing and using bow-mounted electric motors to keep in place.

A blue-and-white boat sports a large-lettered sign, stretching from poles that rest in the bow and the stern pedestal seat bases, that reads, "Good Luck Yamaha Anglers." The boat slowly weaves through the flotilla, easily visible by all onshore. A little farther off the end of the Point are four Pennsylvania Fish & Boat Commission patrol boats, each occupied by three or four armed, uniformed officers.

The sun is rising upriver, cresting over Fort Duquesne Bridge and painting a warm pastel on the boats, the downriver shoreline, and the crowd, which numbers, by my estimation, between four and five hundred people.

Half of them are standing several deep along the fence. Some are pressing forward for autographs, and there's at least a dozen television cameras working the wall, the bystanders, and the pros. Some cameramen are with reporters from local news outlets, but many are roving and associated with one of ESPN's various productions.

Distracted, I nearly bump into a cameraman whose lens is directed at Mark Zona, cohost of ESPN's *Loudmouth Bass* program, which will broadcast live here. Zona has his left arm around the

A crowd lines the Allegheny seawall at Point State Park for the beginning of the 2005 Citgo Bassmaster Classic. The competitor's boats are against the wall, while the spectator and camera boats are away from the wall.

shoulder of a big, smiling, goateed fellow wearing a Ranger Boats shirt, who is talking into the mike.

Nearby, a cameraman with a gray T-shirt that says "ESPN" on the front is sticking the lens of his video camera in front of a wide-smiling, happy-looking Ishama Monroe. A sound man stands behind the camera operator, holding a fur-covered boom mike overhead. From behind, it looks like the cameraman's doing a close-up facial exam, since his camera lens seems to obscure Monroe's face, but from the side, it's clear that the front of the lens is twelve inches away from his nose. Monroe, the only black competitor in the Classic and perhaps one of a handful of blacks in the entire park this morning, is eagerly talking into the lens.

Down the wall a short distance, two television cameras are focused on one competitor. I can't see who it is because one cameraman is standing between the two consoles shooting down, another is in the passenger seat shooting across, and there's a sound tech in between the two of them.

I wonder about this, thinking that such attention must make a guy feel pretty important, and then I look at the next boat in line. George Cochran, a two-time winner of the Classic, is sitting alone behind his steering wheel. He's wearing sunglasses, even though the sun is behind him, and his stone-faced straight-ahead expression suggests that he might be asleep or at least bored.

Next to Cochran, sitting behind the steering wheel of his boat, is Jay Yelas, who won the Classic in 2002. I've previously fished with Yelas, who is astute and engaging. But he, too, has sunglasses on, and the look on his face is not a happy one. Maybe he's focusing on his game plan. Maybe he's worried about how bad the fishing is going to be. Maybe he's looking at the circus around the wall this morning and thinking, *Let's get this over with and go fishing.*

Neither Yelas nor Cochran seem to be of interest to the emcee or the cameras.

Walking along, I pass four college-age girls, dressed identically in blue shorts, white-and-blue sneakers, and white-and-blue sweatshirts that say Yamaha. These are the Yamettes, cheerleaders who have worked events for Yamaha since the 2003 Citgo Bassmaster Classic. They flank angler Bradley Stringer, himself wearing white shorts with the word "Yamaha" stenciled on one leg and a sponsor-studded jersey that prominently says "Yamaha Outboards." Someone is taking their picture, and everyone is in a good mood. Stringer, his arms around two of the girls, looks like he's okay with this perk.

A little farther along, I run into Deb Johnson of BASS, who is coordinating media boat activities. She has assigned me to a boat on Sunday, and she explains that during competition days, boats are made available for accredited media members to go out on the water for a few hours and shoot photos or video of competitors.

"Who are the people who accompany the anglers on competition days?"

"The observers are either media or Federation volunteers," she says. "If no media members want to go, there are volunteers ready, willing, able, and eager to do it."

Sixteen media observers are going out today, she says. Less tomorrow.

"If you want to be an observer, we can arrange that."

I decline.

Then a tall, dark-haired man wearing a black-white-yellow Pittsburgh Pirates shirt that says "Clemente" on the back comes by and stands next to us for a second, looking like he wants to talk.

"I just stopped to say hello because I knew you looked familiar," he says.

"Ken Schultz," I say, shaking his hand.

"Yeah, I know. I've read a lot of your books. I'm Ed Matuizek."

"Where are you from?"

"Right here. Springdale."

He mentions that he fishes a lot on the St. Lawrence and Niagara rivers, perhaps knowing that I've often been to those places myself, as they've been mentioned in some of my books. We talk a bit about bass fishing on the St. Lawrence, the Niagara, and Lake Erie.

"Well, I just wanted to say hello," he says. "It was very nice meeting you."

"You, too. Thanks." I raise my eyebrows at Johnson.

"Well," she says, "a fan."

.   .   .

Johnson walks off. Two fiftyish men and a blond ponytailed woman, all wearing identical yellow baseball caps and yellow, black, and white jerseys, walk by. The woman's hat is covered with autographs. The backs of their jerseys say "PA Southwest Bassmen." I'm thinking that there must be some analogy to be made between basshead wear and the garb worn by tribal people throughout the ages, when the emcee's voice comes over the speakers.

Alan starts the 7 A.M. launch with a tribute to U.S. soldiers around the world, and a woman from Pittsburgh sings the National Anthem while the crowd places hands and hats over their hearts. A guy in one of the media boats is holding a large American flag on a pole.

"Let's light this candle!" shouts Alan. There is a collective rumble as dozens of outboard motors turn on. One by one, each boat moves along the wall as its driver is hailed and briefly but enthusiastically profiled by Alan.

"Go get 'em, Davy," someone screams from behind me.

"Go get 'em, Tim," shouts another.

Most of the boats head up the Mon; a few head up the Allegheny or down the Ohio, all idling until they get past the no-wake zone between the bridges, the PFBC officers watching closely. A local angler standing next to me mentions that there was a petition to the PFBC to let the Classic boats run on plane through the idle zones, but it was denied.

"How often do you usually see one of these patrol boats here?" I ask him.

"Hardly ever."

Soon, the bass boats are gone, the speakers are silent, Alan has left, and the crowd is dispersing. The fountain, which someone told me was under water during last September's floods, is spewing with force and height and looks pretty in the early light.

Standing near the end of the Point, watching and evidently wondering about the whole spectacle, is the only person I've noticed who is wearing a dress shirt, neatly pressed dress pants, and business shoes.

He's Mark McDonel, an accountant whose office is just a few blocks away. He's not a fisherman, just curious.

"It's pretty exciting to have this event come to Pittsburgh." he says. We talk for a bit, and I explain my purpose here.

"What's the universe of anglers to get here?" he asks. "This may show how naive I am, but why is it a *bass* fishing tournament? When I go to a restaurant, I never see bass on the menu."

I explain that you don't find wild bass on a restaurant menu because they're classified by state agencies as gamefish and may not legally be sold. In San Francisco, you can find largemouth bass in the live tanks of Asian markets, but that's another story. Outside of that, I've never seen wild bass for sale or listed on a menu.

Why it's a bass fishing tournament and not an all-species tournament or a contest for other species is a complex subject that I can't answer in a few minutes, except to say that bass are the most popular fish in North America, a subject we'll explore later in this book.

How these particular anglers got here, I explain, is because they qualified. Some BASS tournaments allow for participation by professional bass anglers at the top and the middle ranks, and others by weekend amateurs at the lowest ranks. The system has evolved into one in which anglers must qualify for upper-level tournament participation based on prior performance at lower-level tournaments. A professional bass angler has to do well enough over a season to qualify to be in the no-entry-fee Classic. This is similar to major and minor events in professional golf.

Before leaving, McDonel says that he enjoyed the start. "It's too bad you can't watch it all in one spot. I'd like to watch one of these anglers fish," he says.

He'll get just the briefest glimpse of that on ESPN, I suspect; otherwise, he'll have to get the binoculars out.

The Convention Center and the War Room

The Outdoors Expo—technically, the Classic ESPN Outdoors Expo Presented by Under Armour—is being held throughout the tournament at the David H. Lawrence Convention Center adjacent to the Allegheny River.

Outside the show entrance is a Wall of Fame photo exhibit from past Classics. Perhaps the most notable photograph is from the 1984

Classic in Pine Bluff, Arkansas, showing then Vice President George Bush and then Governor Bill Clinton, each wearing a baseball cap with a BASS patch on it. Clinton's hat looks small for his head and somehow out of place.

Nearly all of the photos from early events depict anglers wearing a few modest patches on their shirts or vests and hats with some company's name on it. Patches and sponsor names are more prominent by 1988, and around 1993, the anglers start to look a lot like race car drivers. From 2000 on, the shirts or the jerseys are nearly all cluttered billboards; they're uniforms. Perhaps this is no coincidence, since it was in April 2001 that BASS and its fishing tournaments came under the ownership of ESPN.

The Outdoors Expo has been billed by BASS as "one of the largest consumer products shows in the country." Having been to assorted consumer shows, I find this claim to be greatly exaggerated, both in terms of exhibitors and attendees. The expo is dominated by exhibits from sponsors of the Classic and the Bassmaster tournament trail, although there are exhibits from some companies that have no tournament affiliation with BASS.

Major Classic sponsor Triton, whose boats are the only ones that anglers can use in the Classic, has a large, open midhall display with many boats on the floor. There's a poster at the edge of the Triton booth that shows a photo of a young couple with Coca-Cola fishing shirts on and the words "Meet Byron and Mary from ABC's *The Bachelor*." Byron is Byron Velvick, a professional bass angler who, in 2004, was featured on the aforementioned program and is now an analyst on ESPN's *BassCenter*.

Berkley, another major Classic sponsor and prominent tackle manufacturer, has a large area for its exhibits, which include a big mobile fish tank used for demonstrating lure action and retrieval techniques. Throughout the day, people stop and watch the tank's bass and bluegills for some time, even when there's no demonstration going on. The Berkley booth sports a poster alerting people to register for a chance to cast for $1 million.

Bass Pro Shops, a BASS sponsor whose nearest store is in Cincinnati, and Dick's Sporting Goods, which is not a sponsor but is headquartered in Pittsburgh, both have retail exhibits. Major Classic sponsor Mercury has a prominent display, but there's no other out-board motor manufacturer here. There are large exhibits by sponsors Toyota, Cialis, Citgo, Busch, Shimano, Lowrance, and Minn-Kota, yet none by any of their competitors.

A small exhibitor, Classic Patterns, sells clothing and video products that bear the names and the endorsements of professional bass anglers. About twenty people are in line there to get the autograph of Claude "Fish" Fishburne, a former professional bass fisherman who was the tournament weigh-in emcee for BASS prior to Keith Alan, before being removed in an evident flap over his association with a boat company that was not a BASS tournament sponsor. Tall and red-bearded, Fishburne is wearing a hat and a shirt with the name and the logo of Skeeter Boats, and he jokes easily with the fans, some of whom are wearing stick-on patches that say, "Where is Fish Fishburne?"

Back near the show entrance is the ESPN booth, where Jerry McKinnis is sitting in a director's chair, microphone in hand, in front of bright studio lights and a camera. McKinnis's production company,

Autograph seekers wait in line at the Outdoors Expo to meet former BASS emcee Fish Fishburne, far right.

JM Associates, is working with ESPN to produce twelve hours of Classic coverage beginning this evening at 7 P.M.

Downstairs in a bright, clean underground-garagelike setting are several white tractor trailers that are, in essence, mobile editing and production centers. I peek inside one, which is crowded and dark. Against the wall, there are at least fifty small video monitors, most showing something different to the headset-wearing people who sit in front of them, watching and working with control panels.

ESPN coordinating producer Jill Frederickson explains what's going on in the war room and notes that this is the first time that they'll be seeing fish caught live on camera and being beamed back to the operations center. The camera on the boats is sending a signal to the U.S. Steel building, she says, which is relayed here.

Frederickson brings me to a makeshift assemblage of boxes located in front of a large projection screen. On top of one box is a laptop computer hooked up to a projector, which is displaying on the projection screen the same thing that appears on the laptop. At the moment, it depicts a map of the Monongahela south of Pittsburgh, from McKeesport to I-70. There are eight red dots on the map, seven of them on the Mon and one on a tributary; each of these is an angler whose name is shown on the map next to its appropriate dot.

In the lower-left corner of the projection screen is the list of competing anglers in the approximate order in which they are believed to be, based upon their estimated catch so far. The computer shows Edwin Evers in first place, having caught and kept four bass that are estimated to weigh a total of 6 pounds 0 ounces. Currently highlighted in the upper left of the screen is Terry Scroggins, who is tied for seventh, having caught five bass and kept two that are estimated to weigh a total of 3 pounds 0 ounces.

There's seven people standing behind the boxes watching the screen, including professional bass anglers Shaw Grigsby and Mark Menendez, who will provide commentary in later broadcasts, and Steve Bowman, a writer for JM Associates.

When each of the forty-seven Classic anglers catches a bass, his observer records the estimated weight, and whether it was kept or released, on a cell phone–GPS device that ESPN calls BassTrakk. The observer, who has completed a mandatory fifteen-minute training session to learn to use the device, punches a button that sends information to the operations center so that ESPN personnel immediately know which angler has caught a fish, approximately how big it was, where it was caught, and how this affects the estimated current standings. The producers use this information to know where the angler is at all times during the day, to track his movements throughout the day, and to depict on their map every place that he has caught a fish. Just as important, if one angler suddenly gets hot, a producer can call a roving camera boat and send it to the hot angler fairly quickly.

Everyone watching this technology is pretty excited about it, and it's likely that this part of the proceedings will be more fascinating than the fishing, especially now that the early results are proving that fishing will be even tougher than predicted. So far, twenty-nine anglers have not caught a fish that meets the minimum 12-inch length requirement, a "keeper" in sportfishing parlance.

"A two-pounder puts you in a tie for twelfth right now," says Menendez, "Gary Klein has caught fourteen, but he only put two in the livewell."

Steve Bowman reiterates the importance of being able to instantly follow what the anglers are doing and explains that there are ten cameras in competitors' boats today and twelve that are on the water, roving.

"So, who knows what you all know in here?" I ask. "You could show this to an audience in real time, no?"

"We have not yet answered the question of whether we want to release this in real time," says Bowman. "We could affect the competition."

Upstairs, there is a large screen that shows how many bass the anglers have caught today and how many they've put in the livewell, but it does not show the estimated weight of these fish or the current estimated standings. The fishermen themselves are not supposed to be able to get this information, at least by phone during the day. A friend, for example, cannot call and tell them how other anglers are doing in the tournament or where they are.

Bowman says that's because the anglers can use a cell phone only in an emergency, and then only to call tournament director Trip Weldon. It occurs to me that there must be some way for the anglers and an accomplice to get around this, which would be cheating and would be hard to do with all of the observers and cameras watching. Still, there's a lot of money and stature at stake here, and where there's a will, there's often a way.

The value to any of these competitors knowing what the others are doing, especially on the first day, when it is crucial to do well (fishing pressure and boat activity often cause the catch to decline in successive days of a tournament) is that most of these anglers fish to their personal strengths and often use techniques and methods that play to their strengths. So, knowing, for example, that John Doe, an expert topwater angler, has caught fish early might provide helpful info to a competitor, who may correctly figure out what and where John Doe is fishing. That, in turn, could lead to a change in another angler's own tactics or locations.

Maybe I've read too many mystery books, but I'm thinking that there's some possibility for hanky-panky.

In any case, I walk away feeling like I've been privy to viewing district or precinct results early on Election Day. And I'm impressed. There was a good buzz in the war room. Everyone is excited about what they're watching.

FOUR

Little Fish, Big Enthusiasm

*A good rule of angling philosophy is not to interfere with any
fisherman's ways of being happy, unless you want to be hated.*
—ZANE GREY

Irrational exuberance, the term that Federal Reserve chairman
Alan Greenspan used in reference to escalated asset values in
1996, might well be applied to the hoopla surrounding the weigh-in
ceremony at Mellon Arena, a facility that was originally built to
house the Civic Light Opera and that features the largest retractable,
stainless-steel dome roof in the world. Here, the seats that can hold
seventeen thousand ticket-buying Pittsburgh Penguin fans are filled
with fifty-three hundred freely admitted bassheads and their friends
and family members, many of whom have been issued Triton-logoed
inflatable noisemakers.

Down on the floor, where the ice rink used to be before professional hockey went on strike, there's a semi-oval track in front of the
stands where the anglers will be towed into the arena in their bass
boats. Inside the semi-oval is a cordoned-off infield, or "pit," where
the ESPN production crew is situated in black cubicles. Next to
them, on one side, is an elevated platform for still photographers,
and behind this is a lighted, elevated tower that shows the current
standings of anglers in the tournament. On the other side is a small

platform where Ron Franklin, a longtime college football announcer for ESPN, sits in a director's chair in front of a teleprompter, his back to the stage. Near Franklin is a tall, circular, bubbling, blue-watered aquarium that holds largemouth bass.

The forward part of the pit abuts the end of the stage, where there's a five-foot-wide, waist-high podium connected to a runway and a large stage. Behind and above the stage to the right and the left of center are two Jumbotron screens. In between the stage and the production area is an SRO area where a few members of the media and between sixty and seventy fans are gathered. Some of the fans were issued passes for this location at Point State Park this morning, while others are lifetime members of BASS who got passes at the lifetime member booth at the Outdoors Expo.

Most of the attending bassheads, however, are packed along the sides of the arena, with a few at the end zone opposite the stage. There's a lot of colored spot-lighting throughout the arena, like in a rock or circus show, and much glitzy blue light around the stage backdrop.

Fishing concluded at 3:00 P.M. today, and the weigh-in show was advertised as starting at 3:15. When I arrive in the upper level seating area reserved for the press, it is 3:35 and Ray Scott is at the podium, saying, "I have never walked down the street where I have met people who were more friendly than in Pittsburgh."

Scott, when he was the owner of BASS, was the emcee for all of the national and Classic tournaments, and although he has not been hosting these events for some time, he was brought here by ESPN to work his charm. Scott is wearing his trademark white cowboy hat and a leather-and-denim jacket devoid of logos. He has been on for a few minutes, evidently, and is now dividing the fans on his left and his right into respective A and B teams and getting them to out-cheer each other.

"Bass fishing in Pittsburgh!" Scott yells. "Let's hear it A Team and B Team."

The crowd roars. Scott welcomes Keith Alan as the Jumbotrons show them shaking hands, then Scott departs, and it is Alan's turn to milk the crowd.

"I hope you guys are ready to get fired up, because the ESPN cameras are rolling, and we will have most of this action live on ESPN and ESPN2."

Alan salutes America and its fighting soldiers around the world. A flag shows on the screens during the National Anthem.

I can't help but think about last night, during a happy hour sponsored by Busch Beer at Austin Henry's Saloon, when I struck up a conversation with a guy who worked next door at the Federal Building, for the United States Army. He did regional advertising buys for the army and was checking out the Classic and the pros. I asked whether the army was thinking of sponsoring this tournament or pros in general.

"We're looking at being involved with bass fishing," he said, then estimated that sponsoring an angler for one year would cost $50,000—"to get them to wear the patches, get up, and say, 'Thanks to the U.S. Army,' and so on, when they are on stage."

I remember that *Bassmaster* magazine ran letters from soldiers in Iraq and an article about some of them fishing at Freedom Dam, aka Saddam's Dam. *BassCenter* did a piece on a similar topic. And Classic spokesman and former BASS owner Ray Scott made a much-touted visit to the U.S. troops earlier this year. I doubt that there's a connection, but I wonder.

Then Alan introduces tournament director Trip Weldon, who is effusive about Pittsburgh and its bass fans. He notes that there were "two thousand-something people" at the launch this morning, calling it the largest first-day launch crowd they've ever had.

Weldon's number differs greatly from my own observation of four to five hundred, but I'm beginning to expect this sort of unbridled math. At the free final-day weigh-in at the Elite 50 tournament at Lake Dardanelle, I had made a weigh-in crowd estimate of three thousand people, counting them in approximate groups of a hundred at a time. It was later announced by BASS, which had no official counting mechanism, that there were ten thousand attendees, bettering the previous final-day weigh-in record of seventy-five hundred, set at the same lake in 2004.

"This may be the closest Classic contest we've ever seen," says Weldon, and, perhaps cynically, I'm thinking that given BASS's penchant for overstated numbers and the fact that fishermen have a historical propensity for exaggerating the size of their catch, it's a good thing that the fish are weighed on scales in front of people. Or sort of in front of them, as it turns out, since the audience can't see the fish on the scales except when an overhead camera shows them on the big screens.

A few minutes later, at four o'clock, the first angler rolls into the arena under circling spotlights and to a cacophony of booming music, cheering, clapping, and the pounding of lots of noisemakers. It's Jimmy Mize, who, ironically, considering the mill history of Pittsburgh, quit his regular job as a paper mill worker in Arkansas a month ago. Mize has a limit of five bass that weigh 6 pounds 2 ounces.

Soon Zell Rowland trudges to the podium with three bass that weigh 3 pounds 10 ounces. Perhaps not wanting to disparage the local fishery, Rowland graciously says that it's a good day any time that he catches just one bass. But when Alan presses him, he darkly allows, "This place will fish real hard this week."

Rowland is followed by Ron Shuffield, who has one bass weighing 13 ounces. Alan announces that Shuffield is tied for third place, then says that we're taking a break and will be right back. People head for the restrooms while commercials run on the Jumbotrons.

We need a break? I'm thinking. This is not being broadcast live. The first Classic telecast—one hour long—isn't until seven o'clock tonight, which means it will be an edited tape of the first day's activities. And all we're seeing now is a bunch of sheepish guys at show-and-tell time without much to show and nothing exciting to tell.

But I have obviously underestimated entertainment production needs. When Alan returns to the podium, he's in whip-'em-up mode.

"The whole world is gonna be watching tonight," he says. "Now, when I give you the cue, I'm looking for a full sixty seconds of mayhem. Here we go, one-two-three, fire it up, Pittsburgh!" There's a lot of cheering and clapping and yelling and noisemaker-whacking as the cameras roll and the boom operator comes in and out of the pit. Over the roar, Alan adds fuel to the fire, "Like the Steelers won the Super Bowl!"

Now I get it. They want the bassheads to act like certain Steeler fans at Heinz Field. The ones with painted faces and wild wigs who are screaming at the top of their lungs and wagging their index fingers at the camera in complete irrational exuberance. The ones you suspect should have been cut off from alcohol about an hour earlier.

But they must not have been exuberant enough.

"Okay," says Alan, "here's the deal. Ron Franklin is over there, and he's doing the lead-ins for the show. . . . The whole world's gonna be watching on ESPN. . . . We want this place rockin'. . . . You guys did an awesome job. They're re-racking the tape, and when I cue you, keep that energy up, we're gonna do it for another sixty seconds. . . . You guys are awesome. You're doin' a great job. We'll let you get a little breather. Take a deep breath."

Half a dozen people yell from different areas of the arena.

"Let's get it on," someone screams.

The producers must be having trouble "re-racking the tape" because Alan has to banter for a few minutes in stall mode, talking about the many people working on this production and all the technology involved, inviting bassheads to join him at the morning launch tomorrow when *BassCenter* is broadcasting live.

"All right, Ron Franklin is ready. . . . Now give me some mayhem, one-two-three, let me hear it!"

And they do. This must be what it's like when Michael Buffer screams at a boxing match, "Let's get ready to rummmmble!"

The bassheads in the pit are especially exuberant, yelling, waving, and jumping. Near the front is a tall fellow waving a four-foot-long bass pillow over his head—it's Ed Matuizek, the guy from the launch this morning who has read my books. He's in the middle of the pit mob, facing the podium, wearing the Roberto Clemente jersey he had on this morning. (Earlier, Matuizek was in line outside the arena when ESPN crew members threw shirts, hats, and a pillow bass to the crowd. The tall Matuizek was able to snare the pillow. Inside, an ESPN cameraman urged him to wave the pillow and help get the crowd excited.)

When the cheering starts to subside, the arena announcer booms in the same deep, important-sounding voice of the announcers who introduce basketball players at the NBA's All-Star game, "Annnd nowww, from Petal, Mississippi, please welcome Cliiiiiff Pace."

As an overhead boom camera records the action, an angler is driven past the infield to the stage prior to weighing in.

Pace's boat is driven down the 120-foot-long lane to the accompaniment of grinding country music, lights flaring, fans waving, pit fans hand-slapping. Ed Matuizek is waving his bass pillow over his head in the direction of Pace's boat as it pulls up to the side of the stage.

Pace has four smallmouth bass, which the Jumbotron shows in an overhead view of the scale, itself embedded in the podium out of sight of the fans in the arena. The fish are flopping, and Weldon has to calm them down before he can confirm a total weight of 3 pounds 13 ounces. Pace is asked to hold up his two largest bass for photos; then he hands them to Weldon and walks through the pit, shaking hands.

Following Pace is Dave Palmer, who has no fish. Alan accompanies him up the stage ramp, saying, "This is kind of like the walk of shame, right here, I hate to tell you." Palmer says he caught twenty undersized bass, but that's all he's invited to say as Alan whisks him off.

"We will come back with more action from the weigh-in stage in just a moment."

. . .

After they come back, three more anglers are paraded through. The first, Aaron Martens, has caught a limit of five bass that weigh a total of 5 pounds 1 ounce, which, though it would be poor in almost any other tournament, is enough to get a big hand from the crowd. People now have an inkling of what's in store for the rest of the weigh-in. Martens is followed by Mike Reynolds, who has a "goose egg," as Alan puts it. Reynolds seems resigned to hunting and pecking for something again tomorrow, but he does draw an ovation with his comments about how great the town of Pittsburgh and the fans are. Reynolds is followed to the stage by Chris Baumgardner, who reaches into his livewell to remove a bag of fish. Alan becomes exuberant, shouting, "Show me something good!" But Baumgardner has just one bass that weighs exactly a pound. He, like Reynolds, is not encouraging about what tomorrow holds or what he can do differently.

Alan then introduces a big-screen video about Rick Clunn, whom he calls "the greatest angler of all time." Then Clunn is wheeled into the Mellon Arena with as much pomp and exuberance as the announcer and the lights and the music—in his case, the song he has requested (all of the anglers get to choose their entrance song), "Get Over It" by the Eagles—can muster.

There's a huge ovation. Clunn has been outfitted with a remote head mike, but when his boat stops at the stage steps, he gets out without a fish bag. The "greatest angler of all time" has zeroed.

Clunn has been through the weigh-in walk at bass tournaments hundreds of times, however, and he is even-keeled and introspective. "This is a tough tournament," he says. "I like tough tournaments. It requires a lot more of your skills. I've never fished a fishery where you could get twenty bites a day and maybe have twenty more fish follow and still not be putting the right fish in the boat."

The screens show clips of Clunn fishing during the day. "I have nobody to blame but myself," he says afterward. "If one person catches a limit, then you have to blame yourself."

A John Deere representative comes to the podium as a four-wheel-drive ATV is brought into the arena and presented to Clunn for winning the Greatest Angler Debate.

. . .

At this point, the weigh-in "show" has consumed forty-six minutes, during which ten of forty-seven anglers have weighed in with less than twenty-five bass.

The eleventh angler, however, is a stark contrast to the others. Alan refers to him as "a legend in his own mind," Californian Skeet Reese. He of the spiked bleached hair and yellow sneakers. At the podium, a balding Trip Weldon gently touches Reese's head, and Alan mentions that "It started out that all the guys on Tour started frosting their hair for some reason, and Skeet would not be outdone. He had to get it as bleach blond as he possibly could."

Reese has five fish that weigh 4 pounds 10 ounces, an average of under a pound apiece.

"That is officially the smallest five-fish limit I have ever weighed in my career," Reese says. "Can you believe that I actually culled up to four pounds ten ounces? That's pretty bad."

He looks embarrassed to hold up two of these bass for photographers.

A little later, Stacey King registers three bass that weigh a total of 5 pounds 1 ounce, tying him for second with Martens. This gets a big ovation, and his biggest fish is placed on the scales. The large screens provide an overhead view of the scales, and the big fish looks like a monster compared to what's come before. The crowd murmurs. Weldon tries to keep the bass from flopping. Waiting for a digit is the biggest drama of the day.

"Two pounds fourteen ounces!" shouts Alan, "That's the Purolator Big Bass of the day so far! How about it, Pittsburgh?"

With less than half of the field in so far, the show is getting old. Many of the media attendees must also feel this way, as the nearby media room has lots of activity. A tray of steamed hot dogs and a cooler of soda were provided, along with about eight rows of folding tables set up for writers. Two dozen of them are seated with their laptop computers open. At a separate table near the entrance, three members of the BASS communications staff, in tan slacks and navy shirts, are entering data and quotes into laptop computers for press info that they will generate as soon as the weigh-in concludes.

Other media and BASS staff, as well as pros who have already weighed in, are milling about and talking in small groups. The wives of a few of the pros accompany them.

In a separate room is a bank of computers where the people running the BASS Classic Web site are located. Ed Scheff and Brett Pauley, both employees of Winnercomm, a Tulsa communications company that produces the BASS and ESPN Outdoors Web sites, are here overseeing the efforts. The BASS Web site contains info and articles about the event and the pros, plus a live streaming-video Web cast during the weigh-in and a real-time leader board. The board started this morning, using the criteria of how many fish were placed in the livewell and what their estimated weight was, which is the info provided by BassTrakk that ESPN producers were viewing earlier at the convention center.

"Internet interest at this particular event has grown in leaps and bounds in the last few years," says Pauley, who reviews some of the features of the site with me. This includes statistical information on anyone who has ever competed in a BASS event, he says.

"Anyone?"

"Give me a name. We'll search it."

I tell him to search my name. Up it comes.

"I didn't know you fished any BASS tournaments," he says with some surprise. "You had a top-fifty finish on the St. Lawrence River in 1977."

"Yep," I say. "Finished four places out of the money."

"I'll be darned."

By 6:20, the weigh-in show has concluded. If everyone hurries, they can get home and watch the ESPN coverage at seven o'clock.

Mize is the leader with a paltry 6 pounds 2 ounces, a new Classic record for the lowest first-day leading weight. King and Martens are tied for second, with Preston Clark and Kevin VanDam, respectively, in fourth and fifth. VanDam and King share "big" bass honors, each having caught a 2-pound 14-ounce fish, which ranks as the fourth-smallest daily big bass ever caught in a Classic and the second smallest day-one big bass.

Just four anglers have caught a five-fish limit. Ninety-six bass were weighed in, having a total weight of 105 pounds 1 ounce, barely a pound apiece. Ten anglers, including previous Classic champs Clunn and Yelas, have not caught a keeper. These are probably low records for the event, too.

Nevertheless, the competition is close, and, as many pros predicted, one sizable fish, or a good half hour at the right place in the right time, could make a big difference in the next two days.

Speaking of the fish, I've been curious about the fate of the bass after their collective weight has been determined. Once the bass are weighed, Trip Weldon places them under the podium, and they vanish.

Rich Lorson, an area fisheries manager for the Pennsylvania Fish & Boat Commission, is overseeing the handling and the redistribution of the fish. I meet him down on the arena floor behind the curtained weigh-in stage and use this opportunity to get his take on the local bass population and the reasons behind the present poor fishing.

"The bass population," he says, "is very good in terms of numbers. The total number of adult fish is lower this year, but that's coming off high adult populations in 2003 and 2004 in our studies. What's making it difficult right now is low water, a dry hot year, and a water temperature of eighty-two degrees. In the last two years we've had high muddy water a lot of the season, and low baitfish supplies, so that's had some bearing. Also, this year, it got warm early, and we've had very low precipitation. . . . We'll have a lot of good food fish coming on for these bass, and maybe there will be a better bite, but not until the water cools down."

Then we look under the stage, where the bass are taken from Weldon and placed in two treated circular holding tanks. The temperature of the water has been lowered by adding ice, and it is being oxygenated and mixed with a chemical designed to benefit the fish by helping them to avoid diseases and keep their metabolic balance.

As we speak, a white PFBC pickup truck backs through the arena hallway. Filling the bed is a large tank with two aerated compartments. Immediately, PFBC personnel begin ferrying five-gallon buckets of bass out to the truck, dumping the contents into the compartments.

Soon, the fish will be redistributed back to the Monongahela, Allegheny, and Ohio rivers in proportion to the numbers that were caught in each river.

Back at the hotel, Triton, Mercury, and MotorGuide are hosting a crowded party in the Steelhead Lounge. Attending are many people wearing Triton and Mercury sponsorwear, plus a few media members, Byron Velvick, and others who, as on the river cruise Tuesday, seem to know one another.

I stand next to a Pennsylvania basshead, Ed Guydon of Bethlehem, who tells me that he met the president of Triton, Earl Bentz, earlier today, and that Bentz invited him and two friends to the party. "He's a great guy," says Guydon, "I'm looking at getting a new boat, and I'll definitely consider a Triton."

He and his friends drove in late today after work and will be here for the weekend. Somehow, the conversation comes around to the people fishing as observers on the pros' boats. "Man, I would pay to be an observer if I could," he says.

Waiting for a drink at the crowded bar, I am sandwiched behind some fellow who seems to be hitting on a woman on a stool next to him but who offers to help get the bartender's attention for both of us. Turning around and looking over my shoulder, he sees a broad-smiling Velvick talking animatedly with a half-dozen people, then mutters disgustedly, "I can't deal with that pretty boy." Of course, this fellow is about sixty years old and weathered like a snapping turtle.

Remarkably, Aaron Martens wanders into the room around nine o'clock. This is interesting since Martens is sponsored by Ranger Boats, which has been prominently displayed on his fishing uniform, and also because I would think that after getting up at 4 A.M., fishing until 3 P.M., waiting for hours to go through the weigh-in show, probably spending time signing autographs at a sponsor's booth at the outdoor show at the convention center, and having to get up tomorrow at 4 A.M. to do it all over again, he would be ready for bed.

ESPN's one-hour show this evening centers around the weigh-in of some of the anglers, including video of them fishing during the day, analysis of the overall and individual efforts, and some fill-in features.

It's a similar format to that used for the live broadcast of many major athletic contests, although there's more exposure for the host city in this than I suspect you'd see if ESPN was covering the NHL All-Star game. And, of course, the show is not live but is what producers cagily call "live-to-tape."

When you see the condensed package of this event on television, you can appreciate how slick the ESPN production is and what it must take to coordinate the anglers, their procession to the stage, the commentary on the stage, and the throwbacks for analysis to either Franklin or the folks "up top," as Alan says on several occasions.

Up top is where anchor Bill Clement presides over short analysis sessions with Shaw Grigsby and Byron Velvick, each in a light blue shirt and tan pants and trying to bring energy, enthusiasm, and insight to the entertainment. Knowing where the anglers have been all day and where they have caught fish, they comment on the results and what individual anglers might do tomorrow.

Being aware of how many fish each competitor has in his livewell prior to weighing in should allow the producers to focus on certain individuals, including those with good results and not just those who play well to the cameras. However, the only weighing-in anglers who will appear on television are those whom ESPN has pre-outfitted with head mikes.

Naturally, one of these is Mike Iaconelli, who shows his exuberance by standing in the boat, waving a towel to pump up cheering fans, reaching over to high-five the bassheads in the pit, and even smacking the bass pillow of Ed Matuizek.

Ever the strategist and marketer, Iaconelli is wearing a Pittsburgh Penguins jersey and a Pittsburgh Pirates hat, and almost before his boat has rolled to a stop, Alan says, "Look at you! You're a marketing genius, dude. How was your day?"

"I had an amazing day," says Iaconelli. "You know, as tough as it is at the Bassmaster Classic, it's the most exciting tournament of your life. And I wouldn't rather be anywhere but *Pittsburgh, baby*! Whooooo!"

The camera follows Iaconelli after he weighs in, vigorously slapping and high-fiving the bassheads in the pit while Bill Clement, in a voice-over, says, "I'm thinking that he doesn't need an extra cup of coffee in the morning."

Just before the producers cut away, the camera catches Iaconelli nearing the end of the pit. He shakes the right hand of wide-smiling Matuizek, standing hatless in his Pirates shirt, then takes the bass pillow from Matuizek's left hand, cuddles it close to his body, turns to the camera, and sighs, "Uhhhhh."

The coverage of first-day activities is buttressed by ads for ESPN's coverage of the World Series of Poker on Tuesday nights, Citgo, Busch, Toyota, Triton, Mercury, MotorGuide, Berkley, and Cialis; in other words, gambling, beer, trucks, fishing, and erections. There are also sponsored segments like the underwater illustrations of Citgo Bass Eye View and the Toyota Rules of the Game.

Pittsburgh gets a terrific boost, not only being shown as the backdrop for many of the angling shots but also being spotlighted several times during the hour. In one segment, Ron Franklin, seated in his director's chair in front of the circular bass tank, opens with a tribute to the city, saying, "They need a huge pat on the back for what they've done to their city as far as cleaning up the water and cleaning up the city itself." That follows with video clips of the same lithographs that I saw at the Heinz Museum earlier in the week, the Steelers celebrating a Super Bowl win, the Pirates celebrating a World Series win, and video of a full-throttle-screaming, bass-clutching Mike Iaconelli (in the Louisiana Delta in 2003) as Franklin intones that Pittsburgh is hosting "the Super Bowl of bass fishing. What was once unimaginable is now reality."

As to the fishing reality, ESPN has done a good job of deflecting viewer attention away from a weigh-in show that was essentially all pomp and circumstance. But it was a bit much when Clement at one point said that the fishing's been better than expected because of the current. Not broadcast were several onstage comments by the anglers about the lack of current, and if this is better than they expected. . . .

But I almost forgot, this is not about the fishing.

As if to reinforce that point, ESPN's coverage of the first day of the 2005 Citgo Bassmaster Classic ends with Clement inviting people to stay tuned for the Alka Seltzer U.S. Open of Competitive Eating, broadcast from the ESPN Zone in Las Vegas.

FIVE

Loudmouths

The average guy can relate to every one of these fishermen.
Not everybody can dunk a basketball or catch a touchdown
pass, but everybody can go catch a bass.

—TWO-TIME BASSMASTER CLASSIC WINNER BOBBY MURRAY

Saturday, July 30, 2005

It's still dark when I get up this morning and look out the window from the eighteenth floor of my hotel. Across the street, all of the boats and trucks that were in the parking lot of Mellon Arena are gone. A neon-red sign in the shape of a fish, with a blinking eye, is visible in the distance next to the highway; the words Bagley Lures glow above the sign.

In the taxi on the way to Point State Park I notice that unlike yesterday, the streets are empty. The driver, on his second run to the park, asks what's going on.

There's a stream of people walking across the field toward the sea-wall. On the right side of the field is a red Toyota pickup whose bed is filled with the front half of an inflated bass, its mouth open and nose pointed skyward as if it were leaping out of the water. A fellow in a red-and-black ESPN shirt is standing face-to-camera in the middle of the field; far behind him, in front of the fountain, bright lights illumi-nate the ESPN stage where technicians are readying equipment and a woman is dabbing makeup on the face of *BassCenter* anchor John Kernan.

Just behind the set, a smallish white woman and a large black man are leaning backward as they hold onto a thick rope that is tied to the top of a hot air balloon being infused with helium. Heels dragging along the ground, they are towed toward the balloon as it quickly inflates, displaying the words "Citgo Bassmaster Tournament Trail" and an illustration of a man and a young girl fishing in a Citgo-logoed bass boat.

Purple on top, layered to the bottom with red, orange, and blue, the balloon looks like a large bulbous Popsicle with a basket. This balloon isn't headed skyward, but wouldn't it be something if Ray Scott or Keith Alan were to get into the basket and lift off over the crowd at seven o'clock, like in *The Wizard of Oz*? Now that would be entertainment.

The only thing that I notice in the sky, however, circling counterclockwise, is a small plane towing a large Yamaha banner with a barely readable trailer that says "Good Luck Classic Anglers!" Beneath the plane, just emerging from the Monongahela, is a coal-laden barge, which could be taking up space at the Ohio River locks soon, if any of the pros are headed that way.

Some of the anglers' boats are still arriving at the seawall, where they will line up on the Allegheny facing downriver. Getting closer to the speakers, I can hear one of the pros saying, "Five years ago, I was driving a truck. . . . "

It is hazy this morning, and Pittsburgh's backdrop doesn't have as charming a patina as it did yesterday. Holding a hand mike and accompanied by a cameraman, Shaw Grigsby stands out against the haze, perched on a ledge to the right of the fountain. Across the river behind him is the Carnegie Science Center, and beneath him on the wall is a sign that warns against fishing in the fountain pool—which contains no fish.

I count forty-eight boats off the wall that are not in the tournament, plus two solo kayaks being paddled by shirtless, hatless bald guys in sunglasses. Maneuvering among the flotilla is Mike Iaconelli with a cameraman who is shooting the fans along the seawall. Some in the crowd yell and clap as he idles by.

Four-time champion Rick Clunn makes final preparations before fishing in the 2005 Citgo Bassmaster Classic.

The volume cranks up on the speakers, which are broadcasting "Crocodile Rock."

Keith Alan interrupts Sir Elton to say that the field will be narrowed down to the top twenty-five anglers after today. Anyone whose two-day weight doesn't make the cut will be standing on terra firma tomorrow—or, as Bachelor Byron later ungraciously says on *Bass-Center*, packing their bags and taking the red-eye home. Alan doesn't mention that each of the twenty-two anglers who places from twenty-sixth to forty-seventh will receive a $7,000 paycheck.

"Kevin VanDam, good morning," says Alan, "How ya doin'?"

VanDam says that he's a little tired from being on the water yesterday and following up last night with obligations. "I'm more or less running on adrenaline."

"Is there any strategy today?" asks Alan.

"My main strategy today is to eat all my lucky cookies right away."

Alan and VanDam talk more, while in the background, "Born to Be Wild" is playing just loud enough to make it hard to hear some of VanDam's words.

There's a little different feel to this morning. It's not just the haze or the rock music, but the fact that there are more people creating a greater buzz. It's a happening. A cross between a wrestling match and a rock concert.

Also different today is that there's a mild protest. Midway along the top of the promenade, a man and a woman who look like college students stand facing the boats and the Allegheny River, silently holding up a professionally made eight- by six-foot banner. White with large capitalized black letters, the sign says "Cruelty Is Not a Sport." Beneath and next to them are spectators, some of whom sport sponsorwear jerseys and hats. Remarkably, no one is harassing the banner holders. People see the sign and pause, then turn away and move on. Essentially, at least for now, they are simply ignored.

More people today are pressing for autographs and hailing the pros. Tommy Biffle answers questions from two bassheads about the speed of the reels he uses. A young sandy-haired girl steps forward and turns her back to Biffle, who places his name among the many autographs on her shirt. Someone asks Biffle which river he likes best, meaning which of the three rivers here. Biffle, who is currently in tenth place and caught three keepers yesterday, immediately deadpans, "The Arkansas River in Oklahoma."

Just down from Biffle, a loose-acting Iaconelli has drawn a crowd of autograph seekers, one of whom is basshead Eric Fularz of New Kensington, Pennsylvania. Fularz is two or three deep in the crowd with a cell phone to his ear. Extending the phone toward Iaconelli, he says, "Hey, Mike! Do me a favor? Just say hello to my fiancée, please?"

Iaconelli, wearing a Ranger Boats sweatshirt and a Toyota hat, takes the phone and in high-pitched voice says, "Whassuuuuuup!" Then bids good morning.

The crowd laughs, and Fularz tells his fiancée she can go back to sleep.

"He's just a great guy," Fularz says. "A down-to-earth guy. All these guys are great."

Fularz has a copy of Iaconelli's new book at home, inscribed with the words "Never give up."

If that is Iaconelli's mantra, then "Get Er Done" must be the motto of nervous-looking pro Jami Fralich, who is just down the wall, evidently standing next to family members. Four women, one man, and three children standing with Fralich, who caught no keepers yesterday, all sport identical T-shirts with those grammatically mystifying words on their backs. Fralich is from North Dakota, which may explain why the shirts say "Get Er Done." Had he been from Texas, the shirts would likely have read "Git R Done."

Nearby, Stacey King grouses to fans, "It's gettin' to be that the fishin's the shortest part of the day."

Welcome to show biz.

The sun is cresting Fort Duquesne Bridge and quickly burning off the haze as the National Anthem plays. Soon I run into Mike Walker, a public relations rep for Yamaha, and I comment about the boat with the Yamaha sign, which is out on the river again today, and also the plane with the banner. He neither confirms nor denies complicity.

"The boat," says Walker, "was a little late getting out this morning. It was stopped first thing by the river patrol and checked for the mandatory safety equipment. Quite a coincidence, huh?"

Then he notes, with what seems to be cat-who-ate-the-mouse satisfaction, that some ESPN folks have commented that with its meandering sign-laden boat, Yamaha is "really pushing it."

"And now," exhorts Keith Alan, who is officially sending the anglers on their way, "meet the newest member of the BASS Millionaire's Club, from Prosperity, South Carolina, Daaavyyyyy Hite."

Hite motors off, and I follow the flow of well-wishers who are moving to the end of the Point. Standing near the fountain is a person in a three-quarter-length bass costume that could pass for a mascot's outfit. Except that this outfit requires the wearer to stand up, so the bass seems to be standing on its tail, its padded pot belly jutting forward instead of down, the person within peering out from the opened

A Saturday morning visitor.

mouth. Next to the mascot are two executive-looking men, both wearing credentials around their necks that say V.I.P. Pass.

I soon spy Trip Weldon hustling along and hurriedly pulling one of the pros over to the wall on the Monongahela side of the Point. It's Iaconelli, who pulls alongside the seawall looking disgusted. He glances at his watch and then faces away toward the river.

Weldon disappears, and a small group of bassheads line the seawall along the Monongahela, wondering what's happening.

Aaron Martens idles by with cameraman aboard, a puzzled look on his face.

"Boat alright?" he asks.

Iaconelli gives him a thumbs-up, then sits for a couple of minutes, fingers tapping on his console.

Weldon hustles back, leans down, and hands Iaconelli his fishing license. As is his custom, Weldon goes through the anglers before the launch and asks each one if he has his fishing license. Iaconelli's was back in his hotel room, so Weldon dispatched someone to get it. The license had not arrived by launch time so Weldon let Iaconelli go through the pageantry but pulled him over and made him wait until the license arrived.

BassCenter airs live at seven o'clock, just as Alan begins sending the pros off one by one in their fishing chariots, which, in fact, they briefly showed after opening with John Kernan and Byron Velvick sitting under a white-canopied stage with the fountain spewing like a geyser in the background.

It's about 7:15 by the time I wander over and stand behind a crowd of about fifty people who line the field and fountain sides of the *BassCenter* stage while Kernan and Velvick finish excitedly reviewing the first-day performance of selected anglers and then cut to a commercial as a camera pans down a line of cheering, waving bassheads.

When the show comes back, they quickly go to a live update from reporter Kim Bain nearby on the Monongahela River. Gary Klein is fishing in the background as Bain, wearing a red, black, and white ESPN jersey that looks at first glance like a Triton Boats jersey, details what Klein used to catch a total of thirty-three fish yesterday, then adds that she's been told that Kevin VanDam has caught a keeper and "taken over the lead."

That ESPN has reporters on the water to offer live comments—it will also have later updates from a similarly attired Robbie Floyd—as well as the ability to say that there is already an unofficial new leader, is groundbreaking in the annals of bass fishing tournament coverage.

Accompanied by sense-of-urgency tones by reporters, the live-on-the-water segments and the real-time leader board on the BASS Classic Web site are meant to heighten suspense and viewer interest but are not without potential side affects. For example, the weight of VanDam's fish, as estimated by his observer, has been used to determine that he is unofficially in the lead. However, yesterday in the ESPN war room I noticed that Edwin Evers's observer had estimated his four-bass catch to weigh 6 pounds, but at the arena those fish tipped the scales at 3 pounds 10 ounces. So, the observers may not have it right.

Also, thanks to the footage being shown on television and at the weigh-in and observed by family, sponsors, and supporters, the pros know what their competitors are using and where and how they are fishing. This could lead to crowding on the better spots in successive days. It might also mean that anglers employ a strategy about under- or overestimating the weight of their catches. In other words, it might be advantageous to "coax" your observer to either under- or overestimate the catch of your fish so that you attract, or don't attract, camera boats.

And the dissemination of current, though unofficial, standings could lead to a scenario where one of the bassheads in a boat following a pro might find out via cell phone that the pro is unofficially in the lead, prompting the fan to holler out that information, which in turn tells the pro something valuable, particularly at a late hour and particularly when he might not otherwise have any idea how well he's doing.

Nevertheless, ESPN seems intent on blanketing the "Super Bowl of bass fishing," as John Kernan repeatedly refers to it. There's a football gamelike atmosphere to this show, and I'm wondering if everyone on camera has been heavily caffeinated this morning or whether their exuberance has been coached or coaxed because they have to force some excitement into the lack of keepers, lack of fish-catching video, and lack of large bass.

In other words, they're using noise and inflection and lots of cutaways to help create drama. Isn't that a definition of theatrics?

This is probably not much different from the coverage of a car race or a big football game, but it seems odd because we're talking about bringing televised drama and excitement to a contest in which the participants are spread over eighty-eight miles of rivers and where the fish are not officially weighed in the boat but later at an off-river ceremony, when there is no longer any estimation and where the real drama unfolds, albeit on a stage in a theatrical environment.

I'm probably alone in this sentiment, but someone needs to invent a device (BasScale?) that trained observers could use to immediately weigh a fish. I think that this real-time stuff would have more television meaning and relevance if the fish were accurately weighed in the boat as they were caught. Yes, this has both positive and negative attributes, but let us know *instantly* who's *officially*, not unofficially, leading; cut out the weigh-in show; and keep us glued to our TV screens until the clock runs out.

Back to the show. The *BassCenter* production team does a good job of covering, evaluating, and hypothesizing the previous day and the day in progress, but not without a few glitches. Once, the "real-time leader board" showed Preston Clark in both second and fourth place, albeit with different weights. They also misspelled Mononga-hela on a sidebar.

Now Kernan is throwing it to the *Loudmouth Bass* hosting duo of Jay Kumar and Mark Zona, who do their schtick with energy and exuberance. When they throw it back to Kernan, the camera shows a wider view of Kernan and Velvick and the background; for a moment you can see in the right-hand corner of the screen a portion of the "Cruelty" banner. Had it been placed more in line with the fountain, there would have been no avoiding it, but for home viewers the airing is so brief that the sign is virtually unreadable.

Each time the show breaks for commercials, the crowd is whipped into yelling and noisemaker banging, primarily by the cheer-leading Velvick but also by a waving female director on stage, who at one time is seen on the set exhorting the crowd while a boom camera pans in from the shadows. Ditto on the return from commercials, which are usually started with crowd-cheering audio and live aerial views of the three-river junction and Point State Park. I have not seen a camera plane or a helicopter, but I have noticed the small plane carrying the Yamaha banner, which keeps circling counterclockwise and, of course, never makes it into the live footage.

The people with the "Cruelty" banner have caused the producers to act fast and reposition the cameras. Once, *BassCenter* returns from a break with the banner moved to a background position almost in front of the fountain, causing the producers to use a stage-right cam-era to shunt the banner to the far right of the frame.

So far, no one has hassled the protesters, and they have said noth-ing, but as *BassCenter* goes to commercial midway in the hour, Velvick turns around to the crowd behind him and gets them hooting and hollering.

"Who's those people over there?" he shouts.

The bassheads boo the protestors.

Velvick throws a hat into the crowd, and there's a brief clamber among young men that is reminiscent of women scrambling for a bridal bouquet. Taking a cue perhaps from Alan the weigh-in emcee, Velvick counts four-three-two-one and points to the crowd of about forty to fifty people as they cheer, yell, clap, and pound on noisemakers, then he wheels around to face the teleprompter while the crowd still cavorts.

Later, near the end of the hour, the show returns from an on-water update report with a high-angle boom shot that removes the fountain altogether and briefly reveals two guys in the background holding a large banner with the words "ESPN The Worldwide Leader in Sports" in front of and blocking the "Cruelty" banner. The people holding the "Cruelty" banner raise it up so the words "A Sport" are barely visible for a moment, but the camera operator quickly tightens the shot to crop the rear banner out.

Moments before the show went back on air, the ESPN banner—which had been tied to the edge of the television stage and then was hastily attached to two poles—had been hustled into blocking position. This was accompanied by cheers from people in the back of the crowd, who then broke out into a spontaneous cry, probably heard many times across the river when the Steelers had a game in hand: "Nah-nah-nah-nah, nah-nah-nah-nah, hey hey-hey, good-bye."

At 3:30, eight antifishing protesters have gathered across the street from the entrance to Mellon Arena. There are three women and five men, all twentyish. Two of them hold the same banner that was at the launch this morning, while the others bear less sophisticated poster board signs, two of which say, "Get Hooked on Compassion, Not Fishing."

Inside, Ray Scott is warming up the crowd.

"I called my daughter," says Scott, "and told her I was here yesterday and that the dad-gum place has got sixteen, eighteen thousand seats in it, and it was about three-fourths full, and we've never seen that in thirty-five years. . . . Tomorrow you better be here early if you want to get in. . . . "

"I wanna say something," he continues. "That lady that sang the

'God Bless America' song awhile ago, that's the best I ever heard it sung in my life."

Then Scott talks about when he was a life insurance salesman and got cussed out for calling someone at home at seven o'clock at night.

"But when I got into the bass fishing business," he says, "I could call a man at ten thirty, eleven, even twelve o'clock at night, and he'd be in bed with his wife or somebody else, and we'd talk for half an hour. That's the difference. We're all celebrating America today because of what we see right here. This is the greatest dream in the world, to be able to fish for a living!"

Now it's Alan's turn. "Look at this crowd! We're going to get you all fired up!"

Indeed, the crowd is already more fired up today than yesterday. There are several thousand more of them here, for one thing (the BASS tally later would be 10,520). And it looks like that includes many more twentyish men and boys, quite a few of whom are shirt-less, with words, letters, or caricatures adorning their bodies.

The back of one such fellow a few rows below me sports the out-line of a fish with the letters BASS underneath, a couple of inches above the smaller words "Old Navy" on the top of his underwear, which is sticking up from under his jeans. The word "Mercury" is painted down his left arm. In front of him is a guy with "Bassmaster" painted across the top of his back, and down in the pit there's a fellow with a big K painted on his chest, presumably for Kevin VanDam. Or Kevin Wirth? Or Gary Klein? Or Stacey King? Or Jeff Kriet?

Alan goes through the same rituals as the previous day, telling the fans that there's live coverage and cameras all over, exhorting raucous-ness at key times, and introducing many of the pro anglers like they were basketball players at an All-Star game.

The producers schedule Scott Rook to be the second angler to weigh in because he has a limit of five bass, which, as they know in advance, is one of only two limit catches today. He temporarily takes over first place, jumping all the way from twentieth yesterday. Rook's catch draws appreciative applause but moderate stage time and no "live" television time. There's more noise and plenty of time a few minutes later for the talkative and flamboyant Gerald Swindle, whose four keepers place him just behind Rook but who gets about twice the stage time. They show video of him fishing throughout the day while Alan draws comments from him, which permits Swindle to get in a plug for his lure sponsor, Lucky Craft.

I wonder whether this extra attention is because Swindle is gabby, with get-in-your-face activeness, and is prone to say, or sometimes shout, what he's thinking. Like today, when, posing on stage with two fish, he honestly says, "It's a bad day when you're holding up thirteen-inchers." Or because he happens to be a member of the Citgo fishing team, and this is, after all, the Citgo Bassmaster Classic. Perhaps not coincidentally, Swindle gets nearly four minutes of face time later on the televised weigh-in show.

The producers roll the anglers through at a noticeably quicker pace today, dispensing fairly quickly with those who've caught few or no fish but giving them at least a little time to get people to see the logos on their fishing uniforms.

There is much cheering a little later for another flamboyant angler and a local favorite Mike Iaconelli, who once lived in Philadelphia. Iaconelli caught four keepers for the second day in a row and temporarily takes over the lead, which is cause for fist-pumping celebration and extra remarks. He gets to show off his electronic belt buckle, which scrolls the words "Never Give Up" across in red letters, and to comment on big-screen footage of him fishing today that runs for ninety seconds, during which he gets in a plug for Berkley, one of his major sponsors.

A second video clip shows him getting his boat stuck in a few inches of water late in the day, a situation that he caused but which he was rescued from by being given a camera boat to get into. I wonder whether this would have happened for someone else who was less charismatic or not being trailed by a camera boat. Or even whether it's proper at all for him to be given such assistance.

Iaconelli tells the crowd that overcoming this obstacle, and catching two keepers in the last hour, shows that people should never give up in fishing or in life. Before Alan can say anything, Iaconelli adds, "Real quick, I would like to say that I wouldn't be here today if it wasn't for my sponsors, Ranger Boats, what an amazing bass boat, and Yamaha Outboards, the best engine in the world. Whooo!" He's the only one so far who has taken such liberties or had this much time on stage to be able to get his plugs in. And he's managed to verbally do for Yamaha what the Yamaha plane and boat banner could not: get a live promo.

In addition, all five minutes of his weigh-in performance are shown on television, preceded by a two-minute feature on his past accomplishments and earlier struggles. Talk about exposure.

By contrast, the more subdued and even-keeled Gary Klein immediately follows Iaconelli onstage to the accompaniment of country music and modest applause. Despite a few upbeat and articulate comments and his temporarily moving to fifth place from seventeenth, he's announced, weighed, and dispatched in under two minutes, which includes about twenty-five seconds of on-screen highlight video that is also covered on television. This is more than many anglers get but less than some, especially Iaconelli.

And that's not counting the arena face time that Iaconelli got earlier when the big screens showed a video in which he gave a mini-seminar on how on-the-water bassheads should behave, even asking them to leave the pros' fishing spots alone until after the tournament and not fish them during the event. Applause was muted after that video, and I thought it was arrogant to assume that what any of the pros is doing in this event—angling on a publicly accessible waterway for fish that belong to all of the people and that are managed with public resources—is more important than the right of an individual to fish in the same place at the same time for the same fish. In other words, he suggested what crowd and fan etiquette should be. If this was a private lake, that might be okay, and it might be okay on public water for many adoring bassheads who are there specifically to watch the pros, but I wonder what Iaconelli would do or say if someone in a $300 johnboat, who doesn't care that some pro is fishing for a large paycheck, pulled up and anchored where he was fishing, which he or she has every right to do.

I didn't check all of the stage time given to each angler, so perhaps some others got special time. Maybe VanDam, who was on stage and on television for more than three minutes. But it seems apparent that ESPN shows preference to "personalities" like Iaconelli, Swindle, and Reese and to an icon like Clunn and a heavyweight like VanDam, all of whom have presence and are reliable for articulate or zany sound bites.

It occurs to me that many of the other anglers could use a media or acting coach, someone to guide them on how to behave, what level of charm they need to exude when they get in front of the camera or the mike, and how to squeeze every drop out of their moments in the spotlight. Chad Morgenthaler later admits that he got chewed out by his parents for not smiling onstage yesterday. He wasn't smiling because he was disappointed at catching two 1-pound bass.

Because these are fishermen, not actors or media pros, a lack of camera presence is understandable. Their problem is compounded at this Classic, however, where, given the paucity of keepers and the small size of the fish, there is less of interest to talk about with regard to the fishing. Nevertheless, although almost all of the pros have good-size egos, most of them are likable, personable, and gracious. Many of them, over the last two days, have made a point of paying tribute to Pittsburgh, even if they don't get time to plug a sponsor. For most anglers, it's genuine, and the bassheads respond warmly.

The feel-good moment of the weigh-in occurs while Alan is talking to Arizona pro Andre Moore, who has caught a few fish each day and whose girlfriend is ESPN reporter Kim Bain, herself a tournament bass angler. Alan brings up the blond-haired Bain, whose attractive looks and Australian accent make her the nicest-sounding and nicest-looking person to appear on the stage so far. Bain is now off-duty, wearing a sleeveless and logoless green shirt, and Alan asks her about providing encouragement to Moore, which is a set-up question the answer to which is followed by a nervous Moore saying that he didn't think he could go on without Bain. So, with the Jumbotron showing both of them, he takes a knee and proposes, she accepts, the crowd cheers, and Alan exclaims, "It's a family show. . . . You got a good catch there, guy."

Tape of this moment, complete with Moore slipping an engagement ring on Bain's finger, will make the highlight reel later on *SportsCenter*, ESPN's marquee daily all-sports news show, with the anchor commenting, "They did not weigh her in. You can catch a bass with a topwater lure that looks like a bug, but if you want to catch a woman, you've got to bring a diamond ring or something."

. . .

In the media room, VanDam is telling eleven reporters and one cameraman how he is trying to make the fish react, primarily by jerking a minnow plug around the bridge piers. This is producing slightly larger keepers on average. This explains why he has weighed in just six fish, three less than the leader, but is only 15 ounces behind.

It is busier here, too, than yesterday, with more people at the press tables near a battery of cameras broadcasting the weigh-in live.

VanDam is still talking. "It's mentally tough. . . . Most guys are up the Mon in the same general area. . . . The key is to capitalize on opportunities and get those fish that bite. . . . A limit with a quality bite will make you look like a hero."

One of the reporters later mentions to me that he was an observer today in one of the pro's boats and that unpleasant words were directed at Larry Nixon by Tim Horton, the latter being displeased with the fact that the former was fishing in the same area. Horton at one point came close to where Nixon was fishing and discourteously fired up his outboard and roared away.

Of more significance, however, is the subplot over water rights that may have caused a huge tumble for first-day leader Jimmy Mize, who returned in the morning to the same patch of grass on the upper Monongahela that he had caught five bass out of yesterday. The problem was that George Cochran went there, too, and stayed the entire time on the upper part of the grassbed. So did David Walker. Mize did not catch a keeper today and fell to twelfth, while Cochran caught four and moved up to eighth, and Walker caught five and leaped from thirty-fifth to tenth.

Yesterday, former Classic champ Jay Yelas, who did not catch a keeper on the Allegheny River, inferred on stage in front of the crowd that the Monongahela was the place to be, but that he would not go there today and get in the way of the leaders.

"Most of the guys play by an unspoken etiquette," said Yelas at Friday's weigh-in. "So I'll stay away from the Mon tomorrow so I don't get in anyone's way. They did that for me when I won the Classic."

It was a subtle but prophetic point, and perhaps one that was meant to give a lesson, had Yelas's fellow pros been paying attention or cared. More than 75 percent of the keepers weighed in on Friday were caught on the Mon. The Ohio and the Allegheny simply are not producing, which is what Wayne Lykens had predicted because the Mon is murkier and warmer.

Friday's fishing results mean that many pros who did not fish the Mon or who had spent most of Friday in the other rivers were likely to go to the Mon today. Indeed, this morning at the launch, it appeared that less than twenty of the forty-seven boats headed away from the Mon. The problem is that with Pittsburgh's waters fishing small (only a few places are producing), the pros can get stacked up on one another with the same few productive places being hit by numerous boats throughout the day. No wonder Iaconelli had asked fans not to fish.

So, did Cochran and Walker deliberately fish in Mize's spot because that's where Mize did well on Friday? Or did they consider it their spot, too? And did Cochran's and Walker's presence throw Mize off his game and cause him to blank today? There is no such thing as having a private spot, but did Cochran and Walker breach the unspoken etiquette that Yelas observed?

Away from the weigh-in crowd, Cochran told reporters that he had been to Mize's grassbed the day before and said that he wouldn't complain if someone was a pound ahead of him. But Mize said that on Friday, he'd had his grassbed to himself, and that Cochran had been upriver and Walker was never in that pool at all.

If Mize is not superstitious, he probably should be. His day started off in a prophetically bad way when the *Courier*, a BASS news sheet distributed in the press room and local hotels, mistakenly displayed a photo of Marty Stone, instead of Mize, holding up a bass and misidentified him in the caption.

When the weigh-in concludes, Aaron Martens's four fish today have placed him atop the standings with a two-day total of 9 pounds 1 ounce. Iaconelli and VanDam are, respectively, 14 and 15 ounces behind. Jeff Reynolds is 1 ounce behind VanDam, and Scott Rook is 2 ounces behind Reynolds in fifth. Jimmy Mize, Stacey King, and Preston Clark, who were in first, second, and fourth yesterday, failed to catch a keeper today and dropped to twelfth, sixteenth, and eighteenth places.

Today, the results were poorer than yesterday. Sixteen pros did not catch a keeper, eleven caught only one, and six caught only two. Just two of forty-seven anglers caught a limit of five bass. The leading weight at the end of the day was the lowest leading weight ever after day 2, by a full 4 pounds. There were 23 percent fewer keepers caught than in the previous day, and the average weight of keepers was even lower, at just 16.4 ounces per fish. The largest bass of the day, 1 pound 15 ounces and caught by fourth-place angler Jeff Reynolds, established a new record-low "big" bass for the Classic. Perhaps not coincidentally, the previous top-three smallest big-fish weights were set in 1983 on the Ohio River, when Cincinnati was the host.

I am reminded of two things that Marty Stone had said three days earlier at the media event in the Steelhead Lounge. "There's two words that never go together: good fishing and the Ohio River." And, "When we look back at this years from now, we'll say we went to a great sports town, a city that treated us like royalty, and it was one of the toughest places I ever put my boat in to fish."

From an exposure standpoint, Pittsburgh is making out very well on TV. From a fishing standpoint, it is hard to make lemonade from this lemon.

SIX

Hooking Viewers

Maybe more bothersome than this genteel vs. barbaric
argument of what fishing is or should be is the notion
of televised fishing. It seems too many people are
more interested in watching than doing.

—USATODAY.COM WRITER JEFF ZILLGITT

Sunday, July 31, 2005: The Launch

Less people are gathered at Point State Park than in previous days. Perhaps this is due to the low catch, today's smaller angler field, the fact that local bassheads have already been here once, or other factors.

The crowd is quieter, too, with distinctly less buzz. Missing are the protestors and their "Cruelty" banner, but more individuals brandish poster board signs, especially exhorting Iaconelli and VanDam, and the Yamaha boat with its banner is again weaving back and forth. Many cameras are stuck in the faces of the pros; classic rock music blares between emcee interviews; and sponsor representatives are eagerly handing out hats and noisemakers.

On the promenade steps, four fiftyish men accept free hats from a fellow wearing a Triton jersey and Mercury hat. He skips one, who says, "Hey, how 'bout a hat?"

The Merc guy looks up. "You got a Yamaha hat on!"

"'Cause they gave it to me."

"Well, take it off. Here's a Merc hat."

The Yamaha boat and banner mingles with kayakers, media boats, and other spectator craft on the second morning of the Citgo Bassmaster Classic.

The fellow accepts it and changes hats. Others come over—like fish being lured to bait—and the Merc rep is quickly depleted. He's about twenty feet away when the Yamaha-hat guy yells after him, "Hey! How 'bout a shirt?"

Keith Alan is on David Walker's boat, asking him how he adjusted to bounce back so well from a poor first day. Walker talks in a low voice about fishing conservatively yesterday instead of aggressively the day before. There is no comment from either man about the controversy surrounding water rights and how Jimmy Mize was crowded.

Ironically, a few minutes later Alan advises bassheads on how to avoid interfering with the pros while following them on the water. He closes with the comments, "Don't get too close. . . . Don't cut off an area that they're going to. . . . Please give them their distance. They're fishing for their careers and maybe for $200,000 cash." It's advice that some of the pros might well heed.

Alan moves to the boat of tournament leader Aaron Martens, who looks like he'd avoid all of this hoopla if he could. Referring to the fact that Martens finished second in the 2004 and 2002 Classics, Alan asks about getting the second-place monkey off his back. Martens deflects the issue, saying that he's getting lots of bites although he's never been leading before going into the final day. Then Alan asks whether Martens, a Southern California native, still considers himself a West Coast angler. Revealing a smidgeon about the life of a top pro angler, Martens mentions that he moved to Alabama in December 2004 but still has a California driver's license and is hardly ever in Alabama.

"Aaron Martens, everyone," says Alan, "the 2005 Citgo Angler of the Year, tryin' to git-er-done." He walks off as the speakers immediately crank up the Doobie Brothers' "China Grove."

Next on the mike is the smiling Andre Moore—Dr. Dre, as Alan calls him—who admits that he's glad that now-fiancée Kim Bain didn't turn him down last night. Alan asks, "When did you think to yourself, 'I know it's kinda redneck, but why not propose on the Classic stage?'"

"I got a problem with the redneck thing," says Moore. "It would have been redneck if I'd have done it at a tractor pull."

The fountain begins spewing a geyser at 6:40, just before I get into media boat number 59, which is tied to the seawall along the Monongahela side of the Point. So far, I haven't read or heard of anyone mentioning this, but it was along the lower Monongahela that Meriwether Lewis and William Clark launched a fifty-five-foot-long keelboat on August 31, 1803, which they would take on an eight-thousand-mile, twenty-eight-month journey to the Pacific, doing more hunting than fishing along the way.

That, of course, occurred in what is figuratively the Jurassic era. Imagine telling Lewis and Clark that Pittsburgh would one day spend one-fifteenth of the cost of the Louisiana Purchase to host a sportfishing competition in which people used glossy yellow boats that went seventy miles an hour to catch a precious few small brown fish, and that more people would line the shoreline of the Point to cheer them on, while bodacious music played in the background, than were on hand to see the beginning of their now-celebrated epic expedition.

. . .

The sun is rising above the Allegheny River bridges now. Several dozen boats are away from the wall, including media boats with photographers or video camera operators who are shooting the crowd and the boats of bassheads who will be following and watching the pros. Keeping their distance downriver are two Pennsylvania Fish and Boat Commission law enforcement boats, each with three inflatable PFD–wearing officers in it.

Along the seawall, bassheads are clustered around the leading anglers, especially Iaconelli and VanDam, some getting autographs, others taking pictures, a few holding up signs. VanDam evidently has many family members, friends, or both, here; one of them is holding a sign that says, "KVD Git R' Done," which deflates my Southern lingo theory, since VanDam is from Michigan.

The view from the water shows a homogenous group of perhaps four hundred people, which includes some BASS-ESPN staff, as well as sponsor representatives, media, and friends and family of the pros. Maybe 15 percent of the crowd is female, and likely half of those are family or friends. The other 85 percent is seemingly made up equally of white men who are in the mid-twenties to early thirties age group and men who are forty-five and up. It appears that there are no blacks in the crowd and few if any Asians or Hispanics.

At 6:50, the music is interrupted by Alan, who tries to heighten suspense prior to the sendoff by noting that the pros are getting their weapons "locked and loaded."

"Let's send these guys out with emotion and energy," he adds.

Alan talks briefly to Marty Stone, who, in light of the past few days' results and his twenty-fourth-place standing, shows completely irrational exuberance by claiming that today he's fishing to catch a 5-pounder and a few small ones and "change the whole deal."

Alan tells the anglers to untie from the wall, and the music cranks up the Rolling Stones' "Brown Sugar."

With this song's driving beat, if not the words, freshly assailing everyone's ears, it's perhaps fitting that Alan immediately steals a few seconds from Iaconelli.

"When you ran aground, dude, what happened yesterday?" asks Alan.

"One of the things you always try to do in tournaments," says Iaconelli, "is get to fish that nobody else gets to. I tried to do that yesterday. Bottom line, I'm gonna fish hard, and I'm goin' out to *win this Classic*."

The bassheads crowded around him roar, which is maybe what he wants to help him get further pumped. But the river-facing speakers can be heard better out on the water than along the seawall, and I wonder whether the emphasis on "win this Classic" is actually meant to send a message to his fellow pros.

Show Time

7:00 A.M.

Alan sends the boats out, one by one, in the order of their current standings. This is timed to coincide with ESPN's day 3 coverage, which commences with a live hour-long *BassCenter* that opens with a spectacular overhead panning shot framed perfectly to keep out the show's own stage but to include the fountain, the tip of The Point, parts of the crowd, and myriad boats and white wakes moving up and down the rivers. The beautiful shot is exuberantly accompanied by an introductory voice-over by John Kernan, who exclaims that today someone will be headed to "bass fishing immortality."

That opening is followed and contrasted by a dizzying seventy-second, thousand-cut, rock-tempo, intro-video segment that is sure to get viewers swallowing their grits and gravy quickly and bound to make anyone think that this bass fishing thing is race-car hot and rock-concert cool. All the cameras produce gobs of hook-setting, fish-yanking, boat-racing, crowd-waving, fish-posing, fist-pumping footage to cram into a heart-pumping promo.

As usual, a gesturing, yelling, foot-hopping Iaconelli gets the most video time, followed by Swindle, who points and yells at the camera like he was taunting an opposing player in a football game. There are short-clip nods to Martens, VanDam, Omori, and Horton and microsecond cameo clips of several others, but you can tell who and what they are selling.

The first taped segment shows quick morning comments, recorded moments earlier, from Swindle, Reese, and Iaconelli, each of whom would seem to be trying to outdo one another in pump-it-up verbiage were it not for the fact that they were each recorded separately.

The show turns to brief comments from its field reporters and analysts, and when Shaw Grigsby throws it back to the anchor booth, Byron Velvick is still turned partly away from the camera, gesturing with his right arm to the crowd behind him. People obligingly yell, wave, and lift banners while Velvick exclaims, as if he is surprised, "This is crazy out here!"

On the other side of the set, Jay Kumar and Mark Zona are several notches above excited, as is the smaller group of bassheads gathered behind them, who are whipped up by Zona yelling and Kumar tossing them hats.

What's crazy is that all of this exuberance is not for the fish, the fishing, or most of the fishermen, but for the sake of being part of the entertainment. It's no different than the crowd at a pro football game, fresh from tailgating with their wieners and brewskis.

7:16 A.M.

My media boat is driven by Dean Summerville of Butler, Pennsylvania, an avid bass angler and a member of the Pennsylvania BASS Federation. After the last angler departs, we nose into the seawall on the Monongahela side of the Point and pick up photographer Dave Rentz. He's shooting images of fishing in the downtown area for the Pittsburgh Convention & Visitors Bureau. Then we idle through the no-wake zone.

Rentz is a newcomer to the bass fishing tournament phenomenon and is amazed at how fast the boats go. "I was on a bridge Friday morning and saw one come by," he says. "Then, wham, it was gone in an eye blink."

"Yesterday I had an Associated Press reporter out who was in a bass boat for the first time," says Summerville. "He thought he was going to get seasick." Summerville says he also had Pennsylvania's secretary of tourism in his boat yesterday, members of the Japanese press, and a photographer for the *Pittsburgh Tribune*.

We pass the idle area, and Summerville launches the boat on plane, where we remain for twenty seconds before coming to a stop before the Smithfield Street Bridge, still in downtown Pittsburgh. Ahead, a crowd of boaters is watching Iaconelli, who has a cameraman in his boat. My sense of Iaconelli's self-marketing cunning is such that I wonder, perhaps unfairly, whether Iaconelli stopped here first because he knew that many basshead boats and camera boats would be on top of him, or because this was exactly where he wanted to be fishing. In other words, is this stop for stage effect or fishing strategy?

One of ESPN's live camera–feed boats pulls up next to us. In it are Kim Bain, a boat driver, a cameraman, and a producer who is already on his two-way radio informing the war room that they're on Iaconelli. The cameraman is shoulder-holding a video camera that sports an eighteen-inch-tall white tubelike cylinder that is fastened to the upper back of the camera—the device used for live transmissions.

Suddenly, Iaconelli yanks up his electric motor, rushes to the driver's seat, jumps the boat on plane, and roars away. The motors of about a dozen boats nearby crank up, but they don't need to roar off, as Iaconelli has already stopped and coasted to the shore in front of Station Square, immediately putting his electric motor down and casting along the shoreline working down the river.

7:22 A.M.

There are forty-seven fishermen in this tournament, twenty-five left in the field today, and Iaconelli has already had more TV face time this morning than probably all of the others put together. In fact, right now, thanks to Bain's cameraman, *BassCenter* is showing him live, casting in front of the Sheraton and down toward the Gateway Clipper fleet. Iaconelli's cameraman is in the bow with him, his lens almost in Iaconelli's face as the angler casts, then gets on his knees to pitch his lure under mooring ropes.

BassCenter cuts to a three-minute canned segment of Iaconelli commenting on winning the Classic in August 2003, accompanied by footage from that event. As Iaconelli's extraordinary luck—or good judgment—would have it, he hooks a bass alongside the Clipper fleet's *Majestic* while Bain's cameraman is rolling and the segment is in progress.

We're close enough to see the catch happen and hear him scream, "Yeahhhhhh!"

Reporter Kim Bain, kneeling, provides a live television update while Mike Iaconelli fishes behind her on the Monongahela River in downtown Pittsburgh.

"Nice going, Mike!" one of the bassheads yells. Several people cheer.

But after unhooking the bass and pointing it to the camera lens, boasting, "Seven twenty-five and I've got one in the boat!" Iaconelli measures it and unceremoniously dumps it overboard. A short.

At 7:29, Bain's boat moves closer and is positioned so that the cameraman can shoot Bain in the foreground and Iaconelli, now casting behind the stern of the *Majestic*, in the background. We're close enough to take a photo that includes both of them. Moments later, she has the mike in hand and is providing a live thirty-second update on Iaconelli's progress.

7:35 A.M.

We move up the Monongahela, stopping at the head of a bridge pier being fished by Gary Klein, who has a lone spectator boat watching him and is accompanied only by an observer.

Four minutes later, Iaconelli goes flying by at full throttle on his way upriver.

"You've got to watch him," warns Summerville. "He'll run right into you."

Seconds later, a group of spectator boats roars by as if a race is on.

Shortly afterward, Robbie Floyd comes up in an ESPN camera boat for a live update for *BassCenter*. He reports that Klein, who finished second behind Iaconelli in the Classic two years ago—the same year that he was shot at—has yet to catch a fish this morning, and that there's been a lot of boat traffic and boat wakes along this section of river.

As far as I can tell, the postlaunch boat traffic he's referring to belongs to Iaconelli, his basshead followers, and ESPN's camera and media boats.

7:48 A.M.

We have moved upriver below Lock and Dam 2, whose green light switches to red just as we arrive, indicating that we'll have to wait awhile to enter. Presumably, Iaconelli, other pros, and a flotilla of bassheads are in the lock and headed farther upriver, since we have not seen them on the run here.

The hair was standing up on our heads during the ride here, and the wind whipped around my ears, making the sound of a large flag flapping in a gale, as Summerville had the yellow Triton skimming along at sixty-five miles an hour until we hit a speedbump in the guise of a boat wake, and he dropped it back to sixty. People on the bank, who probably could not tell our boat from that of a contestant, waved.

Fishing midriver below the dam is Davy Hite, and nearby below him is Stacey King. Behind King on the high banks loom several roller coasters in Kennywood Park. Their precipitous drop gives credence to the thrill-ride reputation that was partly responsible for designating this 107-year-old fun site as a National Historic Landmark.

Across the Monongahela and slightly below Kennywood in North Braddock, the shoreline is dwarfed by the Edgar Thomson Works steel mill, which on this morning is discharging five smoke plumes straight up into the air. It was on August 22, 1875, that the new Andrew Carnegie–owned Edgar Thomson Works discharged its first steel-production smoke plumes, as its new Bessemer Converter began production of an order of two thousand rails and led America into the age of steel. For decades, this mill, and others in Pittsburgh, ran around the clock 365 days a year, employing many thousands of tough workers and supplying the steel that built much of America.

Such trivia is probably no more on anyone's mind, however, than are the trials and adventures of Lewis and Clark.

After a short while, Hite puts a fish into the boat, drawing cheers from nearby bassheads. Like Klein, Hite has an observer but no cameraman, although there are six spectator boats nearby, one of which contains three men, two of them lying back in foldable field chairs.

Someone tells us that Hite, who appears to be using a crankbait, had previously caught a keeper, so he now has two in the livewell. Summerville finds that interesting because he was here the other day with an ESPN cameraman who was filming Rick Clunn.

"Clunn spent two days up here fishing real fast with crankbaits and topwater plugs in shallow water and didn't catch a keeper," he says. "But I was sitting in deeper water, and I saw three or four fifteen- to sixteen-inch smallmouths breaking around us. Clunn never saw it. Of course, I couldn't say anything."

8:01 A.M.

Sitting in the boat, I have from time to time been calling my wife, Sandy, to get an update on what ESPN has been reporting on television. Now, one minute after *BassCenter* has concluded, and as ESPN is beginning four hours of live Classic coverage hosted by Tommy Sanders from the stage atop the convention center, she informs me that they're reporting that at least three of the leaders—Martens, Iaconelli, and VanDam—have not caught a keeper yet.

The circle of information and technology at play here is pretty astounding—and amusing. I am on the Monongahela, talking by wireless phone to Sandy in New York, who is watching a live broadcast of an event in which update reports are being made by people in camera boats near me on the same river in Pittsburgh.

Those people are in communication with ESPN's production brain trust a few miles away in the convention center, who know exactly which anglers have caught bass and where, and are televising updates every half hour. The updates are being beamed twenty-two thousand miles into space, where a satellite is catching them and sending them back to my home television, which is being watched by my wife, who is talking to me via my cell phone.

Certainly, television producers use this technology network all the time at football games, baseball games, car races, and the like. And how many times have you seen someone on his cell phone, standing behind a reporter and waving at the camera because whoever the person is talking to is watching the event and telling him that he is on camera?

But what's so special about ESPN employing modern technology here is that the players in this event are not on a relatively small field or a short track. They're scattered over nearly ninety miles of water. No spectator is in the "stadium" watching the entire event unfold. According to Jill Frederickson, it is "definitely the largest thing that we cover."

ESPN has three production centers in Pittsburgh, one at the convention center, one at Mellon Arena, and one at Point State Park, staffed by more than 250 personnel. Every hour a courier boat visits the roving camera boats, as well as those of pro anglers who have cameramen with them for the entire day, and picks up their current videotapes. Tapes are transferred at a dock or a launch ramp to a person who drives them to the convention center, where they are given to a courier who brings them into the war room. There they get reviewed on dozens of monitors in production trailers while technicians look for the best clips to show as highlights, the objective being to get footage into production and on the air as soon as possible.

Tommy Sanders puts his finger on the significance of the changes when he comments, "In most of the years gone by, you had to wait for the weigh-in to see anything. Now we've got technology that allows us to comment on it like we were watching a ballgame over at Heinz Field."

However, I am still wondering what would prevent me from yelling out to Davy Hite, "Hey, Davy, ESPN just reported that John Doe has caught four keepers on a white soft plastic jerkbait along the shoreline." Which might send Hite to the banks with a similar lure, something he may not have done otherwise, whereupon he limits out with a few larger fish than he'd previously been catching and I—and ESPN—have actually influenced the outcome by putting out information that contestants would not otherwise have but which theoretically could be relayed to them.

What's at stake for the winner—two hundred grand, the value of future endorsements, and solidifying a professional fishing career—is plenty of incentive to try to get information you wouldn't otherwise have. Obviously, these factors have already affected the more mundane question about sportsmanship. Ask Jimmy Mize.

On a deeper issue, the potential exists for the Classic, and perhaps the final day of other major bass fishing tournaments covered by ESPN, to be radically changed. The game would be altered from being a situation where the pros don't necessarily know what the others are doing to one in which they could all be aware of this. It would be like in NASCAR, where each driver always knows where he is in the field and what his fellow drivers are doing, either because he can see them or because he has a crew telling him.

The question is, might the evolution and use of technology result in taking some of the skill out of the bass fishing competition in order to enhance its television appeal and make it more viewer friendly, like a game played on a smaller field?

Part of the attraction in bass fishing and in other such contests is the ability to find bass and, when found, to use the right lures and methods to catch them. On a given day, one person is always a little bit better or luckier than the others at putting this all together. But if, on a given day, outside technology allows everyone to know where and how one or two individuals are having the most success, then hasn't the playing field been artificially leveled? Haven't you given the knowledge of one angler to all of his fellow anglers?

It is not apparent that any of the spectators gathered here are clued in to what is going on elsewhere, but, surely, I am not the only person to have the idea to call someone who is in front of a TV set. And, from time to time, some of these spectators are talking on their cell phones. Why couldn't a basshead following Hite call a basshead friend who is following VanDam to get an idea of what he's up to? A group of guys could get together and form their own private cell phone reporting team, if only for the novelty of it.

And at the risk of getting a little too deep into paranoia or *Mission Impossible*–like espionage fantasies, is there some other way to intercept and rechannel information transmissions? Like sending it to a wristwatch, or sonar, or an iPod, or a spectator who flashes Morse code signals. Yes, that requires a number of conspirators, many people are watching, and there will be an observer, a cameraman, or a co-angler present. Still, there's been less sophisticated cheating in bass tournaments, including BASS events, before.

8:17 A.M.

We move downriver to the Rankin Bridge, where leader Aaron Martens is working one of the upstream piers with a dropshot rig and a four-inch worm. About this time, Tommy Sanders and Mark Menendez are in danger of turning the Bassmaster Classic television coverage into the Mike Iaconelli show, as the "brash and confident" pro, as Sanders calls him, is all over the beginning of their day 3 footage.

The anti-brash Martens, as we arrive, is repeatedly casting from the bow, as his accompanying cameraman follows his every movement lest he miss Martens setting the hook and landing that all-important bass.

Eight spectator boats are 100 to 150 feet away, being kept in

With a cameraman virtually in his face, and first place at stake, Aaron Martens fishes a bridge on the Monongahela River.

position by one of the occupants manipulating the bow-mounted electric motor. When the bassheads talk to each other, it is in a whisper, and things are dead quiet except for the occasional *whop-whop* sound of car tires rolling across the bridge up above. "It's like golf," observes Summerville, then chuckles, "redneck golf, with the whooping and hollering."

Soon there is something to whoop about, as Martens puts a fish in his boat, and five bassheads, all in one large Crestliner cruiser, cheer while three others in a nearby white bass boat exchange high fives. Martens measures the fish and puts it in his livewell.

"Yeah!" shouts one of the bassheads. "That's what I'm talkin' about!"

At 8:20, Martens's cameraman gets into another boat to take footage of Martens from outside the boat. Acting as the observer as well as a cameraman, he has already punched the news into his BassTrakk, which soon causes Tommy Sanders to note that Martens is unofficially back in the lead, after having fallen out of the lead to VanDam, who already caught a keeper.

The unofficial standings now show VanDam in second and Swindle in third, each having put one keeper in his livewell. But instead of showing some footage of either Martens or VanDam at this time, the producers drop in twenty-two seconds of past-event footage of what Sanders calls a "demonstrative" Iaconelli screaming, cavorting, and screaming some more.

8:33 A.M.

Kevin VanDam and an entourage of twelve or so boats have arrived at the other pier on this bridge. VanDam is watching the bridges and moving from one to another every time he sees that a bridge pier has had twenty or more minutes of rest, which is difficult at times as many of the anglers are stopping to fish these piers.

It is likely that VanDam will know if Martens catches a keeper, and vice versa, thanks to the reaction from spectators.

At 8:38, VanDam's engine comes to life, and he quickly shoots upriver. Three boats immediately do likewise, and within fifteen seconds, ten or twelve more follow, creating a bevy of roostertails as they rapidly fade in the distance.

Left in the exodus is the camera boat of Robbie Floyd, who soon holds his mike up to do a live report. His update was preceded by one from Kim Bain, who is upriver, where Davy Hite has caught a third keeper and unofficially jumped into third place. Interestingly, Bain is shot by the cameraman from such a low angle that all that is visible behind her is a backdrop of treetops and blue sky.

Because the producers didn't want to show the world exactly where Hite was? Or because they didn't want the dam, the roller coasters, or the smoky plumes of the mill works in the shot?

8:53 A.M.

We've run downtown so that Dave Rentz can take photos of anglers with the city skyline in the background. Gary Klein is under the Smithfield Street Bridge, where Iaconelli started out this morning. We watch him for about ten minutes before he heads upriver, then we motor around the Point. Suddenly, we hear a siren and look back to see a PFBC boat on plane, blue lights flashing, bringing a non-Classic bass boater to a halt.

We accelerate and head up the Allegheny, crashing into a few boat wakes that jar my kidneys and make me wonder how the pros manage to pee with all of this attention focused on them.

At 9:06, we are up near the South Shore Marina, which provides a terrific view of Pittsburgh on both sides of the Allegheny. Terry Scroggins, with a cameraless observer in his boat and no entourage, is fishing in open water near the downstream side of the marina's dock. We stay about eighty yards upriver of him so that Rentz, with long lens, can photograph Scroggins and the Pittsburgh skyline and the yellow-painted 16th Street Bridge, which are nicely bathed in light. From a distance, to the naked eye, the bass boat looks small by comparison to the large cabin cruisers and pontoon boats docked on the outside of the marina.

About thirty yards above us is a white PFBC cabin cruiser with the word "Enforcement" on its port side and carrying four brown-uniformed officers, one of whom has binoculars trained on the Classic boat downriver. Across the Allegheny along the bank, several kayakers paddle downriver. A pro's boat whizzes past us, also headed downriver, followed by Kim Bain's camera boat, which stops briefly to watch Scroggins and then departs. Both are probably headed to the Monongahela.

9:30 A.M.

Jeff Reynolds, who finished yesterday in fourth place and is flying under the radar of attention and publicity, is now fishing the upstream edge of a 16th Street Bridge pier. Evidently the only top-ten angler not on the Mon, he has a cameraman in his boat and one spectator boat nearby. Reynolds has yet to boat a keeper, and four minutes later, he and the spectator boat depart.

At 9:39, we move downriver to the Roberto Clemente Bridge just above PNC Park to photograph Gary Klein, but he soon picks up and motors slowly past us, smiling and cupping his fingers into a goose egg pattern. When he stops at the 9th Street Bridge, near the towering Alcoa Corporate Center building, we move up above him.

Klein, who ranks fourth in total appearances in the Citgo Bassmaster Classic (twenty-three) and second in number of appearances without a win (behind Roland Martin), has an observer in the boat, a hatless man in a white shirt who sits in the pedestal seat on the rear deck, watching. There are no spectator or camera boats accompanying him.

From a distance, however, Klein is being watched by many eyes. There are two-hundred-some people along the shore and on the outside deck of the convention center, which is directly across the river. They are waiting for the doors of the Outdoors Expo to open at ten o'clock and probably cannot tell who they're watching several hundred yards away near the north shore.

But Klein is perfectly situated for attention from ESPN's cameras on the convention center roof, where, at this moment, they're delivering live morning coverage from the outdoor set occupied by host Tommy Sanders and analyst Mark Menendez. By now, Menendez has gotten rid of his yellow Labrador retriever, Barkley, who inexplicably sat next to him earlier in a hokey move that required Menendez to keep his left hand under the table to hold onto Barkley's leash.

In fact, at this moment, ESPN is returning from a commercial break with a roof-angle live shot of Klein working the bridge pier, allowing Tommy Sanders—who excels at small talk, ad libbing, showing relevance, and smoothing over glitches—to talk about Klein and his history and how important the bridge piers are to this event. Klein gets seventy-five seconds of attention throughout this.

The producers immediately follow with earlier video of Kevin VanDam, who has just caught a second keeper and is unofficially leading Aaron Martens by 1 ounce. It is at the end of this segment that I happen to call Sandy on the cell phone.

"They said that VanDam is now in first place," she reports. "They just showed earlier video of him, and some guy in a red shirt just gave an update from the water. Are you still out?"

"Yeah, we're almost finished, though. We're over on the Allegheny watching Gary Klein."

"They're showing him right now. They showed him a few minutes ago, too, in the same place. By a bridge."

"Do you see another boat there?" I ask.

"Yeah, but now they're coming in tight on Klein."

"That was us in the other boat. Had to be. We're the only boat near him, just upriver."

In fact, while Menendez is talking about the high number of non-keepers that Klein has caught the past two days, Sanders is looking over his shoulder down at Klein.

"Come on, Gary, do it for us right now," he urges. "Catch one for us right now. Catch a keeper. Wouldn't that be great? Let's take a look at Gary Klein, the most appearances, as we said, in a Classic without a win. Gary Klein, super frustrated in New Orleans where he finished second to Mike Iaconelli."

The screen shows a list of anglers who appeared in the Classic without a win, with Roland Martin first and Klein second, contradicting what Sanders has just said. He probably meant that Klein had the most appearances without a win of anyone fishing in this Classic.

The cameras are no longer on Klein at 9:50, when he catches a nonkeeper. As we prepare to return to Point State Park, I notice Klein's observer dutifully recording the catch on BassTrakk, which transmits that information to ESPN's production headquarters downstairs in the building across the river, which in turn relays it up to the roof and the set of Sanders and Menendez—who have gone to a break while a commercial airs touting ESPN's X Games.

Television Afterword

Watching tapes of the entire live Classic coverage on this day, I am struck by the over-the-top exuberance and the frenetic cheerleading of the *BassCenter* and *Loudmouth Bass* crews broadcasting from Point State Park, which contrasts markedly with the measured exuberance of Tommy Sanders, who is by far the best of the on-camera talent. I'm also struck by the emotional tone of their production, which contrasts with the more tempered and diversified show emanating from the convention center roof.

At one point, when reporting on the unofficial and therefore hypothetical changes in standings, Byron Velvick shouts, "It's a war zone out there!" This ridiculous wrestling-match type of analogy is insensitive in light of current events around the world and the relationship of people fishing for extraordinary amounts of money to people who are risking their lives for freedom, being paid little, and sacrificing much in the process.

Can Velvick naturally be that excited about this contest? Is he hoping to incite the few bassheads who have stuck around the set? Or is a producer saying into his earpiece, "Energy, Byron, we need energy. Smile. Show how excited you are."

Many of ESPN's announcers—Kernan and Sanders, in particular—have called the Citgo Bassmaster Classic the "Super Bowl of bass fishing" so many times that I'm wondering whether ESPN has a deliberate mission to ingrain this into the minds of the public, the media, and, most important, the major marketers. I wonder whether the NFL minds.

Thanks to BassTrakk, ESPN has an excellent handle on how the final field of twenty-five is doing, although, again, this is based on observers' estimated weights, which, in an event where the fish are so small and in which ounces will separate finishers, is prone to inaccuracies. There is also a lag in getting the *BassCenter* production team updated; each time the team members appear, their standings chart is not as current as the one that was shown moments earlier by Sanders's production team. And while it seemed like the producers crammed a lot of commercials into the last hour of coverage, occasionally throughout the production they provided good graphics in the form of underwater simulations and map tracking of the places visited by some of the anglers.

There is proportionately much less of Iaconelli after the opening half-hour of *BassCenter*, perhaps because he hasn't registered a keeper all morning and has nothing to scream or dance about. Much more time and video are later devoted to Martens and VanDam, accompanied by short segments on some of the pros who move up and down the unofficial leader board. By late in the morning, George Cochran has caught several keepers and leaps from eighth to an unofficial second-place standing. He seems to be in a position to win, yet while the announcers talk about Cochran, they show virtually no footage of him from this morning or the two previous fishing days, instead filling in with clips from his two prior Classic victories.

Cochran started the day in eighth place and doesn't have a cameraman with him, but I wonder whether he is not among the personalities that ESPN favors. Quiet, unemotional, and older than most of the other Classic anglers, Cochran was part of the still-unraveled water rights dispute with Jimmy Mize yesterday. No announcer has said anything about the dispute today; ESPN probably doesn't care about it or looks upon the issue as a blemish that the producers would rather not highlight.

Just two weeks earlier, however, Cochran won another tough fishing event, the *other* Super Bowl of bass fishing, the Forrest L. Wood Championship, owned by FLW Outdoors, a fact that Sanders carefully references in generic terms, never stating the name of the event, the location, or the fact that winning paid Cochran $500,000, which is currently the largest first-place award in professional bass fishing and $300,000 *more* than he would get if he won the Classic this year. Furthermore, Cochran stated that in 2006 he would fish only the FLW tournaments, thereby snubbing BASS-ESPN and its new eleven-event professional series.

No wonder he doesn't have an ESPN cameraman with him. Perhaps the ESPN brain trust is desperately hoping that he does not win.

The segment that is least about the contest but most interesting is a live interview that Jerry McKinnis conducts at the Outdoors Expo with the parents of Aaron Martens. Martens's father tells about taking his son backpacking at an early age and how Aaron took to outdoor activities while very young. His mother talks about fishing with him for crappies from the shore, where he saw bass fishermen racing by in big boats and said he wanted to do that, and about the two later winning many bass fishing tournaments together.

A mother and a son successfully fishing together for fun and competition is almost as rare as finding a gay black man fishing a bass tournament in Georgia. Is that not a story?

Watching the interview, I realize that one of the things that's missing in ESPN's production is more insight into the pros and their lives, personalities, and backgrounds—insight that comes from other people, rather than strictly from the pros talking about themselves. It should be something that viewers can relate to their own stories and that gives them reason to care about the performance of certain anglers, which in turn provides a motive for continuing to watch other than to learn about the technicalities of catching bass. Almost everything that I've seen ESPN do along these lines is either feel-good or superficial, strictly related to fishing performance and competitive attitude, and doesn't come from other sources. ESPN certainly has the broadcast production technicalities mastered—but not the journalism.

Ironically, earlier in the weekend, ESPN showed a compelling feature on the likable Menendez, who was deathly sick with viral meningitis a year earlier. He got better with the assistance of his then new spouse and won a fishing tournament while still weak and recovering.

Many of the forty-seven pros have been virtually invisible on ESPN's thirteen hours of Classic-related coverage. Yet some of the lesser known ones, who are in this event for the first or second time and don't have much of a track record or accomplishments—particularly the Federation representatives—have achieved their greatest dream in sportfishing just by making it to this event. They're not screaming when they catch bass, they're not yelling at the cameras, they're not dancing in their boats, and, thus, they are not getting noticed.

Of course, features have to be planned in advance, and these individuals may bomb in Pittsburgh or may never be heard from again after this event, so the producers take a risk by investing prepro-duced features in them. But in turning their lenses away from these contestants, they are probably overlooking some compelling stories and interesting personalities.

Another problem is the coziness of the analysts to the subjects being analyzed. Several times, Sanders looks to Menendez to provide some insight into what makes certain anglers tick, but Menendez, though level-voiced and knowledgeable about bass fishing competi-tion, is not a journalist and too often centers his comments on each competitor's drive to win, which we can take for granted, but it reveals nothing and does not advance a storyline. He treats the pros gently (as do Grigsby, Velvick, and Zona), undoubtedly because he competes with all of them in tournaments, is a fellow pro staff team member with some of them, and is friends with many of them.

This deference is especially obvious in the case of Iaconelli, when Sanders offers Menendez an opportunity to opine and provide per-spective about the controversial angler. Iaconelli is intensely disliked by some fellow pros, many bassheads, and others in the fishing indus-try, but Menendez tap dances around the subject without offering his personal view or even summarizing others' opinions. This, and the general performances of Grigsby, Velvick, and Zona, makes the broadcast team akin to cheerleaders.

The state of Pittsburgh's bass fishery is also a story, and ESPN has done less with this than it could, especially given the twelve hours that is has devoted to Classic coverage. The announcers and the analysts are all correct in pointing out what a tough competition this is and how close the final results are likely to be, but they often mention what a great bass fishery there is in Pittsburgh because of all the undersized fish caught. No one disputes this. Yet no one would do a marketing campaign on the theme: "Come to our lake, we've got lots of undersized bass."

Nor do they bring in a Pennsylvania Fish and Game Commission representative to explain what's happening here, why the fishery is the way it is, or what the future holds.

The hosts, the analysts, and the reporters all bend over backward not to insult the city that has paid for this event. In doing so, they avoid an underlying truth: no matter how many small bass are caught, forty-seven of the "world's best bass fishermen" have landed just 170 keepers in the past two days, which is 1.8 per person per eight-hour day, proving what locals Lou Anderson and Wayne Lykens said earlier in the week: right now, the bass fishing in Pittsburgh stinks.

As a result, every viewer who knows anything about bass fishing recognizes the silliness of grown men on TV practically jumping out of their seats in excitement about the course of events. Although there may be something fitting about these results—even the best bass anglers do no better than the common guy under the toughest conditions—and while there is much merit to having a tight, competitive event, it's rather pitiful to see that all of the excitement is theatrically produced. All of the energy in the television coverage of the Classic is staged. The excitement is not created by the contest or the current standings; only production techniques and the raised voices of the announcers—based on estimated weights and unofficial standings, no less—create an illusion of excitement.

I'll bet that when producers at ESPN in Bristol were first handed the assignment of televising a bass tournament, they groused about how boring it would be to watch someone fish. Then they resolutely figured out how to turn their production into a spectacle and fit it into the same overheated mold that is applied to other sports telecasts. I'll bet that few of the main producers have ever fished or are fans of fishing. Not knowing what is at the heart of anglers' passion, they devise an agenda of jazzing up the production to wow the viewers, molding it like so many other television programs that focus on the sizzle and forget the steak, while talking heads blather about the contrived madness.

The ultimate in staging is yet to come this evening, of course, at the weigh-in. But that's a slightly different beast—part revival meeting, part pep rally, part rock concert, part wrestling match. Here, ESPN is trying to hook viewers, keep them on the line, then release them in the hopes that they'll bite again for the grand finale this evening. Because what's at stake is the number of viewing eyeballs and the future televised advertising value of this event. That's where the money is.

Many of the pros who are competing in this Classic will also be in the 2006 Classic, which will be held at Florida's Lake Tohopekaliga, a well-respected bass fishing location. Something tells me that at this event, one or more of the pros will be in front of the media or the weigh-in crowd saying, "My first fish in the livewell today weighed more than my total catch in Pittsburgh last year." Or, "Man, you don't know how good this feels after last year."

I wonder how the approach to the bad-fishing, bad-locale subject might differ if ESPN did not own this event but was covering it from a journalistically pure angle and had paid for the rights to televise it. Would one of its analysts then have the nerve to question why this event was held in such a poor bass fishing venue?

Speaking of nerve, what this team of cheerleaders needs is a Howard Cosell–like persona, or at least a person with his "tell it like it is" approach to sports. Someone with the sense and the cojones to ask tough questions of Cassius Clay. No less a sports programming icon than Roone Arledge, the chairman of ABC News (part of the Disney empire now) called the acerbic, loved-and-hated-but-often-dead-on Cosell, who did *Monday Night Football* games for many years, "the garlic that makes the stew work." That's what ESPN needs here, some garlic.

Another thing bugs me. In spite of the reality of the fishing situation in Pittsburgh, couldn't ESPN have turned the volume and the rhetoric down a bit without sacrificing viewers? Was it really necessary to pump so much hot air into this balloon as a smoke screen for 1.8 small keepers per person per day?

My guess is that the Citgo Bassmaster Classic will not be coming to such an unimpressive small-bass venue again. Big fish impress. Big fish sell. Look at any outdoor magazine and try to find a photo of someone holding up a 12-inch bass, unless it's a kid or the fish has some deformity of note.

To showcase competitive bass fishing, ESPN needs more anglers catching more keepers. More bass that impress. More bass that producers can put into a dizzying, ass-kicking, hook-setting, flopping-in-the-boat, rock-tempo'd montage. One way to do that is to go to places where the fish will be spawning, which is how it will be in Florida next February—although that is not without some pitfalls.

The future lies in having television events that *more people* will watch, which attracts the event and television production sponsors who pay for this high level of coverage. If ESPN has to do it by having announcers become actors, it's got a problem. I'll be shocked if ESPN brings this event back to Pittsburgh anytime soon.

Nevertheless, ESPN has done a terrific job of showcasing Pittsburgh. Well, some of Pittsburgh. We haven't seen any views of industrial sites along the rivers, like Neville Island or the Edgar Thomson steel mill. Nor have we seen many views of pros fishing one of the few places that have been productive besides bridges—discharge pipes, which Jay Kumar says on camera are sending sewer effluent into the river. He's right, but, come to think of it, I never saw one of the health department's orange warning flags at these pipes this week. Perhaps that's because there was no rain other than the thunderstorm on Tuesday evening, or perhaps it's because having the warning flags down would be good for the image and would reduce questions from curious out-of-area media.

Yet we have seen many, many bridges, often bathed in delicate low morning light; lots of carefully tailored overhead views of the Point and downtown regions and the water around them; long-lens views of attractions like Heinz Field and PNC Park and the Duquesne Incline; and tight, nicely lit scenes of boats and people fishing.

As a friend who's an avid bass angler and a businessman, and who watched most of the televised coverage, commented, "Whatever Pittsburgh paid, they got their money's worth."

SEVEN

Fulfilling a Dream

This is the perfect championship event for one reason.
The guy who fishes the absolute best will win this tournament.
That may not be true if we go to a place like Toho where a
guy who fishes the best tournament may end up second
because a guy catches a 10-pounder on him.

—FOUR-TIME BASSMASTER CLASSIC WINNER RICK CLUNN

The Weigh-In

Fishing concludes at three o'clock and the weigh-in show is supposed to begin at three thirty, but at two o'clock people are already bunched up outside the entrance doors to Mellon Arena, waiting. There are quite a few women here, one of whom, in front of me, wears a sleeveless light-blue top with the words "Bass Fly Tourney" on the back and is accompanied by a man wearing a white T-shirt that says, "Booyah Bait Co." and a white BASS-patched baseball cap covered with autographs. In front of him is a paunchy fellow wearing a black messageless shirt and a gray Bass Pro Shops hat that is equally covered with autographs. Near him are a tall man wearing a red sponsor jersey and another in a white T-shirt, the back of which depicts a large multihooked bass plug and the words "Bite Me."

At 2:45, the arena is far more crowded—and festive—than yesterday. Its semidarkness is punctuated by well-lit signs for BASS and the Citgo Bassmaster Classic over the stage, bright camera lights in front of Ron Franklin, the lighted tower that shows the day 2 standings, and a string of plastic fish-shaped lights attached to the lower railings.

A BASS staffer checks my credentials and ushers me around the stands and onto the infield, where I join a mob of bassheads in the pit, hoping to take the pulse of the most fanatic of them. Someone grabs my arm and says, "Ken, I want to introduce you to my friend."

It's super basshead Ed Matuizek, who's wearing his Clemente Pirates shirt and a white hard hat with an American flag on the front. He's also carrying the four-foot-long green bass pillow that he got Iaconelli to hug on Friday.

"This is Ron Mateer."

Mateer, trim-looking and a little shorter than Matuizek, has his sunglasses tucked into the top of a white T-shirt, partially obscuring the words "God Bless America," which circle around two American flags.

"I've waited all my life for this to come to Pittsburgh," says Mateer, a lifetime BASS member.

Matuizek also has a VIP Pass tag hanging around his neck.

Super basshead Ed Matuizek, right, with his bass pillow and friend Ron Mateer.

"Do me a favor?" he asks. "Take a picture of the two of us?"

I take a photo of them, smiling broadly and horizontally holding the pillow, which, as I check it quickly afterward in the digital camera window, looks like they're holding up one hell of a big fish.

I notice now that Matuizek's hard hat also has BASS and Steelers decals on it, and I suspect that he's the only person here with some type of headgear other than a baseball cap.

"Nice hat, Ed."

"I'm gonna try to get Ray Scott to wear it."

Nearby, standing along the railing that separates the pit from the entrance track, is a fortyish couple who are taking everything in. They're Mark and Joni Pearly, who live three and a half hours away in central Pennsylvania. He is wearing a logo- and messageless red-collared sport shirt, and she's wearing a pink top covered by a but-toned pink shirt. Except for their neck tags and his Berkley-logoed cap, they could be at a company picnic or the church social.

"You having a good time?" I ask.

"This is the best vacation ever," says the attractive, wide-smiling Joni.

"Get out!" I blurt, thinking she's pulling my leg.

But she talks about the Outdoors Expo and the weigh-in cere-mony in glowing terms, convincing me that she means it. "You can interact with these people that you see on TV," she adds. "He has the TV on every Saturday. These guys are on our television every week."

"Have you ever been to a Bassmaster Classic before?"

"No," says Mark, a contractor. "But we've been to a few divisional events."

"We like the people involved in this," adds Joni.

I turn to Mark. "Is this something you'd want to do? Be a profes-sional bass fisherman?"

He shrugs.

"I would like him to," pipes up an enthusiastic Joni. "But it's a pretty tough job I think."

Walking around the pit, I encounter the three Pennsylvanians I met on Friday night who were guests of Earl Bentz's at the Triton party:

life member Ed Guydon, and his pals Eran Boyer and Roberto DeJesus. Mid-thirtyish, all three are Federation members and they fish bass tournaments.

"How're you enjoying this?" I ask.

"We're lovin' it!" says Ed emphatically. "It ranks way up there. This morning we were down at the Point at the end of the wall, and every one of these guys went right by me."

"Yeah," says DeJesus, "these guys are all very friendly and approachable. They'll talk to you. That's great. And Pittsburgh is a great town."

Nearby, facing the stage, are two boys standing by themselves and dwarfed by the older, taller crowd. They are Nick Argenas, thirteen, and his brother Aaron, ten, of Pittsburgh. Nick wears a white Skeeter Boats T-shirt that bears the words "Eat. Sleep. Fish," plus two stickers, the larger of which says, "Where is Fish Fishburne?" Both are wearing black baseball caps stitched with the words "BASS—ESPN Outdoors" on the front and a BASS patch on the side.

"You fellows do any bass fishing?" I ask.

Pittsburghers Aaron, left, and Nick Argenas in the VIP area at the final weigh-in.

"We do all kinds of fishing," says Nick, "with our uncle and our mom."

Mom, he says, is up in the stands. They could only get two passes to the pit.

I take a photo of the brothers, who smile readily.

"What do you think of this event so far?"

"It's awesome," says Nick, as Aaron nods.

"Would you like to be a bass fishing pro?"

"That'd be really cool," beams Nick.

I walk away, wondering whether maybe I'll see one of these boys in the Classic one day, an emcee announcing to the crowd, "Back in 2005, Nick and Aaron's mother took them to the Citgo Bassmaster Classic in Pittsburgh, and that's when they knew they wanted to be professional anglers."

The Argenas brothers probably thought it was cool a few minutes later when the Jumbotron kicked to life as *Star Wars*–theme music played and block-lettered words scrolled into the star-filled universe, "Pittsburgh is crumbling under the attack of anglers from all over the galaxy. . . . Evil is Everywhere. Lord Darth Vader. . . . A small band of Jedi Knights fight to maintain peace on the lakes."

What lakes? Which evil? Crumbling?

It's hokey, but it gets everyone's attention, and there's much cheering and noisemaker banging, followed by current host Steve "Lurch" Scott doing some crowd-revving and motherhood-and-apple-pie shtick, including asking veterans in the crowd to stand, which produces a huge ovation. At the singing of "God Bless America," a huge flag unfurls over the stage, after which someone in the upper seats screams, "Ray Scott for president!"

I'm standing in the less-crowded back of the pit, just below the photographer's section, taking in the almost surreal production. Comedian Henry Cho is onstage, perhaps the only Korean American in the arena and certainly one of the few Asian descendants here who is not a member of the Japanese media besides Takahiro Omori. Born in Knoxville, Tennessee, Cho bills himself as an Asian with a Southern accent but seems to have no special connection to the fishing fraternity or material that is relevant to the event, and he does not register huge guffaws.

Standing next to me is current Knoxville resident Bob George, one of the more subdued people in the pit, who is not part of the headset-wearing production team. The national account manager for United Cutlery Brands, mid-fortyish George is a native of Pittsburgh who has been a member of BASS since 1978 and used to fish in bass tournaments.

"This blows me away," he says. "The size of the crowd, the environment here, everything. I saw the Steelers win the Super Bowl, but this is unbelievable. This is going to get bigger and bigger."

"Would you like to be a bass pro?" I ask.

"If I had my druthers, I'd love to be a bass pro," answers George, "but I knew early on that I wasn't good enough. I have a buddy who fished with these guys in the early days. The average Joe can look at this, though, and say, 'I can do it.'"

At 3:35, Cho is finished. Off to my right in the back of the pit on his elevated platform, the stage-lit Ron Franklin is talking into the camera. He has a piece of paper in his hand, and ten feet in front of him are two large television monitors at knee level, both showing the rules of the tournament.

Looking around the arena, I notice that above the upper seats, there's a row of black-and-white banners bearing the names of the past Classic winners. There's a banner, too, for Ray Scott. The upper seats in the back of the arena, which is directly above the truck and boat entrance, are virtually empty, but elsewhere the stands are crowded. The arena looks about 80 percent full.

It's 3:42 now, and the crowd is revving up. Onstage, the announcer yells, "Mercury Marine is offering a big prize for the most enthusiastic fan."

The crowd kicks it up a few notches as AC DC's "Thunderstruck" blares.

A Triton-and-Mercury-jerseyed Roland Martin is running on the track around the pit, looking up into the stands. Loads of bassheads stand and yell, wave, and bang noisemakers.

The announcer is talking excitedly, but his words are indistinct because the crowd is getting louder and louder. Martin is jogging now on the other side of the arena, looking into the stands.

Yamaha representative Mike Walker walks by me at this moment, camera in hand and eyes rolled upward. "This is insane," he says.

Right now, this place sounds like a football stadium where fans are lustily cheering for their home team after a last-second, game-winning touchdown against an arch rival.

Martin is in the pit now, his antics being played out on the Jumbotron. The announcer is shouting something that is even less audible than it was before. Then Martin puts his arm around his chosen most enthusiastic fan: pillow-holding, hard-hat-wearing Ed Matuizek!

The decibels are a little lower, and I can now hear the announcer scream, "Roland, bring him on up here."

Then there's Matuizek on the stage, minus the pillow and with hard hat in hand, towering over Michelle Kilburn, Mercury's manager of tournaments and events, who is handing him something and excitedly proclaiming to the arena, "A 9.9 Mercury engine is now all yours."

Matuizek would later describe the Classic weekend as "one of the highlights of my life."

Matuizek and Kilburn are barely off the stage when Ray Scott is at the mike, talking about the growth of BASS and celebrating the work of retiring thirty-four-year employee James "Pooley" Dawson. "Get-It-Done Pooley" Scott calls him.

"No one has ever been to more tournaments than Pooley and me," says Scott. "He secretly convoyed bass boats under the darkness of night for Bassmaster Classics when they were held at mystery lakes. . . . He's fed two hundred fifty people on almost a moment's notice. . . . He's pitched fishing camps in Canada and Mexico. . . . Pooley's eaten lunch with the president of the United States in a small dining room next to the Oval Office."

When Scott presents Pooley with BASS's fourth Outstanding Achievement Award, the fans respond with such fervor that you'd have thought he was Willie Stargell or Franco Harris. One of their own.

Looking un-bassheadlike in a collared white casual shirt and a white driver's cap, Pooley thanks God for sixty-six years of living, which elicits cheers, and also thanks Ray Scott. He reminisces for a few moments before Scott brings up Earl Bentz of Triton. Bentz presents Pooley with a fishing towel signed by all of the Classic anglers, a year's supply of Purolator oil, a bunch of Berkley fishing tackle, twenty cases of Busch beer, and $500 worth of Citgo gas. When he pauses before his next sentence, someone screams, "Hey, Earl, give him a boat!"

The crowd cheers wildly, and Bentz does just that as they tow in a new Triton. The cheering continues for a long time, with an emotional Pooley being placed in the seat of his boat while a portion of the crowd chants, "Pooley, Pooley, Pooley."

This has to be the best moment of the entire Classic.

Shortly after that, Keith Alan, now on stage with the mike, elicits another round of applause for Pooley and says, "That may be one of the most emotional things I've ever seen at a weigh-in."

As far as I can tell, Pooley is the only black person in the arena. This native of civil rights–torn Montgomery, Alabama, who went to work for Scott in the same year that the Supreme Court upheld court-ordered school busing, effectively integrating public schools, is now receiving adulation from homogeneously white bass fishing enthusiasts who don't even know him, is exiting in a glittering bass boat that costs more money than Pooley's annual salary for much of his BASS employment, and is retiring with a pension from Disney, a company ranked 54th in the 2005 Fortune 500.

Only in America.

At four o'clock, the Pittsburgh Color Guard of the National Guard presents the National Anthem, followed by a huge ovation. I have moved up to the stands in the media section off the press room, which is packed with friends and family of the anglers, a few pros, some sponsor representatives, BASS staff, and media.

George Cochran is one of the early anglers to be showcased, being towed into the arena to the rhythm of Fleetwood Mac's "Don't Stop Thinking about Tomorrow." He quickly gets to the scales with five bass that weigh a total of 4 pounds 4 ounces. Catching five keepers is commendable, as Alan notes when he congratulates Cochran for "getting the job done." However, the bass average 13.6 ounces each, producing a total weight that is almost as small as a five-bass limit can be. This would probably be a record if BASS cataloged records for such achievements.

Surprisingly, Alan references a water-rights incident involving Cochran and another angler earlier in the year in a BASS tournament, then mentions that Jimmy Mize suggested that Cochran encroached on Mize's water yesterday and asks, "Why do we keep hearing this about you, George?"

"They're scared of me," says a grinning, nonplused Cochran.

Some bassheads howl at this bold statement.

"What *is* too close?" asks Alan.

"Well, I saw Jimmy about a quarter of a mile away, and I caught four and he didn't catch any yesterday, so it was my fault. But anyhow, there's about six or seven of us that are locking two pools up, and we're fishing milfoil, grass, and weeds. Three of the top twenty-five were there today, and I think all of us caught fish today, but we never really got close to each other. But his camera crew got in the boat with me after I caught four, and I think that's what made him mad."

Some in the crowd laugh, but others jeer. Alan says, "Ouch, man," and sends Cochran off to applause that is light, considering that he's leading in the clubhouse and could be the winner.

Clearly, many of the attending bassheads fish in bass tournaments, they know what is and what is not encroachment, and they suspect that maybe the veteran Cochran did move in on the Classic rookie Mize's water. Also, many of them have watched this event on television before, and they realize that ESPN "stages" it. Alan would not have brought Cochran up early, before nearly all of the other anglers, if he was going to be the winner or even come close to winning, and thereby sacrifice last-minute drama.

Nevertheless, this is the furthest that Alan has ventured away from fluffy questions, and a devil in the back of my head reminds me that Cochran has rebuffed BASS's tournaments in 2006. Although, if he finishes in the top ten today, he will automatically get a berth in the 2006 Classic. Right now, that looks like a certainty.

For the next seventy-five minutes, the weigh-in production crew quickly parades all but six of the field through, interspersing the anglers with promotional theatrics. Dave Wolak, a Classic rookie and the only Pennsylvanian still in the field, weighs two bass and astutely comments that a lack of experience may have been taken over by an excess of enthusiasm. The spike-haired Lurch scoots around the arena doing a promo for Purolator, asking the crowd, "Who wants to be on TV today?" Many people obligingly cheer. Another spike head, Skeet Reese, dubbed the "West Coast style maker" by Alan, is wheeled into the arena to cheers, although he's more subdued today with his modest catch of "two little anchovies."

During a break in which the crowd is being revved up, the long-armed boom camera, which provides an unobstructed view of bassheads in the pit as well as those in the seats, swings along the lower stands to the waves and cheers of the crowd. Then it sweeps up toward the section where I'm sitting and goes right past me. The movement of the camera face and its reaching arm remind me of the long-necked moray eel–like alien in *War of the Worlds*—the one with the oval face that was menacingly seeking Tom Cruise and his daughter in the basement of the field house where they sought refuge. Except that here, everyone waves and cheers at the alien.

Lurch is back in the stands with a lame, drawn-out trivia routine and is followed onstage by a baby-faced Tim Horton, who also caught two keepers. He takes time to suck up to the crowd—the fans in Pittsburgh, he says, "blew away" the fans in all five of the other places where he previously fished in the Classic—and suck up to his sponsors, mentioning half a dozen of them in a blatant self-marketing move. As if his jersey doesn't do enough marketing for him.

Then Chad Morgenthaler thanks his sponsors and the fans and gets a nice hand, but Preston Clark gets a bigger ovation seconds later when he comes to the stage with a video camera in hand and shoots his own memories of the crowd and the arena. "Thanks for making this one of the greatest weeks of my life," he most sincerely tells the crowd, drawing a huge, appreciative ovation.

Then Lurch is under the stage at the livewell tanks, talking about oxygen maintenance and getting two little kids to "scream like Ike." Andre Moore, whose onstage marriage proposal yesterday, we are told by Alan, made *SportsCenter's* Top 10 highlights, weighs in three bass. Edwin Evers grandstands with two of his bass, which are both less than 2 pounds, and takes a long two minutes just to get the fish from the livewell to the scales before they can be weighed and sent down under for some much-needed oxygen. A fishless Stacey King says that Pittsburgh should be called the City of Brotherly Love because the fans have been so good.

Davy Hite comes to the stage with four small bass, which temporarily jumps him to third place. Alan asks how he did it, while the Jumbotron shows tape of him catching bass earlier in the day. Hite, who is sponsored by Berkley, says, "Well, you know I've been fishing a three-inch Berkley Power Tube. The first two days I could fish it really quick, and the fish would react to it. But today I really just had to soak that bait in there. There was not much current at all. But I got it going early."

When I watched Hite before eight o'clock this morning, he was "soaking" a crankbait, and the footage shown on the screen here clearly shows him landing two bass with a bone- or shad-colored shallow-running crankbait in its mouth. Perhaps he was using a Berkley Power Tube, which is a vastly different soft jiglike lure, for the first two days or sometime during the event. But anyone who looked carefully at the big screen—and many of these bassheads would have—could see that Hite was catching keepers on a plug, not a tube.

Professional anglers have often told the media and fishing fans that they were using a sponsor product for tournament (and nontournament) success when they were not using their sponsor's product (lures especially) or not using the particular type of sponsor's product that the sponsor would like to sell. But to do so on the biggest stage, with the truth being shown over your shoulder on the Jumbotron and then later on television, begs for clarification, if only because it is exactly this information—what the successful pros use and where and how they use it—that wannabe pros and adoring bassheads seek. Yet analysts Grigsby and Velvick, who knew where, how, and with what Hite had been fishing today, say nothing. Perhaps not coincidentally, both analysts are sponsored by Berkley or divisions of Berkley.

It's almost five o'clock when Jimmy Mize comes to the scales without a keeper to weigh in, causing a few people in the crowd to sigh in sympathy, realizing the disappointment Mize must feel in having been the first-day leader of the Super Bowl of bass fishing and then not catching a single keeper in the following two days.

Keith Alan brings up the encroachment issue, telling Mize what Cochran said almost an hour earlier and asking for Mize's take on the matter. The resigned Mize, like the fish he did not catch, doesn't rise to the bait.

"I'm not gonna get into that," he says in a low, level voice. "I'm a better man than that."

The crowd cheers and gives him a good hand as he leaves the stage, after which there's a funny pretaped segment shown on the Jumbotron leading up to the Berkley Million Dollar Cast, in which a fan, whose name was drawn earlier by lottery, assisted by Byron Velvick, has one chance to make a perfectly accurate sixty-foot cast for a big payday. The angler has a casting weight to toss, but his effort stops far short of the target because his line seems to be coiled up or to have a knot in it, causing the weight to stop prematurely short. There are groans and laughs from the crowd, and the cameraman tries to stay tight on the caster, but you can see on the Jumbotron that his line looks messed up.

Near five thirty, it's time for the Super Six, who, it turns out, are in the upper arena near the entranceways as spotlights find them during introductions and follow them down to the stage, high-fiving assorted exuberant bassheads along the way. They are Martens, Iaconelli, Van-Dam, Reynolds, Rook, and Swindle, the top six finishers yesterday.

Again, there's a devil in the back of my head suggesting that ordinarily, it would have been the Top Five instead of the Super Six but not for favored son Swindle, who was in sixth place and is also the highest-placed Team Citgo member. Not to mention that the producers know he's got four keepers and is in the hunt.

At about the time that the Super Six, all wearing head mikes, are making their way down to the weigh-in area, the Worldwide Leader in Sports is concluding its television presentation of one spectacle, the quarter-final round of the Alka Seltzer U.S. Open of Competitive Eating, and jumping directly into ninety-minute coverage of the 2005 Citgo Bassmaster Classic.

The program starts with a snappy but less frenetic and more pertinent opening video montage, followed by an arena camera panning over ecstatic bassheads. The familiarly solid voice of Ron Franklin energetically says, "You're looking live inside Mellon Arena in Pittsburgh, Pennsylvania. It is packed to capacity. Not a seat to be had for this final day of competition."

Then Franklin, at his seat in the arena pit, with bass swimming behind him in the cylindrical tank, reviews the standings and narrates video of the leaders fishing during this day, after which he describes the rules of the tournament—which is what I took a photo of him doing about two hours earlier.

Franklin said that the arena is packed, but that's not exactly true; it's crowded, but there are a lot of seats to be had (BASS later reports 13,413 attendees; the arena's highest attendance ever was 18,150 for a 1999 World Wrestling Federation event). He also said that this final-day broadcast from Mellon Arena is live. In fact, it does not have the "Live" tag in the upper corner and is actually *live-to-tape*, which is a cheeky term that producers use for a multicamera production in which a live occurrence (event, interview, concert, etc.) is recorded on tape and broadcast later, edited or unedited. It's an industry-wide practice, and if the initial broadcast occurs fairly close to the actual taping, most viewers cannot tell.

This is entertainment, after all, and perhaps I'm quibbling about these inaccuracies, but they underscore a persistent recurrence of hyperbole.

After some analysis and commentary from the blue-and-tan crew of Bill Clement, Shaw Grigsby, and Byron Velvick, the producers cut to the stage where Cochran is weighing in. They include all of his encroachment comments, which must seem a little puzzling to some viewers; it could have been clarified by the analysts but is not explained as they break for commercials. On the other hand, after five commercials in a row, they follow with a brief segment on Aaron Martens, temporarily deposed to second place, that focuses on his two second-place Classic finishes and ends with Martens prophetically saying, "How many seconds [in the Classic] can you get? I don't want another one."

Before getting to the final theatrics, the show intersperses analysis and commentary with stage weigh-ins, showing Skeet Reese, Tim Horton, David Walker, Davy Hite, and Marty Stone (a Team Citgo member who had two small fish, like many of the anglers who were not given TV time and who rained high praise on Pittsburghers) and yielding just the briefest nod to Edwin Evers, whose four fish, weighing 6 pounds 2 ounces tied him with Mize for the largest single-day catch of the tournament. Mize's weigh-in appearance does not make the broadcast.

It is 5:51 P.M. in real time, and the Super Six are seated in chairs on the stage. Alan takes a minute to chat with the anglers and references the daily crowds at the Point, which gives Swindle an opportunity to inexplicably make redneck fun of the Yamettes.

"I've got a cheer," taunts Swindle. "Ya-ma-who? Ya-ma-what? My Triton-Merc will smoke your butt!"

The crowd howls, but this bit of Swindle-the-vaudevillian is appropriately edited out of later television coverage, which builds toward an apex when the analysts hand proceedings over to Keith Alan. He references the hot seat; a seventh chair that is reserved for the current tournament leader. The hot-seat thing was probably borrowed from game or reality programs and was used at the final weigh-in of the Lake Dardanelle tournament, except there the hot seat was on a platform out among the bassheads, while here it is onstage near the scales.

The hot seat is empty now. George Cochran is supposed to be in it, but he's MIA. Alan says, "I don't believe he's in the house. I think he's scared of the Super Six."

So he asks Swindle to go to his boat and bring up his catch, which Swindle does in what for him is a subdued manner. Trip Weldon dumps four bass out of a black bag onto the Plexiglas-boxed scale. The fish flip and flop while Weldon tries to get a correct weight. Four pounds 1 ounce puts Swindle in the lead and draws plenty of cheering and clapping from the crowd. On television, the cameras show him pumping his fist and then quickly switch to his clapping wife in the stands. But this is not the outburst that you'd expect from the G-man, as Alan calls him, if he really thought he could be the winner. He evidently realizes that others have enough weight to beat him.

Alan keeps Swindle by the scales as the screen and the television show video of him on the water today, catching four keepers and losing one. Three of the five, if you looked closely, were hooked on a white crankbait, while the other two appear to have been caught on a grub or a tube.

The same routine will be followed for each of the remaining anglers, and the pacing is all in Alan's hands. Scott Rook is weighed in next, but his one fish and quiet demeanor don't generate much excitement. The same is true for Jeff Reynolds, who failed to catch a keeper.

Kevin VanDam gets a big ovation when introduced and a bigger ovation when his limit catch of five bass, weighing 4 pounds 13 ounces, puts him in the lead over Swindle by more than a pound. Accustomed to the spotlight and the hoopla, VanDam is cool onstage as he fields a few of Alan's questions, thanks his extensive family sup- port network, and watches today's video of him catching bass.

VanDam takes the hot seat as Swindle walks down the stage steps, and a camera follows him hand-slapping the bassheads at the front of the pit, one of whom is young Nick Argenas, who reaches for Swindle but misses him.

The crowd's roar is even greater when Iaconelli is introduced, and he gets them to pump it up a notch by exhorting them while reaching into his livewell. But his three-bass catch weighs just 3 pounds 2 ounces, and there will be no break-dancing or wild antics.

While the screen shows his efforts today, which includes landing several fish on a white crankbait, Iaconelli mentions that he used two lures, an ultralight crankbait and a brand-new prototype Berkley Gulp soft tube that he calls "most amazing." Iaconelli is also on the Berkley pro team.

I'm wondering how come nobody is mentioning the name or the brand of crankbait that he's been using. Berkley makes such lures, too, but it's a good guess that these anglers have not been using a Berkley crankbait. Before Iaconelli is dismissed, he gets in a mention of his book and DVD and says, "This is the most amazing group of fans I've ever seen in my life." Iaconelli really likes the word "amazing."

Alan drags the suspense out by sitting with Aaron Martens, the reigning Angler of the Year, a title he earned by having the best overall results throughout the season, and asks him how it would feel if he added the Classic Championship to that. Only one other person has done so in the thirty-five consecutive years that this event has been held.

Finally, Martens goes to his boat, which has been towed into the arena, and I suddenly realize that these anglers have been separated from their boats and their fish for over a half hour. I wonder what the security mechanism is to make sure that the fish are properly aerated, and, more important, that no one can remove a bass from someone's boat, add one to it, or otherwise manage some hanky-panky. It strikes me that this detachment is like asking a pro golfer in the Masters to be separated from his unchecked and unsigned scorecard for a while before it is turned in to officials. Maybe I'm a little too suspicious, but there's $200,000 on the line for the winner, and, as Davy Hite said in an on-water interview that ESPN broadcast earlier, winning is worth a million dollars or more to someone over the next year or two. That's a lot of reason for mischief.

There appears to be no skullduggery or evident concerns about this, and in a prescient move that intensifies the drama, the producers have Weldon hold the fish before weighing them while the Jumbotron and home TV screen show a video of Martens on the water today, during which he agonizingly lost several would-be keepers.

Weldon puts three bass on the Plexiglas-lined scales.

Martens needs 3 pounds 15 ounces to win.

VanDam is off the hot seat and standing, swinging his hands together in nervous anticipation.

Martens is looking at the scale, his left hand raised over pursed lips as he already knows that it's not going to happen for him.

Alan yells, "Three pounds eight ounces!" while Weldon simultaneously turns and points decisively to VanDam, who jubilantly pumps his right fist into the air three times while the crowd erupts into wild applause and cheering.

Amid the ensuing hoopla, a camera shows Martens shaking hands with pit fans upon his exit, Takahiro Omori handing over the championship trophy, and VanDam triumphantly holding the trophy overhead while pyrotechnics burst forth, confetti and streamers rain down, and the crowd's roar drowns out the background music. Mellon Arena is rocking, perhaps as it has before at climactic moments of the Rolling Stones or Grateful Dead concerts.

Kevin VanDam and family take a victory lap in Mellon Arena.

The celebration continues while VanDam, accompanied by his wife and young twin sons, makes a trophy lap around the arena pit in a Triton boat, the victor sitting in the rear deck seat while balancing the trophy on his lap and waving an American flag, handed to him by an ESPN staffer.

Afterword

ESPN's television production ended with live-to-tape video of VanDam wheeling around the arena in triumph, with a summary voice-over by Clement, Grigsby, and Velvick, the latter twice selfishly commenting on his disappointment over Martens finishing second. The weigh-in spectacle concluded with Alan bestowing the Purolator big bass award for the day to Evers for a record-low-tying 1-pound 15-ounce bass, and someone winning a fully rigged bass boat.

The top-ten order of finish was VanDam, Martens, Swindle, Cochran, Iaconelli, Evers, Hite, Reese, Rook, and Horton. VanDam's margin of victory was 6 ounces, which is about half of the weight of one Pittsburgh keeper, or equal to a bass from its nose to just behind its pectoral fins. While not the lowest margin in Bassmaster Classic history, VanDam's three-day total of 12 pounds 15 ounces set a new record-low winning weight.

He and others had predicted that whoever caught a limit on the final day might win, and that a big bass was the wild card. They were right about the limit, as only VanDam and Cochran scored five keepers on the final day. No truly big bass were caught on any of the days; however, VanDam shared lunker honors the first day by catching a 2-pound 14-ounce bass, which was so much bigger than the average fish caught by others that since he caught one less bass overall than Aaron Martens, it did make an enormous difference. And while Martens lost a number of potential keepers, particularly on the final day, many of the anglers lost fish that were momentarily hooked as well, so it can be argued either way as to whether that cost him the championship.

Jimmy Mize, the first-day leader who failed to catch a keeper on the second and third days, finished in sixteenth place. The top-ten finishers were all guaranteed a berth in the 2006 Citgo Bassmaster Classic, meaning that all of ESPN's preferred personalities, as well as the inscrutable Cochran, would be in play for the early story lines on that event.

The payouts for first through fifth place, respectively, were $200,000, $50,000, $40,000, $35,000, and $25,000—a far cry from the first Bassmaster Classic in 1971, when the winner won $10,000, fifth place paid nothing, there was no television coverage, and ESPN had yet to be created.

A few analytical flaws aside, ESPN's final television production was entertaining. It was crowded with forty commercials, although the final twenty-three minutes of the event, featuring the weigh-ins of all Super Six anglers, ran uninterrupted by commercials or commentary. Overall, the production was well done, aided greatly by compacted footage of each angler fishing during the last day, by the inclusion of close-up shots of the anglers and family members, and by adhering to a tightly run schedule.

Perhaps with such a large contingent here, ESPN should be

expected to have a good final production. Nevertheless, it must have taken a tremendous amount of work to get this accomplished and coordinated. Moreover, ESPN succeeded in making good and somewhat dramatic entertainment out of an event that covers an enormous playing field and in which the on-site drama occurs in a compressed time period and only when each angler lays his catch on the arena scales.

Of course, in the last production and through all twelve hours of ESPN's coverage, Pittsburgh was a big winner.

Although it was VanDam's second Classic victory, he later said that winning again was "a dream come true." He also told reporters that he was tired, not having gotten to bed each night before eleven o'clock. Indeed, I had been surprised on the previous night to see VanDam at the Professional Bass Fishing Hall of Fame banquet. Some day, he'll be inducted into that hall.

Coincidentally, also on this day, former third baseman and prolific hitter Wade Boggs was inducted into the National Baseball Hall of Fame. Boggs, an avid angler who often participates in charity saltwater fishing tournaments, said in his speech, "I am living proof that dreams come true."

EIGHT

Why Bass?

Calling fishing a hobby is like calling brain surgery a job.
—PAUL SCHULLERY

Why Bass?

Ten years ago, it was generally agreed by fisheries experts that there were 23,000 species of fish on this planet. Today, some sources put that number at 25,000. A lot of these are members of very large groups, or families, as ichthyologists call them. For example, worldwide there are 30 families of catfish and an estimated 2,200 species. There are more than 2,000 species in the minnow family alone and more than 1,000 in the cichlid family.

Impressive as these numbers are, perhaps more surprising is the fact that only 60 percent of the world's fish inhabit the oceans, which contain 97 percent of the earth's supply of water. Saltwater species are arguably more diverse than their freshwater relatives, as evidenced by the fact that there are fewer species in individual families. For example, worldwide there are about 400 species of fish in the sea bass family, more than 300 in the rockfish family, and about 100 in the snapper family.

North America, which was largely discovered by Europeans because of the abundant cod that existed in the western North

Atlantic Ocean, is estimated to have more than 1,000 fish species swimming in its Atlantic coastal waters, some 500 species off the California coast, and approximately 800 freshwater species in the United States and Canada.

With so many fish to choose from, how did bass get elevated to alpha status?

In part, the answer to this question lies in what's important to people who fish for sport. Of all the fish species in North America, only a small percentage are pursued by anglers for sport. A minority of these, including bass, are freshwater species.

In terms of maximum weight potential, most of North America's fish species are small, growing to half a pound or less. The maximum size of many species ranges from a few pounds to several dozen pounds. Relatively few grow to more than 50 pounds. Most large-growing fish are piscivorous apex predators living in an eat-or-be-eaten environment; this makes them susceptible to sportfishing efforts.

Bass, which are freshwater fish historically capable of reaching a maximum documented weight of 25 pounds but usually found in the 1- to 5-pound class, are indeed an apex predator. Yet that alone does not explain their attraction to anglers. In fact, the freshwater fish that anglers call "bass" are actually large sunfish, and they are among those few North American freshwater fish that are considered gamefish *and* widely available to the masses.

There is no indisputable definition of *gamefish* or *sportfish*, which are interchangeable terms. American states and Canadian provinces, which oversee the management of freshwater fisheries on public bodies of water within their political boundaries, have enacted laws designating some species as gamefish to preclude them from commercial capture and prohibit their sale by anglers. This status is reserved for species that are not only popular and intensively sought, but that are viewed as having more desirable sporting virtues than nondesignated species and are also viewed as being more vulnerable.

In general parlance, however, and as the result of evolving cultural attitudes and local customs, the term *gamefish* refers to freshwater and saltwater fish that are sought by recreational anglers and valued for their willingness to take an artificial lure, an artificial fly, or hooked natural bait and prized for their fighting virtues when caught in a sporting manner.

Most species that are considered gamefish are predatory and carnivorous, which makes them likely to strike at the offerings of anglers. Species with such highly esteemed traits as ability to jump, strength to make long runs, aggressiveness in taking a lure, and attainment of large size tend to be the most popular gamefish, especially if they are abundant.

Edibility is not often a factor in whether a fish is considered a gamefish, although many top predatory fish—such as walleye, salmon, tuna, halibut, and striped bass—are excellent to eat. Likewise, some fish that make good table fare are not among the species that are viewed as gamefish; rays, mullet, monkfish, tilefish, and tilapia are among these.

All freshwater bass, but especially largemouth and smallmouth bass, are considered gamefish because they are aggressive animals that often ambush prey; they are prone to jump when hooked, although not all do; they are usually located in or near cover or objects, which often requires skillful casting and adroit lure or bait presentation; they strike a broad array of lure types and can thus be caught by many methods and with different equipment; and they are widely available.

About Bass

For scientific purposes, ichthyologists classify all fish according to the family they belong in and subgroups thereof, using an ordering system that dates back to the 1700s. Latin names have been given to all species for accurate identification. The common names used by laypeople often bear no resemblance to the Latin names, and there may be many different common, or colloquial, names for the same individual species based on regional preferences, societal custom, language, dialect, or sheer inventiveness. A lot of confusion has resulted.

Many freshwater and saltwater fish species are referred to as "bass." Some are truly bass and some aren't, but all have a physique and a profile that are generally similar, thus causing them to be called "bass." True bass are members of the Serranidae family of sea bass, which in freshwater includes the white bass and the yellow bass and in saltwater includes the black sea bass, the striped bass, the giant sea bass, the kelp bass, and many other species.

The primary quarry in bass fishing tournaments are the fish that have historically been known as "black bass," a group of darkly colored freshwater fish that are native only to North America. The term *black bass* refers to all species and subspecies of the genus *Micropterus*, which actually belong to the Centrarchidae family of sunfish. Black bass species include largemouth bass, smallmouth bass, spotted bass, redeye bass, Suwannee bass, and Guadalupe bass. All are strictly freshwater species and are more elongated and generally larger growing than their other sunfish-family relatives.

The Suwannee and the Guadalupe bass are relatively uncommon and have very limited ranges. The redeye has a slightly larger Southeastern distribution but is relatively small. The spotted bass, which looks a lot like a largemouth, is fairly common in some Southern and Western waters but is usually smaller and less abundant than the largemouth.

Largemouth bass, *Micropterus salmoides*, and smallmouth bass, *Micropterus dolomieui*, are by far the most abundant black bass species and the primary targets for anglers who participate in the Bassmaster Classic and its qualifying events. Their relatives in the Centrarchidae family include crappies and numerous sunfish species. All thirty-some members of this family are classified under the order Perciformes, which, ichthyologically speaking, connotes a large group of advanced perchlike fishes that have spiny fins.

This gives some credence to the supposition that European settlers are responsible for the "bass" terminology. It is believed that the word *bass* is derived from the Middle English word *basse*, which is either a corruption of the Old English word *baers*, meaning "bristly or spiny," or of the Dutch word for perch, *barse*. Anatomically, largemouth and smallmouth bass are definitely spiny.

One of the first encyclopedic-like books on fishing, *The Art of Angling* by Richard Brookes, published circa 1740 in London, contains an entry for an English freshwater fish called pearch, which is also described as barse. It also contains an entry for an anadromous fish called bass, later to be called the European sea bass, which is still found throughout the United Kingdom and is especially popular in Wales. This book and its descriptions predated the standardized scientific classification of fish, and the adoption of Latin names, which was initiated in 1758 by the Swedish naturalist Carl von Linné, known as Linnaeus.

Whether appropriately or inappropriately named, the largemouth is the biggest and most renowned Centrarchid and the one species that people in North America think of when they hear the word *bass*. This generic word has also come to be used in reference to boats, rods, reels, lures, and other gear specifically used in pursuit of these fish.

As a result of widespread introductions throughout North America, the largemouth bass—often referred to as a "bigmouth bass"—has become available to more anglers than any other species of gamefish. Its native range was generally the eastern half of the United States and southernmost Ontario and Quebec in Canada. It was originally located across an area from Iowa south to Texas and northeastern Mexico and east to the South Atlantic Coast, including western New York and western Pennsylvania, but it was absent from most of the Appalachian and Ozark ranges, most of the northeastern United States from Maryland to Maine, and easternmost Canada. Since the late 1800s, its range has been expanded to include major or minor portions of every state in the United States except Alaska and most of the southern fringes of Canada, as well as numerous countries in Europe, Asia, Africa, South America, Central America, and the Caribbean.

Considered a species that prefers generally warm water, the largemouth bass thrives in relatively fertile environments, primarily being found in reservoirs, lakes, ponds, and large slow rivers with quiet backwaters. In all of these places it is one of the top predators, with a wide-ranging diet, and is a species that seeks numerous forms of weed, rock, or wooden cover that it can use for ambushing prey.

Throughout their range, most largemouth bass encountered by anglers average 1 to 1½ pounds in weight and from 10 to 13 inches in length. They are commonly caught up to 5 pounds and less commonly from 7 to 10 pounds. A largemouth bass weighing more than

Bass pro and ESPN analyst Mark Menendez with a largemouth
bass from Lake Fork in Texas.

5 pounds is uncommon in northernmost waters but quite common in
southern-region waters, where fish can grow faster quicker and have
longer growing seasons. A 10-pounder is viewed as a trophy anywhere
and, with few exceptions, is harder to come by in modern times.

The maximum size attainable for largemouth bass is theoretically
between 23 and 30 pounds. The naturalist William Bartram, exploring
Florida's St. Johns River in 1773, reported catching a 30-pound bass,
yet only a dozen largemouth bass of more than 20 pounds have ever
been formally recognized (ten of them from California), with the
largest being the all-tackle world record of 22 pounds 4 ounces,
caught from Montgomery Lake, Georgia, in 1932. This is one of the
longest-standing freshwater records, and certainly the most coveted.

Largemouth bass are suitable for a wide array of fishing techniques and thus dear to manufacturers of fishing equipment. A
generally shallow-dwelling species tailor-made for casting, the

largemouth has probably spawned more artificial lures, and variation upon variation of lures, than all other freshwater sportfish combined. And its short-lived but action-packed fight, replete with aerial maneuvers and explosive bursts for cover, keeps anglers coming back.

In sum, the largemouth's adoption of varied environments, suitability to diverse fishing techniques, and penchant for aggressive behavior have helped to elevate it to the most popular sportfishing target in North America.

The smallmouth bass is the second largest Centrarchid and is generally considered a species of more northerly environs. The original range of the smallmouth bass was from the Great Lakes and St. Lawrence River drainages in Canada south to northern Georgia, west to eastern Oklahoma, and north to Minnesota. It has since been widely spread within and beyond that range, across southern Canada west to British Columbia and east to the Maritimes, west to the Pacific Coast states, and into the southwestern United States. It has also been introduced to Hawaii, Asia, Europe, and Africa.

Although it has also been widely dispersed geographically, the smallmouth bass has more specific habitat requirements than the largemouth does, and within this broad range it is not as widely abundant or distributed as the largemouth is. The most abundant smallmouth populations occur in cool northern waters, although a great number of big smallmouth have been caught in the southern portion of their range. Naturally a fish of both clear rivers and lakes, it has been widely introduced to other water types.

Smallmouth bass—whose mouth is small only in comparison to that of its bigger cousin—prefer clear, quiet waters with gravel, rubble, or rocky bottoms. They live in midsized, gentle streams that have deep pools and abundant shade, as well as in fairly deep clear lakes and reservoirs with rocky shoals. Although they are fairly adaptable, they are seldom found in murky water, and they avoid swift current.

Most smallmouths encountered by anglers are about 1 to 1½ pounds in weight and from 9 to 13 inches long. Specimens of more than 3 pounds are considered fairly large but not uncommon. Most anglers have caught few, if any, smallmouth bass weighing more than 5 pounds, although some waters do produce 5- to 8-pound individuals annually. The largest smallmouth known is the all-tackle world

A 5-pound smallmouth bass.

record, a fish that weighed 11 pounds 15 ounces when caught from Dale Hollow Lake in Tennessee in 1955.

In gross numbers, there are far fewer smallmouth bass than largemouth bass in North America. Smallmouths are more highly respected for their fighting ability, however, because they have a friskier disposition when hooked. When caught on appropriate tackle, they put up a longer and more-determined resistance and are more likely to be repeat acrobats.

The Growth of Sportfishing in the United States

In the latter part of the nineteenth century, there was a special zeal for transplanting and stocking fish in North America. In 1870, five commercial fish hatcheries were operating in the United States, and the newly formed federal U.S. Fish Commission, in conjunction with nineteen state fish commissions, eagerly undertook fish propagation and distribution, aided greatly by railroad development.

Among the most notable and consequential occurrences: striped bass and American shad were transplanted from their East Coast environs and established in California. Rainbow trout, native to the western United States, were transplanted to the Midwest and the East. Brown trout, native to Europe and previously unknown in North America, were imported from Germany. Carp, native to Asia but well established in Europe and unknown in North America, were transplanted from France and England. At the same time, and for decades afterward, the range of black bass was expanded by bucket and barrel, through the documented efforts of various agencies and the furtive efforts of eager anglers.

The champion of all things related to black bass fishing was the Cincinnati physician James A. Henshall, who is also credited with developing the first rod for use with a baitcasting reel. The pioneering Henshall was precocious yet prescient with the knowledge, advice, and opinions that he presented in his groundbreaking *Book of the Black Bass* in 1881, which he dedicated to the Culver Club of Cincinnati for its fish and game preservation efforts.

"This book owes its origin," Henshall wrote in the first paragraph of his preface, "to a long-cherished desire on the part of the author, to give to the Black Bass its proper place among game fishes, and to create among anglers, and the public generally, an interest in a fish that has never been so fully appreciated as its merits deserve, because of the want of suitable tackle for its capture, on the one hand, and a lack of information regarding its habits and economic value on the other."

In *Book of the Black Bass*, Henshall noted that black bass had exceptional sporting virtues, were very "assertive" fish, had the vigor of trout and the leaping ability of salmon, and were highly eclectic in their fondness for flies, lures, and natural baits.

His comment about the black bass, "I consider him, *inch for inch* and *pound for pound,* the gamest fish that swims," has become one of the most famous in U.S. angling literature.

In light of later developments in fisheries management, angling equipment, river impoundments, and American society, Henshall was a prophet, as the following quotation from his chapter "The Black Bass as a Game Fish" demonstrates.

> That he [the black bass] will eventually become the lead-
> ing game fish of America is my oft-expressed opinion and

firm belief. This result, I think, is inevitable; if for no other reasons, from a force of circumstances occasioned by climatic conditions and the operation of immutable natural laws, such as the gradual drying up, and dwindling away, of the small Trout streams, and the consequent decrease of Brook Trout, both in quality and quantity; and by the introduction of predatory fish in waters where the Trout still exists.

Another prominent cause of the decline and fall of Brook Trout, is the erection of dams, saw-mills and factories upon Trout streams, which, though to be deplored, can not be prevented; the march of empire and the progress of civilization can not be stayed by the honest, though powerless, protests of anglers.

Henshall was nearly dead on. He did not foresee the importation of brown trout (first introduced in 1883), which would become more widespread and popular than brook trout, and it was not until the middle of the twentieth century that black bass would become more popular nationally than the various trouts. Ironically, while dam construction helped to diminish brook trout populations, it was the erection of dams in the twentieth century that greatly helped black bass become "the leading game fish in America."

The popularity of black bass increased through the decades after Henshall wrote his book, spurred on by the development of more tackle suitable to bass fishing, not the least of which was non–fly style artificial lures, especially wooden lures, which got their start at the dawn of the twentieth century. Improved fishing lines, new types of reels, and much better fishing rods evolved through the middle of the century, and more people took up angling for all types of freshwater and saltwater species.

Sportfishing interest especially exploded after World War II, as Americans became more prosperous and had more leisure time. In the Northeast, trout still held the upper hand in popularity, although the word *trout* then primarily meant brown trout, followed by brook trout and the widely transplanted rainbow trout. Anglers diversified their efforts, however, and bass were generally regarded favorably even in trout country.

Many sportsmen of that day were all-around outdoorsmen who fished for various species and hunted for several types of game; devoting some effort for bass, along with trout and maybe walleye, pike, or muskies, was common, especially in northern states. Nevertheless, many snooty trout purists, especially those who fished with flycasting gear in streams, disdained bass. As recently as the 1970s, it was not uncommon to find a stalwart trout and salmon aficionado in New England who thought that bass were "trash fish."

In the southeastern and southwestern United States, few waters were suitable to the coldwater requirements of trout. There, warmwater species prevailed. The various black basses, largemouths in particular, plus the rest of the sunfish clan, were the major freshwater sportfish to be had other than catfish. In these regions, angling for bass was increasingly popular, with Florida rivers and lakes being the most esteemed places to catch largemouth bass and generally producing the largest specimens, thanks to a year-round growing season.

What really changed the United States' freshwater sportfishing landscape, however, and gave a huge boost to bass fishing, was the mid-twentieth-century construction of dams on scores of major rivers, creating large reservoirs that allowed populations of baitfish and predators to explode. The result was fast fishing and an explosion of opportunity.

It started in the Depression with the policies instituted by President Franklin D. Roosevelt. The Works Progress Administration of the New Deal and Roosevelt's creation of the Tennessee Valley Authority in 1933 initiated federal construction of dams to harness cheap hydroelectric power, provide water management, improve farming techniques, aid river navigation, and construct hospitals and schools. New industries, attracted by cheap electricity and labor, diversified the Southern economy.

In June 1938, *Field & Stream* magazine reported, "At the present time, the entire Tennessee Valley . . . is undergoing one of the greatest face-lifting jobs in history . . . being transformed into a series of inland seas . . . every farmhouse with electricity . . . such vast bodies of water will support more fish and game than ever existed. . . . It should be a sportsman's paradise."

It wasn't just the Tennessee Valley, nor was this phenomenon confined exclusively to the South. Major cities and agricultural areas needed water in addition to power. The Colorado River was impounded to help grow the West, and reservoirs were created from Maine to Montana to help prevent flooding.

The taming of rivers and the development of reservoirs, hailed by business interests but attacked by conservationists, became a major factor in bringing people to fishing. The numerous reservoirs created from the late 1930s into the 1970s caused an explosion of forage and warmwater gamefish populations. For many older anglers today, the 1950s through the early 1970s were fishing's "good old days." Abundant and not-too-sophisticated fish, expanded opportunities, newfound circumstances, and increased demand sparked rapid and ripple-through developments in boats, motors, fishing accessories, tackle, angling techniques, retail and mail order suppliers, and on and on.

The changes that took place in sportfishing from immediately after World War II until about 1980—a virtual microsecond in the time line of human history—dwarfed everything that had happened in the previous seven thousand years.

NINE

Fishing for Inducements

Build it and he will come.

—THE WORDS HEARD BY FARMER RAY KINSELLA
IN THE MOVIE *FIELD OF DREAMS*

A lthough the history of sportfishing, and especially its development in North America, is well documented in literature, that same literature is remarkable for its absence of information and commentary—indeed, nearly complete ignorance—regarding fishing contests or competitions, particularly in freshwater. This is especially notable given that today there are tens of thousands of such events.

Fisheries biologists Steven Kerr and Kendall Kamke, who conducted a survey of competitive freshwater fishing activities in Canada and the United States in 2000–2001, estimated that there were more than twenty-five thousand competitive *freshwater* fishing events in those countries in 2000. A 1989 survey of freshwater and saltwater competitions (which included all of North America, plus Puerto Rico and the U.S. Virgin Islands), conducted by the American Fisheries Society (AFS), estimated that there were thirty-one thousand competitive fishing events in both freshwater and saltwater that year.

Fishing competitions range from small, one-species, eight-hour events sponsored by a local fishing club to multimonth, multispecies,

large-area events run by a group and including thousands of participants. Prizes range from a token individual or team trophy (or simply
the accumulation of points) to $1 million-plus cash purses.

Such wide disparity underscores a fundamental lack of definition
regarding what constitutes a fishing competition, what distinguishes
more formal events from less formal ones, and how to separate them
by the value of prizes offered.

Event organizers seem to follow no particular rule regarding
nomenclature. Thus, competitive fishing events in North America
are predominantly called tournaments, derbies, and rodeos, and in
some cases festivals. In Europe, the word *match* is most commonly
used for competitive events, although this is seldom employed today
in North America.

The AFS survey report, issued in 1991, broadly defined competitive fishing as "organized events in which a group of anglers fish for
inducements, such as awards, prizes or public recognition, in addition
to the catch or the satisfaction of catching fish."

Sportfishing events that offered inducements prospered after
World War II as the popularity of recreational fishing grew, and as
fishing clubs and business interests saw a benefit to organizing or
hosting these events, or both. The records of fishing competitions are
replete with references to tourism development and promotion, with
saltwater events (especially in the Gulf of Mexico) dominating in the
early years.

Who started the first fishing contest, and where and for what, is a
mystery. There may have long been informal competitions based on
wagers between friends and small groups. And there were likely
always prizes offered by fledgling tackle companies seeking to promote their goods.

An advertisement by William Shakespeare of Shakespeare Fishing Tackle, in the June 1903 issue of *Field & Stream*, noted, "I offer
$100 in prizes for largest fish caught in your locality this year. Write
for particulars and let me send you free books on 'How to Catch Bass,'
'The Art of Bait Casting,' and my hundred-page Catalog of Fine Fishing Tackle."

Shakespeare's company would become one of the premier U.S.
fishing tackle manufacturers, and it's still in existence today. Although

now situated in South Carolina, Shakespeare in 1903 was located in Kalamazoo, Michigan, the hometown of 2005 Citgo Bassmaster Classic winner Kevin VanDam. Its fishing tackle subsidiary, Pflueger (an early twentieth-century contemporary of Shakespeare), made a reel that was used in 1932 to catch the all-time world record large-mouth bass.

While it may be a stretch to call Shakespeare's prize offer and what similar inducements may have then existed a "contest," sportfishing competitions evidently existed at intra- and inter-club levels in England and France in the late 1800s. According to author John Essex, writing in the April 2000 edition of the British magazine *Classic Angling*, formal competition in England between clubs started with the formation of the National Federation of Anglers (NFA) in 1903. The NFA consisted of clubs throughout England that sought to "formulate rules and suggestions for the improvement of the sport, the prevention of pollution, and the furtherance of anglers' interests in general."

According to Essex, the *Daily Mirror* newspaper put up a cup, and the NFA held the first All-England National Championship in 1906 on the Thames at Pangbourne, near Reading. Essex didn't specify what the anglers fished for; although Atlantic salmon still migrated up the Thames at that time, it is reasonable to assume that the quarry was coarse fish, which are the staple of nearly all European match fishing competitions.

Seven teams and eighty-four competitors participated, with the Mirror Cup being won by a team from Leeds and individual honors going to Fred Beales of Boston (England). The winning team received medals. The English National Championship, also known in later years as the All-England and the National, was, and still is, the premier fishing competition in that country, with participants qualifying through trial matches. Essex, quoting a past president of NFA, notes, "To be chosen to fish in this match, or to win the right to fish, is perhaps the dearest desire of many thousands."

The last of these events to be held as an "open" competition occurred in 1971 on the Severn River. The event was reorganized in 1972, with teams being classified into several divisions, the most skilled and accomplished teams having to qualify to compete in the top division. The English National Championship match competition continues today under NFA administration. The winning team from Division One annually represents England in the world championships, administered since 1952 by the Confederation Internationale de la Peche Sportive (CIPS), or International Sport Fishing Federation. Although virtually ignored in the United States (U.S. tackle manufacturers and television networks have declined to support it), the world championship is the premier competition for match anglers throughout the world and was most recently scheduled for September 2006 in Portugal.

In 1910, *Field & Stream*, then a fourteen-year-old national sporting magazine, reported at length on a mano-a-mano contest in Ohio. The contest was between Chicago lure manufacturer William Jamison, who manufactured a bass lure called the Coaxer, and Ans Decker, of New Jersey, who manufactured a bass lure called the Decker Hopatcong.

In 1908, Jamison had run an advertisement in *Outdoor Life* for his Weedless Coaxer that stated, "We claim that the weedless 'Coaxer' will catch more bass than any other bait on earth and we stand ready to prove it at any time." He later followed that up with this challenge in a *Field & Stream* advertisement: "I offer to meet any angler on earth, manufacturers of artificial baits preferred, in a three days' fishing contest on any lake within 500 miles of Chicago to prove that the sportsmanlike Coaxer, with its humane armament, will catch more fish than any other bait on the market, or than the live frog or minnow."

The contest between Jamison and Decker took place on June 16–18, 1910, at Congress Lake, a private lake belonging to the Congress Lake Club and located near Canton, Ohio. There were three judges, one of them being a *Field & Stream* representative identified as Mr. Macy in a later Jamison catalog.

Jamison caught twenty-eight bass to Decker's sixteen, and there followed a slew of letters in the magazine from early-twentieth-century bassheads who, according to a 1955 article by *Field & Stream* fishing editor A. J. McClane, thought that the lake was too weedy for Decker's three treble-hooked plug versus the single-hooked Coaxer, that Jamison was simply a better fisherman, or that various other lures would have done better.

Perhaps sensing the readership value of a contest, *Field & Stream* initiated a national fishing contest itself in the spring of 1911, offering $1,500 worth of prizes for the largest fish caught in each of a large group of freshwater and saltwater categories. The following year the magazine offered $2,000 in prizes and expanded the categories.

The annual contest underwent many changes over the years and was enormously popular, even after it switched to nonmerchandise and noncash prizes. *Field & Stream* editors Hugh Grey and Ross McCluskey, in their 1955 book *Field & Stream Treasury*, stated that the contest "has continued ever since as the *big* American fishing contest."

Many of the winning entries in the *Field & Stream* Fishing Contest became world records (some still exist), and it is likely that the contest led *Field & Stream* to undertake the job of certifying both freshwater and saltwater world sportfish records. When the International Game Fish Association (IGFA) was formed in June 1939 as a predominantly saltwater organization, *Field & Stream* gave it the saltwater record–keeping business.

On March 23, 1978, to satisfy the cost-cutting efforts of its accountant, the magazine turned over both freshwater record–keeping responsibility and its fishing contest to the IGFA. It was one of the dumbest moves in the annals of American sportfishing. While the IGFA has done a far better job with record keeping, *Field & Stream* gave away what could have become its greatest marketing and self-promotion tool. The 1977 fishing contest, which was the magazine's sixty-seventh, was its last. The IGFA ran the fishing contest for twenty-four years and discontinued it in 2000.

Perhaps the oldest ongoing organized fishing competition in the United States is the Alabama Deep Sea Fishing Rodeo, sponsored by the Mobile Jaycees and held for the seventy-fourth time in July 2006.

Created by a group of Mobile businessmen who got the idea for this contest while fishing together one summer day in 1928, the Alabama Deep Sea Fishing Rodeo was intended to popularize that city's saltwater fishing. The first event, which attracted 260 anglers, was held in 1929. The anglers paid $5 each, which covered their accommodations and prizes. The organizers headquartered the event at Fort Gaines Pier on Dauphin Island, then accessible only by boat, and used carrier pigeons to transmit daily catch news back to town.

The event was taken over by the Mobile Jaycees in 1948. Event literature says that more than a hundred thousand spectators are drawn to its current Dauphin Island site. More than thirty-two hundred anglers participate in this three-day event, seeking the largest individual specimens in thirty inshore and offshore categories and paying a $40 adult entry fee.

West of Mobile, Texans got into saltwater fishing competition as early as 1932 at Port Aransas and in 1934 at Padre Island.

The Port Aransas Deep Sea Roundup, which is billed as the oldest tournament on the Texas Gulf, was founded by a group of fishing guides, headed by Barney Farley, in 1931. The first event, held in 1932 and then called the Tarpon Rodeo, attracted 22 anglers. Port Aransas took the competition over in 1933. A record number of 853 entrants participated in the two-day July 2005 event, which awarded trophies only in bay/surf and offshore divisions. Entrants pay a $75 entrance fee, and the money raised funds a scholarship program— every senior in the local high school receives a $1,000 scholarship— and assorted children's programs. The seventy-first Port Aransas Deep Sea Roundup was held in July 2006.

The Texas International Fishing Tournament (TIFT) was begun in 1934 to stimulate the development and growth of tourism in the Rio Grande Valley. Currently the largest saltwater fishing tournament in the Lone Star State, TIFT is a nonprofit corporation that funds scholarships and promotes area sportfishing. Headquartered at Padre Island, the event awards a hundred trophies to anglers in bay, offshore, and tarpon categories; charges a $75 adult entry fee; runs for five days; and attracted a record 1,501 participants in 2005. The sixty-eighth TIFT was held in August 2006.

East of Mobile, Floridians were fishing in club competitions since the early 1930s, if not before. A day-by-day account of the December 1933 competition among members of the Florida Year-Round Club, fishing out of Key Largo primarily for sailfish and dolphin, appeared in the "Rod and Gun" column of the *New York Herald Tribune*.

Author Donald Stillman participated in the event along with Dudley Siddall of the *New York Sun*, Earl Roman of the *Miami Herald*, and Lynne Bogue Hunt, one of the greatest wildlife illustrators of that day. Roman won the dolphin division, Hunt won the sailfish division, and Stillman noted in his column that "the competition bids fair to become the angling classic of the Sunshine State."

That did not happen, but two years later saw the birth of an event that bills itself as "the oldest, largest, most successful and respected fishing tournament in the U.S." Respected it is; largest it may be by some definition; oldest it is not. Nevertheless, the Metropolitan South Florida Fishing Tournament—the MET—is distinctive in that today it runs for five months, is open to anyone free of charge, provides more than five thousand noncash awards, and has been release-oriented from its inception.

Henry H. "Hy" Hyman, a manager for Miami Electric, conceived the idea of a free fishing tournament in 1935 to promote tourism in the Miami area. It ran for two weeks, included about a hundred anglers, and was supported by tackle manufacturers, a local newspaper, and assorted tourism interests. Five years later, it was so successful that tournament directors described the MET as "the most important participation contest in America."

While this statement is typical of the unchecked hyperbole and enthusiasm that is often associated with many fishing contests, the MET was nonetheless praised by some prominent figures. In 1965, Joe Brooks, then the fishing editor of *Outdoor Life*, wrote, "After 31 years of operation, the Metropolitan Miami Fishing Tournament remains the outstanding angler's contest in the world."

John Alden Knight, creator of the Solunar Tables and one of the most prominent American outdoor journalists, wrote the following one year earlier: "The very idea of fishing tournaments and rodeos (an awful word) is contrary to the basic spirit of fishing. . . . The pressure of keen competition rests heavily on your shoulders and the normal blessings of fishing are nullified. The one outstanding exception to this condemnation of tournaments and rodeos is the Metropolitan Miami Fishing Tournament."

Today the MET is owned and run by a nonprofit corporation, encompasses eleven South Florida counties plus Cat Cay and Bimini in the Bahamas, has 150 weigh stations, and receives more than 18,000 annual entries. The seventy-first tournament concluded in May 2006.

In 1935, the same year that the MET started, the angling author, socialite, and saltwater fishing editor of *Field & Stream* from 1937 to 1972, S. Kip Farrington Jr., got the idea for an international tuna fishing "match" patterned after the U.S. Davis Cup for tennis. This arose after he and Michael Lerner, fishing in separate boats, caught some of the first bluefin tuna on rod and reel in that province, and in front of an audience no less.

Lerner, a wealthy, world-traveled angler who was friends with royalty and many top industrialists, is considered the grandfather of modern big-game fishing. He was one of five people (another of whom was Ernest Hemingway) who met at the American Museum of Natural History in New York City on June 7, 1939, to form the IGFA. Lerner and Farrington, and their wives, pursued big game fish all over the world during the golden era for those species.

On September 1, 1935, Farrington joined Lerner in Wedgeport, Nova Scotia. "That Sunday there were more than four hundred people on sightseeing boats," wrote Farrington in his book *On the Trail of the Sharp Cup*, "and craft of all description were out to see the fun. Some of the boats had orchestras on board."

Lerner caught 275- and 390-pound bluefin tuna. Farrington wrote, "The crowd roared, the orchestras played and the whistles blew." Farrington later caught a 165-pounder, and at the end of the day they were mobbed onshore. "From this experience, and especially the fact that the spectators' craft could see the launches, the boats being all together when the strikes occurred, I got the idea of starting a Davis Cup of fishing," wrote Farrington.

With the assistance of the Nova Scotian government and the donation by Boston businessman Alton B. Sharp of a trophy designed by Lynn Bogue Hunt, the first International Tuna Cup Match was held in September 1937 between teams representing the British Empire and the United States. Later events would include teams from the United States, Canada, England, Spain, Mexico, Cuba, France, Argentina, Chile, Scandinavia, Venezuela, Brazil, and the Netherlands. The winning team received the Sharp Cup and the event was held annually, with a hiatus during World War II, until Nova Scotia ran out of giant bluefin, ending with the 1976 event in which not a single tuna was landed (only one was landed in 1975 and none in 1973).

When the match was called off, Lorne Baker, the federal director of fisheries for the Maritime provinces, lamented, "As a publicity medium for Nova Scotia, the tuna tournament was more effective than even the famous schooner races of thirty years or so ago. There is no denying the importance of the tournament to [Nova Scotia]."

Farrington's book claimed that the success of the first match and those that followed was the "inspiration for all the other fishing tournaments that have since been held in many waters around the world." More hyperbole but perhaps true with respect to some later international big game fishing competitions fished by a small, elite group of wealthy anglers who traveled the world.

It did not take much traveling or wealth to fish in the plethora of competitions that blossomed after World War II. Nelson Bryant, the outdoor editor of the *New York Times*, commented on the competitive explosion in a February 12, 1982, article about fishing contests in that publication.

"Once regarded as an essentially contemplative endeavor perhaps overlaid with the desire to refine one's angling skills as a meal or two was gathered, much sport fishing is now enmeshed in the same razzle dazzle one finds in organized athletic encounters," wrote Bryant.

"Angling tournaments blossomed in this country after World War II with the rise in the standard of living, increased leisure time, increased mobility and an awareness on the part of chambers of commerce, state fish and game agencies, boat, motor, and tackle manufacturers that if substantial prizes and prize monies were offered it would attract a great many more anglers, who would also have need of food, drink and lodging while on the scene."

Bryant lived on Martha's Vineyard, where, in 1946, Nat Sperber, a public relations representative for the new ferry service, was commissioned to come up with a fall promotion. His brainchild: the Martha's Vineyard Striped Bass and Bluefish Derby. Sponsored originally by the Martha's Vineyard Rod and Gun Club, the first derby drew a thousand fishermen from twenty-nine states and the province of Ontario. The top prize was $1,000 and a one-week stay at a local inn. Second place was a building lot in Gay Head.

By 1949, two boats were awarded as top prizes, and spinoff events included a derby dance, a derby marshal, and a derby queen. In 1951, the event was taken over by the Martha's Vineyard chamber of commerce. Today the five-week event has a nonprofit structure, charges $40 for adult entrants, and funds scholarships to island high school graduates. More than three thousand anglers participated in the sixtieth derby in the fall of 2005, and a record $350,000 in cash and prizes was awarded.

Many other events that are still in existence began about the same time, particularly saltwater contests. The International Light Tackle Tournament Association (ILTTA), an organization of fishing clubs, was formed in 1946 and held its first contest, dedicated to using light tackle to catch billfish, as part of that year's Sailfish Rodeo in Acapulco, Mexico. The ILTTA tournament is held annually in a different location, emphasizes release, awards a team replica trophy in lieu of cash prizes, and was most recently held in October 2005 in Puerto Rico.

The entire month of October is the period for the Destin Fishing Rodeo, which was held for the fifty-seventh time in October 2005. According to tournament organization literature, the event was started in 1948 by a small group of Destin, Florida, fishermen and businessmen, primarily to enhance tourism. The rodeo, which is run by a nonprofit corporation today, claims that more than thirty thousand anglers participated in the last event, which is free to anglers who fish aboard boats that are registered in the rodeo, and it awards more than $100,000 in prizes.

These are a few of the more prominent saltwater events that occurred immediately following World War II and that still continue. Later to come would be such prestigious events as the San Juan International Billfish Tournament, which started in 1954; the Hawaiian International Billfish Tournament, which hails itself as the "grandfather of all big-game tournaments" and was started in 1959; the Masters Invitational Angling Tournament, a light-tackle billfish event started by legendary boat builder John Rybovich in 1963 and now held annually in Cancun, Mexico; and a number of club events that were started out of Palm Beach or Miami.

Tournaments were so pervasive by the middle of the twentieth century that in 1951, the *Wise Fishermen's Encyclopedia*, edited by A. J. McClane, said the following, under the entry titled "Tournaments": "Due to their incalculable number and geographic dispersion, no attempt is made herein to comprehensively list all the fishing tournaments . . . currently taking place throughout the world."

That holds true even more so in 2006. An advertisement in late 2005 for Monroe County in the Florida Keys listed sixty-nine major saltwater events in 2006 just for that area alone, which doesn't include smaller events hosted by restaurants, tackle shops, fishing clubs, or others. Want to see how many ice fishing contests there are? An early 2006 Google search under "ice fishing tournament" yielded 23,300 results. Refine the search by specifying "2006" and you're down to 16,000, one of which is the single-day, 10,000-participant Brainerd Jaycees $150,000 Ice Fishing Extravaganza (where they drill 20,000 holes on a bay in Minnesota's Gull Lake and award a 4x4 truck, ATVs, snowmobiles, and cash).

What is noticeably absent in the annals of long-lasting fishing competitions is events that were or are solely devoted to freshwater species. Freshwater fishing competitions existed before World War II and prior to the first Bassmaster Classic in 1971; there are oblique references to unnamed freshwater contests in various types of literature of the 1950s and 1960s. But given that today the overwhelming number of competitive fishing events in North America are held in freshwater (according to the surveys noted previously), the lack of truly long-running freshwater contests is surprising.

In fact, the Bassmaster Classic, first held in 1971 and presented for the thirty-sixth time in February 2006, is one of the oldest continuously held freshwater fishing events in North America. But it's not the oldest.

The community of Rio Vista, California, has been holding a striped bass derby since 1933, scheduling its fifty-ninth event in October 2006. Held on the Sacramento River and the Sacramento (or California) Delta, this is a mostly freshwater, partly saltwater event, as the area fished is tidal and the lower portions of the derby's fishing boundaries extend through Suisun Bay to Benicia.

Started by tourism interests, the Rio Vista Striped Bass Derby is believed to be the oldest fishing derby on the West Coast (the promoters call it the oldest striped bass derby in the West). Today it's part of the tourism-oriented Rio Vista Bass Festival, presented by the Rio Vista chamber of commerce, complete with car show, fireworks, parade, carnival, and thirty-five thousand attendees. The three-day 2005 fishing competition drew eleven hundred anglers for a $25 entry fee, with a boat, a motor, and a trailer as the prize for weighing in the largest striped bass, a species that was transplanted to California in the late nineteenth century.

The Tip Up Town USA Ice Fishing Contest run by the Houghton Lake, Michigan, chamber of commerce is evidently the oldest continuously held *strictly freshwater* fishing competition in the United States. It was conducted for the fifty-sixth consecutive time in January 2006.

According to the chamber's historical account, "It all began in February 1951, when community minded persons realized that Houghton Lake, which produces great ice fishing, was literally a 'Community on the Ice' each winter. Two local businessmen, Bob Sweet and Bob Carmen, conceived the idea of creating a little fun on the ice to relieve the long winter months, and by which they might attract more tourism to the area during the off season. A nationwide contest to name the Winter Festival, as it was then being called, drew more than 500 entries. The contest judges eventually chose Tip Up Town USA as its name."

The trademarked Tip Up Town USA (TUT) is more carnival than fishing contest today, although it all started with an ice fishing event. TUT includes a parade, a dance, a snowmobile race, an ice-carving contest, the election of a mayor, and the crowning of a queen, plus many more activities that celebrate winter and bring a community together.

A few hundred anglers participated in the latest TUT ice fishing contest, but comparing this event to the Bassmaster Classic is like comparing the Pop Warner Football Championships (referred to as the Pop Warner Super Bowl, incidentally) to the NFL's Super Bowl.

Speaking of which, in spite of, or perhaps because of, being repeatedly called the "Super Bowl of bass fishing," and despite the fact that it does not have the largest field of contestants, does not offer the largest overall cash purse or the largest first-place cash prize, is not the oldest continuously running fishing contest, and does not attract a field of powerful and wealthy participants, the Bassmaster Classic is the most prominent, if not the most prestigious, single sportfishing competition in North America and perhaps the world.

How did this happen?

TEN

The Rise of BASS

There are commercial sports in this country and sports that aren't commercial, and that's the way it's always going to be.
—TALK RADIO SPORTS SHOW HOST MIKE FRANCESA

The All-American Invitational Bass Tournament

Ray Wilson Scott Jr., the man who created the Bassmaster Classic, who had the biggest impact on U.S. fishing tournaments and especially bass fishing competitions, who greatly helped to spread a catch-and-release ethic among all anglers, who stimulated the sales of fishing and boating equipment, and who helped to make black bass the most popular sportfish in the United States, was born in Montgomery, Alabama, on August 24, 1933. The Deep Sea Fishing Rodeo in Mobile had just been held for the fifth time, and the Tarpon Rodeo in Port Aransas for the second time.

Four months earlier, the April issue of *Field & Stream* listed additional winners in its 1932 fishing contest with the following notation, "We especially want to call your attention to the first prize–winning large-mouth black bass in the Southern Division—a 22¼-pounder. This is the largest black bass that has ever been entered in the *Field & Stream* contests in a great many years."

The magazine would later determine that this fish, caught in June

1932 by a nineteen-year-old family-supporting farm boy, was the all-time world-record bass caught on rod and reel. That record still stands and is today the most coveted of all fishing records. Ray Scott, of course, did not know about that record for years, but one day, a taxidermist's replica of it would hang on a wall in his building, which was headquarters for Bass Anglers Sportsman Society (BASS), the world's largest organization of anglers.

In 1939, young Scott caught his first fish at Panama City, Florida, on a family vacation at the beach. Later that summer, his uncle showed him how to use a baitcasting reel. He was taken with fishing and would become enamored with angling for bass. Industrious, inventive, gifted in sales, and entrepreneurial from an early age, the postarmy, postcollege thirty-three-year-old Scott had been successfully selling life insurance for seven years in March 1967—two months after the first Super Bowl had been held—when he had an epiphany while on a sales trip in Jackson, Mississippi.

He had been thinking about how to make a career out of fishing and had already tried and rejected the notion of running a fishing tackle store. Scott commented on his dream of a career in fishing in his 1981 book *Prospecting and Selling: From a Fishing Hole to a Pot of Gold*. "I had always been a salesman. And I loved selling. But bass fishing consumed my every idle hour. For so long I had been blessed, or perhaps cursed, with a dream, a fantasy I often indulged in while driving from place to place, or while sitting in some customer's lobby, waiting to keep an appointment. What I really wanted to do was . . . find a way to spend my working hours fishing, and make a good living while I was doing it."

On that trip to Jackson, he had stopped at the Johnny Reb Lure Company, where Don Norton had talked about entering a fishing derby. Scott knew of these derbies, and as he wrote in *Prospecting and Selling*, he said to Norton, "I've even been to a couple of those shindigs, and they're always won by the guy who has the most pounds of fish stored in his freezer." When Norton assured him that this one was clean, Scott nodded and thought, "Those derbies are all alike, nothing more than little old Chamber of Commerce promotions where everybody pitches two dollars into a hat, then finds out who's the smartest at cheating without getting caught. And nobody ever got caught. They weren't worth the trouble. I didn't like those derbies. They give fishing—and honest fishermen—a bad name."

As he had done on other occasions, Scott arranged his Jackson schedule that week in 1967 to be able to enjoy some bass fishing. With his dream and his conversation with Don Norton in the back of his mind, the stage was set. As Scott said in *Bassmaster* magazine thirty years later, "I decided to spend a weekend fishing around Jackson with friend Lloyd Lewis. Our trip was cut short by bad weather, and by noon I was back at the Ramada Inn in Jackson, lying in bed and watching sports on TV. My mind wandered from the golf game. . . . I remember standing up in bed and snapping my fingers: Snap! The idea hit me like a ton of bricks: 100 bass fishermen from all over the country would come to a place where they could bring their skills together and make money doing it. Snap! I was going to hold a bass tournament at Beaver Lake in Arkansas. I'd never been there, but I'd read about it in an article written by Charlie Elliott in *Outdoor Life*."

His idea was not another derby for bass, with the negative connotations that held for him. It was a premier, exclusive fishing competition. He would charge a high entrance fee to attract the very best anglers. He'd eliminate cheating. He'd make it like the best professional golf tournaments, the PGA of bass fishing.

On Monday, Scott was in Little Rock, meeting with the director of Arkansas tourism, introducing himself as the president of All-American Bass Tournaments. A month later, he was meeting with the directors of the Springdale, Arkansas, chamber of commerce, who warily declined sponsorship of the Beaver Lake event but offered a back room in the chamber office from which Scott could operate. He got personal and financial assistance from the owners of a marina and a commercial boat dock on Beaver Lake, whose businesses would benefit from the tournament. And the local Holiday Inn gave him a free room if he would make that hotel his tournament headquarters.

For fifty days, he gathered names and cold-called people who were reputed to be top bass fishermen. From them, as well as from the owners of marinas and tackle shops, he got a list of men who were considered to be good bass anglers in their areas. He called them and

Ray Scott signs autographs at the 2006 Citgo Bassmaster Classic.

told them whom they were referred by, and he made an effort to make the competition be (or at least appear to be) exclusive.

One of the participants in the Beaver Lake tournament was Carl Dyess of Memphis, who was called by Ray, invited to participate in the tournament, and then asked for three boat dock owner references so he could be checked out before getting a formal invitation. Dyess gave Scott the names of three docks that didn't have telephones, yet Scott called Dyess back in an hour to say that he had been highly recommended.

Scott's letter of invitation to would-be participants began, "On June 6, 7, and 8, 1967, the most important event in sport fishing will take place at Beaver Lake in Northwest Arkansas. It is the happening called the All-American Invitational Bass Tournament in which America's greatest anglers will come forth in a rod-to-rod combat of fishing skills."

He got Bob Cobb, then the outdoor editor for the *Tulsa Tribune*, to write up the event in his column and mention that members of a

Memphis bass club were challenging Tulsa fishermen via this event. He also talked Cobb into coming to the tournament to observe it.

One hundred and six fishermen from thirteen states paid their $100 entry fee—unheard of, when derbies charged just a few dollars —and blasted off on the first morning in a motley assemblage of "fishing" boats. The bass they caught were weighed in by uniformed wardens from the Arkansas Game & Fish Commission, cleaned by members of the chamber of commerce, and donated to an orphanage.

After three days, Nashville policeman Stan Sloan came out on top, winning a first-place prize of $2,000 cash and an all-expenses-paid trip to Acapulco. Scott lost $600 in the process but got the respect of the fishermen, the chamber of commerce, and the few writers who covered the event.

Homer Circle, who gave a benediction at the closing banquet of the tournament and who would later become the angling editor of *Sports Afield*, was highly complimentary in his column for the *Rogers Daily News*, as was Charles Elliott, writing in the *Atlanta Journal-Constitution*, who called the event a "tremendous success."

Even more tremendous would be the success to come, both in the conduct of tournaments and in the fortunes of many of the men who were connected with the first All-American and the Ray Scott bass tournaments that immediately followed. In fact, four of the 1967 Beaver Lake tournament's participants—Don Butler, Bill Dance, Tom Mann, and Ray Murski—plus Ray Scott, Bob Cobb, and Homer Circle, are now in the Professional Bass Fishing Hall of Fame.

The die was cast for Scott's future, as well as for the popularization of what some would later describe as the "subculture of bass fishing." Most significantly, a foundation was laid for later tournament success. Ray Scott would masterfully apply and improve upon the following bricks and mortar of that foundation over the next two decades: the interest of people in the tourism business—hotels, chamber of commerce, marinas, and so on—in promoting their areas and drawing visitors. The willingness of state natural resource agencies to assist in some manner, since they could gather information at low cost to themselves while monitoring angler activities. The willingness of companies that stood to benefit from the use of their products to become involved (one lure manufacturer sponsored a contestant and another provided the trophies). The attraction of such an event to members of the outdoor media, who would provide pre- and postevent publicity.

Most important, Scott was assured that there was a market for participants among a diverse and heretofore untapped part of the sportfishing community, especially in the South. There were many bass fishermen who wanted to prove and improve their skills, compete with others, and be recognized for their accomplishments and who dreamed of making a living in the sportfishing business.

The Rise of BASS

Scott took a three-month leave of absence from selling life insurance in July 1967 to plan his next two tournaments, which were held in October 1967 at Smith Lake in Alabama and in February 1968 at Lake Seminole in Georgia. He never returned to the insurance business.

Ready to form an organization, Scott wisely rejected advice to make it one for all anglers; he was determined to attract only specialists. Bass fishing was what he knew, and appealing to the swelling cadre of bass fishermen made sense. With the U.S. population standing at nearly two hundred million, the number of people who were fishing had grown significantly, especially throughout the South, which was bursting with large impoundments that contained exploding populations of bass.

Boat and motor manufacturers were racing to create products that would satisfy the desire to fish, cruise, race, and ski on large bodies of water, while tackle manufacturing was bursting at the seams now that anglers everywhere had embraced fiberglass rods, user-friendly reels, and less troublesome fishing lines. A bevy of accessory products—some revolutionary, like sportfishing sonar and electric positioning motors—were evolving and gaining more widespread use, opening up new frontiers in angling. In most respects, except perhaps for bluefin tuna fishing off Nova Scotia, which was as remote to Scott and his bass pals as fox hunting on horseback by following hounds, this was the golden era of American sportfishing.

Special-interest magazines had also begun to flourish by 1967, and by the end of that year, Scott was working on a bass fishing magazine.

But first he needed an organization name, which he got—Bass Anglers Sportsman Society—from Bob Steber, then the outdoor editor of a Nashville newspaper, the *Tennessean*, who was asked by Scott to come up with words that could be represented by the acronym BASS.

The year 1968 was characterized by great social turmoil in the United States, increasing turbulence over the Vietnam War, and the assassinations of Robert Kennedy Jr. and Martin Luther King Jr. Fishing provided a delightful and healthful diversion from work and social concerns for many people, especially those who lived in rural areas of the country. Growing an organization for passionate bass fishermen became Ray Scott's full-time work that year, which was a make-or-break one for him.

By February 1968, Scott had enticed 150 anglers to pay $125 apiece to compete at his Lake Seminole tournament, which was won by the "highly recommended" Carl Dyess. That month, Bass Anglers Sportsman Society also had a magazine, in the loosest possible definition of that word. Around 2,500 copies of the first issue of *Bassmaster* were printed, and three more issues followed that year. Although grammatically and aesthetically wanting, they contained articles written by bass fishing enthusiasts. As Scott later wrote about the first issue, "At best it was a clandestine collection of stories written for free by fishermen."

Don Butler of Tulsa loaned Scott $10,000 to pay the postage (first-class stamps were then 5 cents) for a BASS membership mailing to people who had sent in warranty cards to Abu Garcia, then the largest manufacturer of fishing reels and rods in the country. Scott's solicitation produced enough checks from new members to repay Butler ten days after the mailing went out. While there was little advertising at first to support the magazine that Scott offered to members, tournaments provided the cash flow that allowed him to press on, and his train was gathering a head of steam.

By December 1969, Scott had the wherewithal to hire Bob Cobb as a full-time employee and the head of communications and to make him a stockholder in BASS. Seven months later, he did the same with Helen Sevier, a direct mail expert who became director of marketing, in charge of growing the membership. Cobb quickly improved the quality and the educational component of the magazine and also began an editorial focus on the growing interest in "casting for cash" and on the personalities who were achieving success on the new "professional bass fishing circuit."

Within two years of Sevier's employment, membership jumped from fifteen thousand to sixty-five thousand. Such growth was in part due to her shrewd placement of ads in major outdoor magazines and to her savvy direct-marketing efforts, but also because Scott was spreading his bass fishing gospel to people throughout the South, one by one, at fishing seminars that he organized. In these, some of his top tournament fishermen talked about their techniques. At one seminar, he drew more than three thousand anglers. At most, nearly 10 percent of the attendees signed up to become members, and all of them went into the database that Sevier was amassing for future mailings.

In mid-1970, Scott hired James "Pooley" Dawson, the man who was honored upon his retirement at the 2005 Classic in Pittsburgh, to work part time at various jobs, making his employment permanent in 1972. In November of that year, Scott hired a former Southern Railroad employee, bass angler, and organizer of the first bass club in Chattanooga, Harold Sharp, to run his fishing tournaments. Sharp had caught the biggest bass in Scott's Smith Lake tournament in 1967, and his Chattanooga bass club became the first to affiliate with BASS, which was the beginning of the Bass Federation, a national association of bass fishing clubs.

Sharp and Scott made sure that BASS tournament rules were enforced without exception and made holding an "honest" contest the first priority, after getting participants. The tournaments they administered, which were covered in *Bassmaster*, quickly began to have an effect on the equipment of the participants, as well as on people who emulated them, and thus on the boating and fishing tackle industries. To counter the negative image of photos of strings of dead bass at the weigh-in, they began and mandated catch-and-release bass tournaments, which greatly helped to foster a conservation ethic among all freshwater anglers, including those who had never fished in a contest.

Looking to draw attention to his fledgling organization in 1970 and 1971, and angered by the condition of the waterways in his own city and state, Scott filed a class-action lawsuit against the Alabama Water Improvement Commission and its director, all 214 of the companies that the commission had given lenient water and sewer discharge permits to, plus the chief of the U.S. Army Corps of Engineers. Using the little-known 1899 Federal Refuse Act, he charged that the commission was a front for industry and polluters.

"I wanted to embarrass them," says Scott. "And get somebody to clean the rivers up."

His efforts to call attention to the threat to public waters landed him on NBC's *Today Show*, where he was interviewed by Joe Garagiola; he also had an interview with Dick Cavett.

"Publicity-wise, it did what I hoped," says Scott. "Today you can drink the water in the Alabama River."

This activity occurred prior to enactment of the Clean Water Act of 1972, and although BASS had grown to ninety thousand members by the fall of that year, it was still a small voice. Nevertheless, in future years such activism would lead to BASS having a seat at the table with national and regional government policy makers and would entrench BASS as a political force.

This seat, and this influence, was something that older, more professionally written publications (i.e., *Field & Stream*, *Outdoor Life*, and *Sports Afield*, which collectively claimed nearly five million readers at that time) did not have, being subscriber-based publications owned by large corporations with no roots in the outdoor world and which counted every expenditure against its effect on the bottom line.

In September 1977, just ten years after he'd started on a shoestring, Ray Scott's organization counted 270,000 members, each of whom received a yearly subscription to *Bassmaster* as part of his or her membership dues. The magazine that month, labeled Volume X, Number 6, had 128 pages, numerous four-color ads and editorial photos, lots of instructional bass fishing information, and an article about the great bass fishing that had just been rediscovered in Cuba. It also contained an article about the environmental activism of BASS members at the state and national level; the Bass Federation was then organized in thirty-five states and had 1,475 chapters, or clubs, which held their own local and regional bass tournaments. If they averaged six events per club, BASS-affiliated clubs alone may have been responsible for nearly nine thousand fishing contests in the United States.

In late 1977, as an editor and a writer in the New York City headquarters of *Field & Stream*, I was summoned into the offices of publisher Michael J. O'Neill, who sought my opinions about Bass Anglers Sportsman Society, Ray Scott, and bass fishing tournaments. Since the spring of 1976, I had been writing most of the magazine's coverage of bass fishing. I had fished in a BASS tournament and had written about it for the magazine, had been a press observer at the Bass-master Classic, and had recently written a much-publicized article about bass fishing in Cuba.

The magazine's accountant, John Condon (the same fellow who would cause the magazine's fishing contest and freshwater record keeping to be donated to the IGFA a few months later), was reviewing the books of Bass Anglers Sportsman Society with an eye toward acquiring the company.

The urbane O'Neill was sophisticated and highly respected in the New York publishing community. He was not a fisherman and may never have caught or even seen a bass in his life, but he saw value in the burgeoning publication *Bassmaster*. He was dubious, however, about the rest of BASS.

We discussed the fact that Bass Anglers Sportsman Society was a membership organization, which meant membership fulfillment and recruitment issues, plus chapter management, which was above and beyond merely publishing a magazine. Not to mention that *Field & Stream* would become the owner and the manager of a bass fishing tournament business.

"There are all kinds of deals going on there," said O'Neill, implying that Condon was trying to sort out all of Ray Scott's complex arrangements and place a value on tradeouts of boats and motors, sonar, fishing line, rods and reels, lures, hotel rooms, airfare, and what-all-else for magazine advertisements and tournament sponsorship.

O'Neill also expressed concern that *Bassmaster* and other proliferating special-interest fishing and hunting publications posed a threat to *Field & Stream*'s advertising.

I asked him why we accepted their advertising, if doing so didn't actually help BASS grow.

"We also sell them our mailing list," he said, meaning that they made direct mail solicitations to our subscribers, probably luring some of them away. "It's good money."

Not only good, but easy. Some of BASS's advertising in *Field & Stream* and its rivals consisted of self-contained, two-sided, one-page inserts. A growing Bass Pro Shops would do the same thing for a number of years. The then most recent edition of *Field & Stream* to contain BASS advertising was the August 1977 issue, which had a full-page ad with a photo of the organization's patch and the large bold words, "Not every fisherman wears this patch. Can you?" It also contained this quote from Bill Dance, identified as one of the country's top bass anglers and a satisfied BASS member: "Since joining BASS, my fishing has improved 500%." So had his income. Dance had won a bunch of the early BASS tournaments and had gotten a lot of publicity. His endorsement quote would be repeated for years.

It was naive of me to ask O'Neill why *Field & Stream* accepted BASS advertising. The magazine, like nearly every publication owned by a corporation with stockholders, took almost any advertising for purely bottom-line reasons. BASS ran a large ad in many issues a year; it was a good, regular customer that didn't need a hard sell by an ad salesman.

In the end, a take-the-money-and-look-the-other-way approach would cost *Field & Stream*. The rise of special-interest fishing and hunting magazines would eat into the circulation and the advertising efforts of the Big Three (which included *Outdoor Life* and *Sports Afield*), as these national magazines were then known. Eventually, *Field & Stream*'s subscription list would not produce well enough for BASS, other fishing publications, Bass Pro Shops, and assorted companies that needed good names to drive their own readership and customer base. They would stop advertising in *Field & Stream*, having plucked all of the best fruit.

O'Neill was right about the erosion of endemic advertising, which steadily worsened. In later years, *Field & Stream*'s prohibitive advertising rates, due in part to publishing such a large-circulation magazine, proved too much for most of the small and medium-size companies in the sportfishing industry. Also a problem was that the magazine was overwhelmed by the task of being all things hunting and all things fishing to all people who hunted and all people who fished. This made (and still makes) the magazine less attractive to, say, the manufacturer of a bass fishing lure, whose advertising would necessarily reach many readers who didn't do any bass fishing; furthermore, his cost per thousand might have been terrific in the large scheme of things, but his gross cost was, well, gross. Similar problems befell *Outdoor Life* and *Sports Afield*—but not *Bassmaster*, which was 100 percent devoted to bass fishing.

With reservations about the real value of BASS, concerned about issues associated with running a membership fulfillment business, and probably wary of a country-talking, wheeler-dealer, bass-fishing evangelist, O'Neill passed on the opportunity to buy Ray Scott's organization.

In 1986, the company would be sold to Helen Sevier and a group of investors. In 2001, it would be bought by ESPN, a television production company that did not exist in 1977.

BASS originally went by the acronym B.A.S.S., but ESPN—itself originally the Entertainment and Sports Programming Network— soon deleted the periods and virtually dropped the cumbersome original name that Bob Steber had given Ray Scott.

ELEVEN

The Birth and Growth
of the Classic

You have to do what you love; otherwise, what's the point?
—NOVELIST ELMORE LEONARD

The First Classic

Ray Scott and Bob Cobb developed the idea for a championship-level bass fishing tournament during a three-hour drive to Atlanta in 1970, primarily as a vehicle for getting media attention for their growing organization. Publicity had been lean, and Scott and Cobb reasoned that they needed a lot of publicity for professional bass fishing tournaments to be taken seriously and to get more people fired up about them, as well as to grow the membership of Bass Anglers Sportsman Society.

Scott and Cobb decided to call the championship the BASS Masters Classic and to hold it in 1971. It was announced before a location had been selected or the execution of the tournament had been planned.

They decided that there would be just twenty-four participants who would qualify for an expense-free entry by virtue of their performance over a season of bass fishing contests. BASS would attract attention by offering a then-unheard-of $10,000 cash prize to the winner and would have fully rigged new boats waiting for the anglers

Competitors and media gather before the start of the 1971 Bassmaster Classic on Lake Mead.

at the mystery location. To make the championship equally demanding on the contestants and to provide an enticing story angle for the media, they would keep the location of the event a secret until the last possible moment.

As for the media (which was actually called the "press" in that era before now-ubiquitous TV cameras and cyberspace), they would invite one member of the media for each angler—to serve as an observer as well as a reporter—and would pay all of that person's expenses to attend. When Scott called outdoor writers from newspapers and magazines, most of whom were referrals from other writers, he pumped up the sales pitch, offering the opportunity of a lifetime to cover this new event, to fish alongside one of the "pros" for four days, to be part of an exciting shotgun-blast start, and to bear witness to the start of something extraordinary.

Some writers were skeptical and declined. A few were already converts, some of them even being on the board of advisers of BASS. Others were curious, perhaps even seduced, figuring that the worst that could happen is that they'd get an expenses-paid holiday somewhere and might actually catch some fish.

Thus, on October 18, 1971, twenty-four anglers, some of their wives, and a like number of media representatives boarded a Delta Airlines plane in Atlanta that had been chartered in the name of the Golden Age Garden Club.

Among the qualifying anglers who would later become prominent in bass fishing were Roland Martin, who was listed as a teacher and a fishing guide from Montgomery, Alabama; Don Butler, who had loaned Scott postage money a few years earlier; Tom Mann, who would start one of America's foremost lure manufacturing companies; Stan Sloan, who was listed as a former law enforcement officer and a lure manufacturer; and John Powell, a retired Air Force master sergeant who had won back-to-back BASS tournaments.

The list of fishermen spanned ten states and included seven representatives of tackle companies, several salesmen, two fishing guides, a resort owner, an undertaker, an attorney, an X-ray technician, a farmer, and men from various other fields. Not one was listed in the media guide as a professional bass fisherman—then a novel new term—although by then several of the men actually were.

The media roster spanned fifteen states and included several outdoor writing icons of the day, among them Homer Circle, then of *Sports Afield*; Jim Hardie of the *Miami Herald*; Charles Salter of the *Atlanta Journal-Constitution*; and Bodie McDowell of the *Greensboro Daily News-Record*. The outdoor editors of major daily newspapers in Fort Worth, Nashville, Chattanooga, Tulsa, Oakland, Kansas City, Chicago, Baton Rouge, Wichita, and Houston were on hand, as was Geoffrey Norman of *Playboy*, television fishing show pioneer Virgil Ward, and *Sports Illustrated*'s Bob Boyle, who in 1999 would write Ray Scott's biography, *Bass Boss*.

The news release that BASS had earlier issued, which had been sent to media around the country, was headed "Anglers Fish Mystery Lake for $10,000 Prize." It extolled the hard work of Roland Martin, ranked number one in the standings, who then had won more than $11,000 in ten BASS events, as well as the benefits to the society's fifty thousand members by "the results, testing of fishing gear and learning techniques that prove successful in out-smarting the crafty bass." It noted how the contestants would fish out of specially designed $4,000 bass tournament rigs, and it called the first-place award a "bonanza," and "the largest winner's purse in bass fishing history."

None of the anglers and the media members who boarded the chartered plane on October 18, 1971, knew where they were headed. Scott waved a hand with several hundred-dollar bills in it and invited anyone to win it by guessing the location of the Classic. None did.

According to an article written about the event by *Fishing World* writer Milt Rosko of New Jersey, "Only after our jetliner lifted to 10,000 feet out of Atlanta did Ray open a sealed envelope and say, 'We've got the best bass fishermen in the world on this plane. You wouldn't expect the World Series to be played on a Little League ball yard. Neither would you expect the world championship of bass fishing to be held in a fish hatchery. We're headed for Lake Mead on the Nevada-Arizona border. It will be the toughest fishing test of your angling careers. But it will be worth it. To the victor goes $10,000 cash.'"

One of the people on the plane was Dave Newton, a writer for the Las Vegas News Bureau, who had contacted Scott about bringing the tournament west as part of an effort to promote Las Vegas as a family vacation destination. Through Newton's efforts, the Classic was hosted by the Las Vegas Convention Authority and the Union Plaza Hotel. Las Vegas put up $25,000 and made all of the airfare, hotel, and meal arrangements.

BASS put up the $10,000 prize money and arranged for boats to be shipped in secrecy fourteen hundred miles from Ft. Smith, Arkansas, a task that was overseen by weighmaster Harold Sharp. Two of the trailers carrying the boats got snowbound in Flagstaff, Arizona, so there were not enough boats for the practice day to put each angler in his own boat with a writer. A nervous Sharp asked Scott what to do and was told to pair a few of the anglers up in boats together.

"We'll shuffle the deck," said Scott. "Don't worry about it."

"What about the writers?" asked Sharp.

"Send 'em to the bar," said the boss.

When the Bassmasters and the media weren't at the bar or on the lake, they could see Liza Minnelli at the Riviera, Don Rickles at the

Sahara, Connie Stevens at the Sands, or Andy Williams and the Lennon Sisters at Caesar's Palace. Or they could try their luck in the casinos.

It was uncanny yet symbolic that the first BASS Masters Classic was held in boom-or-bust Sin City. Scott was certainly rolling the dice that these fishermen, none of whom had previously been on Lake Mead, would not only catch some impressive bass, but that they, and the event, would wow the media.

The group gathered on the first morning of the Classic, October 20, in a congenial way, all of the contestants and the media plus Sharp and Cobb and a bullhorn-holding Scott posing on a floating dock for what would be a historic photo of fifty-four men, many in jumpsuits and wearing BASS patches, standing next to a flotilla of Rebel Fastback inboard-outboard boats and dwarfed in the background by an array of docked cabin cruisers. With their jumpsuits on, many of the anglers looked like the early jumpsuit-wearing NASCAR drivers.

The anglers' boats gathered in a row across a bay near the marina, each with the words BASS Masters Classic emblazoned on both port and starboard rear gunwales and a BASS decal affixed to both forward gun-

Tom Mann fishes on Lake Mead during the 1971 Bassmaster Classic. His media partner is Bob Zwirz of *Sportsfishing* magazine.

wales. Sporting 90 hp Mercruiser engines, forward pedestal seats, bow-mounted MotorGuide electric motors, and console-mounted Lowrance depthfinders, they were state of the art for 1971, although this would be the only time that a boat with an inboard-outboard engine would be used in the Classic, and the only time that this brand of boat was used.

When a flare was shot into the air, the throttles went down and two dozen boats streaked together out of the bay into the open waters of Lake Mead, where 162,000 acres of the Colorado River were backed up by the Western Hemisphere's highest concrete dam, offering 822 miles of undeveloped shoreline to fish. The collective rush out of the bay into the enormous lake was a metaphor for the world of professional bass fishing that lay ahead.

The fishermen returned each day to a weigh-in held at the marina. There was a small crowd of spectators—maybe 150, according to one account. The fish, which were dead and brought to the marina on stringers, were placed on a white metal grocery store scale, and the daily weights for each angler were handwritten on a large board.

After one day of practice and three days of competition, Bobby Murray of Hot Springs, Arkansas, a twenty-five-year-old sales representative for Jim Bagley Bait Company and a former fishing guide, was declared the winner, catching seventeen largemouth bass that weighed a total of 43 pounds 11 ounces, primarily by retrieving a white spinnerbait around heavy shallow cover.

A victory photo of that event shows a jumpsuited, broad-smiling Murray hoisting an impressive stringer of bass—not all of which were his own—over a table and a trophy. He is standing next to a beaming Ray Scott, who is delivering a $10,000 check. The only thing close to an endorsement on Murray's clothing is the Bagley patch on his baseball cap.

The total purse for the 1971 Classic was $12,750, and Murray received $10,850 of that, the extra $850 being in bonuses. Tom Mann, who finished second but earned nothing, caught eleven more bass than Murray did, using spinning tackle and four-inch worms in deep water. Roland Martin, who finished fourth, caught the tournament's largest bass, a 6-pound 9-ounce largemouth that rewarded him with $700 of his total $900 in bonus money.

. . .

Bobby Murray hefts a string of bass, and Ray Scott displays a check for $10,000, at the end of the 1971 Bassmaster Classic.

Bobby Murray graduated from college in 1969 and had done preparatory teaching at Little Rock Central High School. Three jobs awaited him after graduation, but he passed on them and went to Toledo Bend Reservoir in Texas to become a fishing guide.

"That's what I wanted to do," says Murray. "I always thought I would coach football and teach history, but once that fire was in my belly about fishing, I said, 'I can make a living at this. Whether I've got to guide, or whatever, I'll get in the industry somehow.'"

Sound familiar? Ray Scott desired to make a living in the fishing business in 1967 when he was on a sales trip to Jackson, Mississippi. Having such a desire was probably common for most of the other fishermen in that first Classic. Having such a desire is what drives the top bass pros today and is a major reason for the success of the Classic and all of the events that lead up to it. Having a dream to do what the pros do, to do what Murray did, or to do what Scott did, lurks among bassheads from California to the Carolinas. It's the golden dream that drives all of the present-day bass tournament madness. Ray Scott found a kindred soul in Bobby Murray, and they both tapped into a wellspring of desire.

After college, Bobby Murray guided for two years at Toledo Bend, then went to work for Bagley, a rising bass lure manufacturer, less than a year before he fished in the 1971 Classic. After the Classic, he had his own tackle store for a few years, then held a variety of sales and promotion jobs in the fishing tackle and fishing boat business while still continuing to compete in major bass tournaments.

Murray won the Classic again in 1978, which solidified his career, not only as a great angler but as a legend in the sport.

"Then I was not a onetime wonder," he says.

Today he and his twin brother, Billy (who was a cameraman for Jerry McKinnis in the 1970s), conduct promotions and sales training seminars for many of the country's big-box stores.

Murray does not fish major bass tournaments any more, but he still has the competitive desire. He sees what has happened to professional bass fishing today, and the money and the notoriety that go with it.

"Every day I think about being twenty-five years old and in this game. Every day," says Murray, now sixty years old. "Make me twenty-five years old, and let me break-dance on the front of the boat!

"Just think back. Roland Martin, Bill Dance, myself, Ricky Green, Rick Clunn, put us back at twenty-five to twenty-eight years old and turn us loose. Just think what we could do now if our backs didn't hurt and we didn't have back surgery, knee replacements, and prostate problems. There was nobody that had the fire in their belly like that group had. But we can all take pride in knowing that we were pioneers. The Bassmaster Classic would not be what it is today if we had not had the integrity, the love for the sport, and the willingness to sacrifice, in many cases our families, which is a shame, as well as our money and our bodies early on in those boats in that big water. Without that foundation, this would never be here today. That first Classic gave me the credentials to carry the sport on."

As true as Murray's comment is with respect to the early bass tournament stars, there is a greater truth: without widespread media attention, Scott's professional bass fishing tournaments and his Bassmaster Classic would have gone nowhere. Ray Scott created a vehicle that some of the outdoor media would come to love, many outdoor writers being partners, wittingly and unwittingly, in spreading the gospel of bass fishing and, in the process, growing the stature of bass fishing tournaments—in particular, its major championship event.

As one longtime media attendee would later say, "Ray's formula was excellent. He wanted to embed the press within his tournament."

Dave Newton would later be quoted in *Bass Boss* as saying, "Those fishermen and writers gave us more press in a year for our family-related outdoor activities than we could ever have possibly gotten by calling writers individually and saying, 'C'mon and fish with us.' The Bassmaster Classic really put Lake Mead on the map as a bass fishery."

Those writers and many others who attended Classics for the next twenty-eight years also put the Bassmaster Classic and the Bass Anglers Sportsman Society on the map.

The Classic Grows

The 1972 BASS Masters Classic was held in October at Percy Priest Lake in Tennessee. The first dues-paying member of BASS, Don Butler of Tulsa, won a tough event, producing twenty-two bass that weighed 38 pounds 11 ounces, which was more than 13 pounds ahead of second-place finisher Ricky Green, and which became the largest winning margin of the Classic until 1984. After the event, Butler was introduced on the stage of the Grand Ol' Opry by Ernest Tubbs.

Butler owed the win and what is still the largest winning comeback in Bassmaster Classic history to his good friend Green, which is a story that demonstrates the camaraderie and sportsmanship that existed between many of the fishermen in the early days of the Classic, and which appears to be much different today with so much more at stake.

After the first day of the 1972 Classic, Green had a catch weighing 15 pounds, which was more than 7 pounds ahead of his nearest competitor. Butler had caught two small bass and was nearly 13 pounds behind. Green told Butler what he was using and even showed him where he was fishing on a map. The next day, Green went back to his first-day spot and caught only 3 or 4 pounds; Butler went about two miles above Green and caught 22 pounds, opening up a 5-pound lead. On the last day, both men returned to their prior-day spots; Butler caught 13 pounds and won, while Green caught 6 pounds and came in second, 4 pounds ahead of third-place finisher Tom Mann.

"If I hadn't told Butler all that," says Green, who would appear in thirteen more Classics without winning, "I would have been the winner, I guess. I always wondered about that."

That Classic, and the four following, were all held at mystery locations, which the media loved and speculated about, providing bonus publicity. Yet it increasingly became a logistical nightmare as the size of the media corps grew, the difficulty in secretly getting boats to the location became more difficult, and the cost to administer the tournament ballooned.

During those years, there was speculation that Ray Scott might take the tournament out of the country, especially to Mexico. Although that never happened, Scott did have an interest in bringing it to Cuba, whose fishing suddenly opened up to Americans in May 1977.

In January 1977, I began efforts, with the blessing of *Field & Stream*, to gain entry to Cuba for the purpose of fishing for its then legendary Treasure Lake bass. No one had fished in Cuba since the end of Fidel Castro's revolution in 1959. In April 1977, while on a Mako Boats-Evinrude Motors fishing junket in the Bahamas that was also attended by Ray Scott, I openly spoke with several people who had fished in Cuba during the late 1950s, as well as with Clive Gammon, a writer for *Sports Illustrated*, whose colleague had recently written about a big-game fishing tournament in Havana.

Scott overhead one of my conversations and later took me aside, saying that he wanted to bring the Bassmaster Classic to Cuba and had hired an expatriate Cuban lawyer in Miami to see if he could gain entry to that country, but nothing had yet come of this. He offered me a deal to take him to Cuba if I got the chance first and said that in return, he'd take me if he got the chance first. I declined and a month later was fishing at Treasure Lake, later writing the first modern-day article about the tremendous bass fishing that existed there.

When I returned from Cuba, I called Scott and left a message with his secretary about going to Cuba, but he never returned my call and remained unhappy with me for a long time afterward. Although *Bassmaster* ran an interview with me about my trip and the new fishing opportunities in Cuba, Scott later denounced everyone going to that communist country as "trading bass for bullets" and he strong-armed many of the bass pros who later wanted to go there.

My article about fishing in Cuba appeared in the August 1977 issue of *Field & Stream*. Two months later, BASS conducted its seventh Classic. Ironically, it was held in the state that contained most of the Cubans who fled their homeland during Castro's revolution.

The first time that the media and the contestants had prior notice of the location of the Bassmaster Classic was in October 1977 on Lake Tohopekaliga, Florida. Toho, as it is known, had an average depth of five feet, was choked with hyacinths and hydrilla, and was expected to produce a good catch. But the bass turned fickle after a two-week cold spell dropped the water ten degrees. Rick Clunn, who had won the Classic with a record-high weight the year before, repeated as champ with a then record-low total catch, becoming the first person to win two Classics and the only one through the present time to win consecutive titles.

Proving that luck can be a factor even with professional anglers, Clunn virtually won the event with his second cast on the first day of competition. He was heading to his first intended fishing spot that morning, but heavy fog made him a bit unsure of his location, so he stopped, later discovering that he was a hundred yards short of where he wanted to go. Clunn put his electric motor on and started fishing with a buzzbait, which a 7-pound 7-ounce largemouth immediately grabbed. He won the event by 1 pound 12 ounces, taking the $25,000 first prize, which was half of the total purse. The following year he would impressively place second, 8 pounds behind Bobby Murray.

I attended the 1977 Classic as a "press observer," as it was called by BASS, having previously been at the 1976 event at Lake Guntersville. I would attend five more in the following years, my last visit prior to 2005 being at the October 1982 Classic on the Alabama River in Montgomery.

An unpleasant incident with Clunn in 1982 was partially responsible for my not attending future Bassmaster Classics, although a similar episode the following day with another contestant, Ken Cook, put me over the edge.

BASS always had Classic anglers fish one contestant per boat, unlike qualifying events in which two pros fished in a boat. Anglers were each accompanied by a member of the media on every practice day and competition day. In the early Classics, nearly all of the media attendees were newspaper or magazine writers who were rotated so that they had the opportunity to accompany different anglers each day. Writers outnumbered anglers (forty-one fished in the 1982 Classic), which was good because some didn't want to accompany the pros or wanted to go only on certain days or with certain individuals.

To encourage the writers to accompany pros and fill a keep-them-honest observation role, BASS allowed writers to bring a limited amount of their own tackle on the boat and to fish, provided that they didn't interfere with the anglers and did not assist them or provide them with information. A tackle box, lures, some accessory gear, a jacket and a hat, a PFD (personal flotation device), and other items were among the loot annually provided to each media attendee, with a care package containing these items being sent to each writer's home beforehand and other goodies being provided upon registration where there was, according to one writer, "a cafeteria of paraphernalia."

In addition, BASS offered a cash award to the press observer who caught the biggest fish each day. Initially, $500 was awarded only to the press observers. Later, to smooth ruffled feathers, BASS also gave $500 to the fisherman he was with.

Allowing writers to fish and offering them a cash incentive often proved unfair. A few writers were pretty good bass anglers, some very good. Some were decent anglers but not attuned to bass fishing, and they brought tackle that was wholly inappropriate. Some couldn't catch a bass if they were in a hatchery tank that held fish that hadn't been fed for three weeks.

Sometimes the writers couldn't cast well or work a lure properly, and they frequently got snagged, causing the pros to waste time backing the boats up so the writers could get unsnagged (most pros would just make them break the line and keep on going, to the annoyance of the writers). Some writers were noisy, fumbling dunderheads in a boat. And a few seemed to think that they were in a contest with the pros.

Those writers who were capable bass anglers were often asked by the pros to fish a particular lure or fish in a certain way, which in effect allowed the pros to have two things going at one time and help figure out what the bass wanted. Several times, I was asked by a pro to fish with one type of lure while he used other types. If I caught some bass, or a large bass, by doing something different from what the pro was doing, it provided useful information about lure type, lure color, or location that he might not have figured out if he'd kept doing what he was doing.

At times, that is exactly what happened, not only with me but with other media people who were good anglers. This advantage could not occur for a pro who was stuck with a writer who had no fishing ability. Of course, some pros preferred to be with writers who just snoozed all day, neither helping nor hindering. It was a double-edged sword.

Common sense and courtesy dictated that the writer would fish only in the back of the boat and would cast back (not ahead) or fish off the other side of the boat. I spent a lot of time fishing the deeper, open water side of the boat, while the pros I was with were fishing cover along a shoreline.

But not everyone did this. And some writers were especially intent on trying to catch a money-winning bass.

"When they had that five-hundred-dollar thing going," says Ricky Green, "some of the writers could get pretty aggressive. Ol' Reeves Field, he threw up in front of me half the time. Once on a tournament day, I missed one and Reeves just threw right in there. 'Dang! What are you doing?' I yelled, and then he set the hook. It turned out to be a 6-14, I think. At that time the money didn't go to both guys. It just went to the sportswriter."

Most of the early Classic pros could tell similar stories, and while some didn't care to see their writers catch any big fish that the pros might have landed, either in practice or during the tournament, others were pretty generous during practice days. Green was one of them, in fact.

Bruce Holt, then a writer and today executive director of G. Loomis, the premier hi-tech fishing rod manufacturer in North America, proved as much in an incident that occurred when he accompanied Green in 1981.

"It was a practice day," says Holt, "and Ricky said, 'Grab a plastic worm, and I'll throw this spinnerbait.' We're in this creek, and Ricky threw a spinnerbait way back to a stump, and a big bass blew up on it. He yanked his lure away and said, 'Throw up in there.' So I did. I threw in there three times and missed him all three times. After the last miss, Ricky turned and said to me, 'You just blew $500 for both of us,' and he gave me a hard time about it all day. Then he went back in there the first day of the tournament and caught it."

The Alabama River Classic in 1982 was the seventh and last of the early-day events that I attended, and while some had been more interesting than others and had provided better fishing (for the anglers and for me as a press observer), not once had there been a problem with any of the people I'd been paired with, many of whom I had requested. Some days were very enjoyable, and I recall no unpleasantries with any Classic angler whom I fished with, most of whom were gentlemen and easy to get along with. That included Charlie Campbell, Blake Honeycutt, Bo Dowden, Bill Dance, Ricky Green, Forrest Wood, Rayo Breckenridge, and others.

On the second day of the 1982 Classic, I was paired with Rick Clunn, whom I had never shared a boat with. I met him at the launch site and put my tackle in his boat, and we idled out to the starting point. On the way, Clunn asked me not to fish, explaining, politely but firmly, that he thought press observers should only observe, that the anglers had a lot at stake, that my job was reporting and his job was fishing.

Not anticipating this, I was taken aback. In hindsight, I should have immediately demanded to go back to the dock—or jumped out of the boat.

Moments later, we were roaring down the river. Clunn, who had done poorly the first day and was far behind in the competition, headed into an expansive oxbow. Rather than be confrontational, I sat behind the console, very unhappy. Neither of us spoke for three hours, as Clunn fished with the intensity and concentration of a stalking predator. I tried to snooze, counted leaves on the trees, and longed for a good book to read. It was like being in prison.

By midday, with one or two tiny fish in the boat, Clunn may have realized that his chances in this event had evaporated, and he said that I might as well fish, if I wanted to. So I did, not particularly enthusiastically, and generally throwing my spinnerbait in the wake of the boat to be as inoffensive as possible. It was basically something to do, as I was stuck until three o'clock.

A little later, fishing fast and looking for the odd impulsive-reaction strike, Clunn tossed his spinnerbait ahead along the trunk of a large tree lying near the bank. He cast a second time to the tree, and then a third time, the last cast being back and over the outer limbs. Then he turned and pitched up ahead. The boat was now well past the tree.

I looked at the tree as a target, because this is what you do when you're bored and have a fishing rod and you're around lots of objects. You practice making accurate presentations, congratulating yourself on landing the lure right in between those split trees, for example, where a bass, if there was a bass, would be waiting to reward you.

My distant cast back to the tree trunk landed on the far side. I rolled the lure over the trunk and let it flutter, and a bass grabbed it. It was about 3 pounds. I put it in the livewell and, feeling awkward, sat down again. I think I fished some more that afternoon, but I don't remember any talk between us or anything else interesting or pleasantly memorable.

My fish was the largest media bass that day. Clunn finished the tournament in twenty-third place. At the banquet the following evening, he and I both received checks for $500. Clunn's then wife, Gerri, sought me out afterward and thanked me, which made me wonder if maybe he gave her his bonus winnings.

In any case, that marginally brightened the third and last day of the Classic for me, most of which had been spent in excruciating unpleasantness, thanks to Ken Cook, who that morning waited until we had run a half hour from the launch ramp to his first fishing spot to tell me that I could not fish.

Maybe Cook was disgruntled because he had done poorly so far (he wound up twenty-ninth). Maybe he had a problematic media partner the previous day. Maybe his hemorrhoids were acting up. But Cook was belligerently nasty and demanded that I not fish the whole day.

It didn't matter, as I pointed out, that this was not the rule under which I agreed to be an observer. That I promised not to hinder his efforts. That had he told me about this first thing in the morning—which is why he waited until I was a captive a half-hour away from the launch site—the tournament director would have ordered him to let me fish. Or there would have been a major effort trying to get a stand-in observer.

Again, in hindsight, I could have . . . duked it out, swum to shore, forced the issue, and fished anyway. Rather than create an incident that would be bad for us both, I sat on my ass and seethed. I didn't fish all day. He caught nothing memorable. We didn't speak. It was and remains the most unpleasant day I have ever spent in a boat with another human being. And that's counting the time I thought I might die in a storm out in the Gulf Stream or when lightning struck a tree near me on a lake in Mexico.

A few days later, I talked with the editor of *Field & Stream*, Duncan Barnes, about the Classic. For the third or fourth year in a row, he said that he did not want me to do a story about the Classic for the magazine, although I was welcome to write it up in one of their *Fishing Annuals* (one-shot newsstand publications with a fraction of the readership). I told him I would do that and also that I wouldn't go back to the Bassmaster Classic again and that he was welcome to send anyone in my place in the future.

No one from *Field & Stream* went to the Bassmaster Classic and wrote an article about it for the next two decades.

What especially bothered me about *Field & Stream*'s attitude was that Barnes, who disliked fishing contests and wouldn't have gone to a Bassmaster Classic even if Jesus Christ were there, approved my going to the Classic at the expense of BASS, ostensibly to write an article for the magazine, when he didn't want an article about it. What he wanted was me, as the magazine's de facto bass fishing authority, to wave the flag in a PR gesture. He could always tell the ad sales guys that Ken Schultz was there—if and when BASS the advertiser called about our lack of coverage—but that there wasn't enough for a feature story.

I did not want to go through that charade again—and risk being confined all day in a boat with my thumb up my ass. When the next Classic was held, I was catching salmon on Lake Ontario.

Gradually, the Classic changed, though media representation remained virtually the same until 2000. Some of the changes were meant to draw spectators to the event so that sponsors could get better exposure for their increasing cost and to make the Classic, plus major bass fishing tournaments, TV-friendly. In the late 1970s and early 1980s, televised outdoor shows were becoming more numerous, and while most such shows were broadcast locally, cable television was making inroads around the country.

By 1980, the then-fledgling cable network ESPN televised reruns of an old *Outdoor Life* series that was hosted by actor William Cannon. That year ESPN sold airtime in 1981 to JM Associates of Little Rock, Arkansas, a small company then syndicating a program called *The Fishin' Hole*, hosted by one of the company's partners, Jerry McKinnis.

In early 1980, McKinnis called me and asked about places to film for smallmouth bass in New England; he also asked me to join him to do a show. That June, filming for the following year, McKinnis came with me to Squam Lake in New Hampshire, where the popular movie *On Golden Pond* had been shot. We had excellent fishing, and his filming of that became the first episode of *The Fishin' Hole* to air in 1981. It was also the first original fishing/outdoor program ever broadcast on ESPN.

That episode aired countless times in 1981, including on Thanksgiving Day, and received a national award the following summer. *The Fishin' Hole* is currently the longest-running program on ESPN besides *SportsCenter*, and JM Associates is now a large outdoor production company that produces or coordinates most of the outdoor programming done for ESPN.

McKinnis's instant success on cable television, and the need for programming on this new medium, helped stir others to produce outdoor shows or to migrate existing shows from local stations to cable. Within a few years, outdoor programming grew significantly. In 1985,

BASS began its own cable-television show on the Nashville Network (TNN), supervised by Bob Cobb and called *The Bassmasters*.

BASS also started an outdoor-product consumer exhibit in conjunction with the Classic, in order to attract people who could be available for the weigh-in. BASS conducted Classic weigh-ins in auditoriums that could hold thousands of people, instead of holding them outdoors in the parking lot of a state park or marina. Commenting about bringing the weigh-ins indoors in *Bassmaster* in late 1985, Ray Scott wrote, "We're making bass fishing a 'spectator sport.'"

The weigh-in became theatrical so that it would play well on television. Loud music, live entertainment by country music stars, light shows, and glittering truck- and boat-drive-ins became part of the hoopla. Members of the press corps had often been introduced from the stage by Ray Scott, but when BASS stopped doing that, it was obvious that an attitudinal shift was occurring.

The locations where BASS held the Classic were seldom top-of-the-chart bass fisheries. Events in the first decade were mainly held on large lakes, but in the second decade they were top-heavy with rivers. From 1980 through 1990, the Classic was held ten times on rivers: the St. Lawrence, the Alabama (twice in a row), the Ohio (twice), the Arkansas (twice), and the James (three times in a row). Only the St. Lawrence produced good fishing.

The other site during that span was Chattanooga in 1986 along the Tennessee River, although all the fishing took place on Nickajack and Chickamauga Lakes. That was the year that Chuck Yeager and former president Jimmy Carter assisted at the second day's weigh-in.

The November 1986 issue of *Bassmaster*, which reported on that year's Classic, was notable for a subtle change on its contents page. The previous month, Ray Scott had been listed as chairman of the board/president. But this month he was chairman emeritus. Helen Sevier was now president and publisher, and John S. Jemison Jr. was chairman of the board. In July, Scott had sold Bass Anglers Sportsman Society to Sevier and Jemison Investments. Although Scott would remain as a BASS spokesman and tournament emcee for twelve more years, this would be the beginning of new directions in the company, and television would creep closer to becoming the engine that grew and sustained it.

TWELVE

Romancing the Media

Where seldom is heard a discouraging word,
and the sky is not cloudy all day.
—LYRICS FROM "HOME ON THE RANGE"

While Rick Clunn and Ken Cook had a legitimate beef about the media fishing with them in what was supposed to be a championship event and were probably reacting to increasing pressure to do well in the Classic, they were wrong to do what they did to me (and perhaps to others), and in the way they did it. Clunn wasn't unpleasant—but Cook acted like a basshole.

However, those episodes clearly brought into focus a problem that had been gnawing at me anyway—the fact that BASS paid (or arranged through its tourism partners) for my air transportation, accommodations, meals, and even fishing license each time that I went. *Field & Stream* editor Duncan Barnes was fine with that because it cost nothing to have me there on behalf of the magazine.

A similar issue is at the heart of what grew the Classic. Most of the attending media were writers, the majority of them newspapermen, a minority from a disparate array of magazines. Through the 1970s and in the early 1980s, there were few television reporters and cameramen. Only a few of the writers worked for publications—like the *Chicago Tribune*, for example, or a large nonendemic magazine—that required their reporters to pay their own way or at least make a token payment for their transportation, lodging, and food (sometimes it was so token as to be laughable). Everyone else was feeding at the BASS trough.

Very few of the magazine and newspaper writers, especially those from smaller publications or those who were not full-time employees of the publications they represented, would have been at the Bassmaster Classic if Ray Scott and Bob Cobb did not pay their way. Put another way, very few of them would have been there if they had to do it on their own nickel.

Most of the attending media were not salaried. They wrote on a freelance basis for their local newspapers or for magazines— in essence, being self-employed or at least not employed by the publications they wrote for. It was unlikely—in fact, unusual—for a publication to cover much of a freelance writer's travel expenses, except perhaps film and photo processing. Writers who worked for small newspapers were lucky to be getting $50 a column; for smaller magazines, maybe $150 for an article, with photos. They couldn't possibly pay their way, write only for their publication, and just break even, let alone come out ahead, if they had to pay for it.

An enterprising few found the assemblage of bass fishing pros to be good for helping them write a number of how-to magazine articles, and they did make money. That, too, was great for BASS because it helped to create the sport's personalities and "experts" whose expertise was inextricably entwined with the tournaments that BASS operated, thereby promoting and reinforcing the importance of the organization, its events, and especially the Classic.

There was also the question why some writers from really small publications were always at the Classic, and why some came from areas with no great bass fishing constituency.

Bud Leavitt, for example, a renowned outdoor writer from Augusta, Maine, attended numerous early Classics; to this day, no one from the state of Maine has qualified to fish in the Bassmaster Classic. Art Sullivan, an outdoor writer for the *Boston Globe* and one of the most entertaining characters in the annals of outdoor journalism, attended many of the early events, although it would not be until 1986 before anyone from his state was a contestant.

Many writers not only attended the Classic but became good friends with Scott and Cobb, who, in the words of one longtime media attendee, "created a Classic family." That family helped BASS in a variety of ways. Homer Circle, first a reporter for the Rogers, Arkansas, newspaper and then the angling editor of *Sports Afield*, was perhaps the best media friend and confidant that BASS ever had and, according to Ray Scott, wrote the first word of copy in a newspaper about Scott's organization. Fred David, a writer for the *Syracuse Herald-Journal*, not only attended the Classic for many years, even though only one angler from his state fished in the Classic during the first thirteen years, but was a primary facilitator in bringing the Classic to the St. Lawrence River in 1980.

It was ingenious of Ray Scott and Bob Cobb to recognize the importance of the media to the future of the Classic and also to figure out a way to get someone else—the local convention and visitors' bureau, the chamber of commerce, the tourism development agency, and so on—to foot the bill because of the publicity generated and to kick in for the expenses of all or most of BASS at the same time.

Homer Circle of *Sports Afield* fishes as an observer in the back of the boat with Bill Dance, on Lake Tohopekaliga in Florida during the 1977 Bassmaster Classic.

In other words, they got someone else to pay for the entire cost of an event that primarily helped promote their own organization and their own tournament(s), by inviting a compliant horde of outdoor media to what, for many, was an annual holiday.

Like the mustachioed character in the Guinness commercial says, "Brilliant! Brilliant!"

What this also meant, however, is that almost no one wrote anything critical or asked tough, probing questions of Scott or the contestants. Like the early sportswriters who never wrote about the peccadillos of baseball's stars or the dark issues of the national pastime, the Classic writers basically just covered the story of who won the big game, and how. They wanted to be invited back, they had a hard enough time trying to convince their editors that they should be covering a bass fishing contest in Cincinnati or Pine Bluff, and they were given only enough space to cover the basics anyway.

Almost no one took a hard look at the impact of Scott's other tournaments, which often had 250 to 300 participants and were used as qualifiers for entry into the Classic, or investigated the short- and long-term effects of BASS's competitions on the local fishery or reported in depth about the attitudes of local anglers. Few dared to question the delayed mortality effect on the bass that were treated and released after being weighed in or to question other things that went on with the bass, the anglers, and the localities. Most writers swallowed BASS's propaganda hook, line, and toxic lead sinker. Or just closed their eyes.

(Incidentally, BASS routinely kept many of the larger fish after the Classic and its regular tournaments for photographic purposes. Roland Martin and I were given half a dozen 5-pound largemouths the day after the BASS tournament on the St. Lawrence River in 1977. A photo that I took of Martin and one of those fish appeared on the March 1978 cover of *Field & Stream*.)

The writers being hosted by BASS, and in some cases winning $500 of its money, also masked an underlying reality about the event and the media: if most of the newspapers and the magazines would not pay for their writers to attend the Bassmaster Classic, and if most of the writers would not pay out of their own pockets to attend, then they both perceived that the Classic was not important enough to pay to cover, especially in the early days.

But since BASS was throwing the party and picking up the media's tab to attend, more and more writers jumped onto the bus.

By the mid-1980s, a hundred members of the media were attending the Classic. Two hundred showed up when Vice President George Bush was the honorary weighmaster in 1984 and when both he and Governor Bill Clinton were present at the final-day weigh-in. The fisherman standing with the two future presidents on the winner's podium with a trophy and a $40,000 check, who caught a new record-high weight and led from wire to wire, was Rick Clunn.

Thanks to all of the ink, plus radio and increasing television coverage, the Bassmaster Classic grew in stature from year to year in the way that a pack of snow rolling down a hill coated with heavy snow turns into the world's largest snowball.

For many attending writers, as well as many representatives of fishing tackle and boating companies, and the large contingent from

The weigh-ins for the 1980 Bassmaster Classic took place along the St. Lawrence River. Ray Scott, dead center in a white cowboy hat, is at the scales on a table as a pickup truck pulls a contestant and his boat to the table. Spectators are on the hillside behind the flagged rope. After being weighed, the fish were dumped out of bags into the water in the lower left of the photo.

state federations, it was Bass Fishing Festivus. There was an open bar in the press room in the early events, and some members of the media engaged in major elbow-bending. On more than one occasion, last-minute replacements had to be found for press observers who were no-shows at the launch site in the morning or who were too under the weather to go out in boats. The open bar was later ended, but that didn't stop media elbow-bending. At one Classic, several writers nightly signed their bar bills under the name of one writer from Ohio, who upon checkout discovered $1,200 of bar charges on his tab.

Some writers used their spare time to get acquainted with anyone in the area who wore a skirt. One writer for a major newspaper, who'd spent the night away from the BASS hotel with a woman who worked for the local tourism bureau, was dropped off by her at the launch at four thirty in the morning, only to coincidentally step right into the frowning face of Ray Scott. Says a New York writer, the Classic "was a good way to meet girls, from BASS, the hotel, whatever."

After a reception at the Arkansas governor's mansion one time, a then Miss Arkansas was coaxed into joining the media on a libational trip back to the hotel, but the bus was stopped en route by a state trooper who had been dispatched by the governor to retrieve her.

It wasn't just the media, of course. One evening, a writer walked out to the hotel parking lot and saw the media rep for one of the sponsoring tackle companies standing between two cars with his pants down and his index finger pointed first to his lips and then to the tipsy wife of a state federation president. One of the early Classic competitors did more female entertaining than fishing, always presenting his current lady friend to other people as "my nurse."

Don Ecker, who wrote a twice-weekly freelance outdoor column for one of New Jersey's largest papers, the *Bergen Record*, attended the Classic as an invited guest of BASS twenty-one consecutive times, starting in 1980. During that period, he says, only three anglers from his state fished in the Classic. Now retired, Ecker says that media attendance at the Classic "got to be sort of like a reunion every year. You developed a circle of friends."

One year when the tournament was held in Alabama, Ecker and some of those friends were griping about the "rat-trap" hotel food they were eating. So he got a recommendation for the best restaurant in town and called it, telling the manager who he was and why he was in town. He also said that he was with a bunch of "high-powered bass fishing writers" who were looking to see what kind of good cuisine was available locally, since the food was terrible at the hotel, and—no promises—they might be able to give the restaurant some publicity.

"We'll be right over with our limousine," said the manager.

Ecker rounded up a group of writers, and they went to the restaurant.

"I ordered the food," said Ecker. "I told the others to take out their notebooks after each round of food, and we'd vote to see what people liked. I told them to keep a straight face, and it went like clockwork. They served us from soup to nuts, their finest dishes, and it was superb. We didn't order any wine, but every dish that we ate we voted on, and we did it a little vociferously. The limo took us back to the hotel. Three of the guys wanted to marry me after that. As it turned out, some of the newspapers involved did have a little sidebar on the restaurant."

It was the dissatisfaction of anglers, plus an increasing need to accommodate television production, that caused a big change in the Classic media-observer program. BASS eventually did away with media awards and prohibited any observer from fishing with the pros. BASS currently offers media members a chance to go out in the boats for a day or all three days of the tournament, provided they do nothing but observe and eat their lunches—and, in recent years, properly use BassTrakk.

Only a few observers who accompany pros fishing in the Classic today are members of the outdoor media, and those few mainly tag along just on the first day of the contest. Sometimes the observer is a reporter for a non–outdoors news organization and is not an angler and has usually never seen professional bass fishermen at work. Mainstream media like this opportunity because they cannot go to a NASCAR race and get in a car with a driver on a competition day, get on a horse with a jockey in a big race, or get on the scrimmage line during a football game, but they can spend the day on the water when a bass pro is casting to solidify his future career. Never mind that most of them don't understand the technicalities of what they're watching or don't grasp subtle undercurrents; they can certainly spot dedication and determination.

Occasionally, in recent years, an outdoor print media observer accompanying an angler who was doing well has been kicked out of the boat during the middle of a contest day by TV cameramen, who then replaced the media observer in a competitor's boat. This has greatly annoyed, and somewhat disenfranchised, that member of the print media.

Being an observer with one of the tournament leaders on the final day of the Classic is now out of the question. To accommodate the way that ESPN shows this event, the leading six to ten anglers and perhaps a few other favored (i.e., camera-performance-oriented) sons have no observer other than the TV cameramen who have been assigned to them for in-the-boat shots. It's debatable, in fact, whether a TV cameraman makes an astute observer, his job being to get every catch and reaction on tape, rather than to see that the rules are closely followed.

Initially, the change from cofishing observers to sit-on-your-hands observers led to grumbling among outdoor writers, many of whom declined to go for watch-the-pro boat rides, having spent plenty of time in the past observing or fishing with professional bass fishermen. Fortunately for BASS, it found many volunteers among the Federation ranks who wanted to sit in a boat all day and eyeball a pro. Some of them would pay for the opportunity if they had to, which they don't.

There is, however, a liability issue here, and everyone who is an observer in a boat today is required to sign a BASS liability release form. Nevertheless, a Federation observer in the 2003 Citgo Bassmaster Classic sued the pro he observed, Edwin Evers, plus all of his sponsors, BASS, and all of the Classic sponsors, for negligent boat operation that caused him a lower-back injury that required surgery. The matter was scheduled to go to trial at the end of March 2006 in New Orleans.

By the mid-1980s, BASS had its own television crews covering the event. Television began to take on a higher priority and became an increasing irritation to the rest of the media. In the eyes of print journalists, television cameras and TV interviewers have a way of taking over an event and requiring that things be done to satisfy their needs, the rest of the media be damned. That became an issue on the water at times (witness the boat expulsion of print media mentioned earlier), as well as off it. Eventually, many of the media regulars could get their who-what-how story from the weigh-in and the following press conference without having to be on or even near the water. Some daily newspaper writers with fast-approaching deadlines, waiting for a pithy quote and details to complete their stories, have chafed while BASS or ESPN TV crews interviewed winning pros on camera for soundbites to be broadcast much later.

When the writers stopped going out on the water, they were then free until the afternoon weigh-ins. Many of them, without daily deadlines to meet, found other things to do. Some arranged to go hunting in the area where the Classic was held. But when the Classic was moved from the fall to midsummer, ostensibly to make it easier for families to attend, the hunting season hadn't yet started. So they sought other fishing opportunities that might provide them with non-Classic-related newspaper or magazine articles. When the Classic was in New Orleans, for example, some writers went saltwater fishing. Despite the changes in the media's situation at the Classic, with BASS paying expenses to get to the area, "attending" the Classic was still a good deal.

As long as Ray Scott was heavily involved in BASS, this symbiotic relationship with the media—which came to include more folks representing television and radio—continued. In 1998, Scott and BASS parted ways, and Scott went off to promote new ventures, among them whitetail deer feed and light spinning tackle for bass.

In May 1999, George McNeilly, then with CBS radio in Washington, D.C., was covering a Winston Cup race when Tony Dolle of the Nashville Network told him that if he liked the car races, he should go to the Bassmaster Classic.

"I said, 'The Bassmaster what?'" recalls McNeilly, who had covered four Olympics, eleven Super Bowls, and the World Series but had never heard of the Bassmaster Classic.

He attended that July and was greatly impressed with the sport and with the anglers he met. A little later, Helen Sevier hired McNeilly to head up the BASS media and public relations efforts and to help with the company's overall push to grow professional bass fishing.

McNeilly had barely started the job when he found out that most of the media were receiving complimentary travel, food, lodging, and what-all to attend the Bassmaster Classic. He was astounded by the media's hotel bill.

"I think I was the only reporter in 1999 who paid his way," says McNeilly.

Before seeing Helen Sevier about this, he called CBS radio and asked them to keep his old job open, then called his wife and told her they might be going back to Arlington, Virginia, because he didn't know whether he could stand for this.

"My thinking at the time," says McNeilly, "was nobody ever said, 'Hey, George, I'm so glad you're coming to the Super Bowl, I'm going to put you up at the Hyatt.' Nobody ever said, 'Hey, George, you want to come to the Daytona 500 or the Dover race? Here's a plane ticket.' I wanted to grow a sport, not a tackle junket."

Excited about the potential to grow professional bass fishing, McNeilly also wondered why it hadn't attracted more attention beyond the outdoor media.

"Like most sports fans, I'm a pretty knowledgeable guy about generalist sports," he says. "But I had never heard of the Bassmaster Classic. They'd been paying for the press to come for years. What's wrong with this picture?"

McNeilly also didn't like the idea of obligating members of the media to be officials at a sporting event or having them out in a boat all day and being too tired to write a good article later about the event.

So he went to Sevier and told her that BASS couldn't pay the way for the press anymore. He was willing to subsidize the hotel bills for freelance writers, but he felt that the sport had to stand on its own legs.

"Do what you want," Sevier said, but as McNeilly walked out, she warned him that there had better be as many people from the media at the next Classic as there had been in New Orleans.

"We had about one hundred thirty press in New Orleans in 1999," says McNeilly, who had only one other person in his communications department then, "and we had a record three hundred thirty in

Chicago the following year, including the big newspapers and CNN and everyone else, because we really worked on it."

According to McNeilly, an incredible amount of press coverage resulted from that event.

"Helen has often been criticized for going to Chicago in 2000," he says. "And we know the outdoor show lacked consumers. But from a media perspective, it helped put the sport on the map. I think it really opened it up."

To McNeilly, "opening up" means attracting diversified media—that is, nonendemic media. That's part of the secret to getting major corporations to take notice. Not many CEOs and marketing executives for major companies like General Mills and Coca Cola read fishing magazines and outdoor columns in local newspapers unless they happen to be avid fishermen (there are a few).

But they are reading *Fortune*, the *Wall Street Journal*, and *Time*. Attracting a reporter for one of these or similar nonendemic publications—because of the marketing dollars being spent by some companies to appeal to this overwhelmingly white male demographic; because of the novelty of showering someone with a huge check for catching a bunch of smallish fish; because of the many programming hours that ESPN is devoting to it; because of the exuberant crowd of bassheads at the final-day weigh-in; or because bass fishing is as red-state all-American as apple pie—is far more important than comping a fishing writer from the *Mid-Lakes Fishing Gazette*.

"The anglers, the sport, and the products had been treated very well by the outdoor media," says McNeilly. "But I felt that for this sport to grow, we had to get stick-and-ball writers to appreciate it. Over the last five years, we've gotten an incredible amount of generalist press, everything from *NBC Nightly News* to an eleven-page piece in *Esquire* to the *New York Times* a couple of times."

That's not exactly stick-and-ball writers. In fact, stick-and-ball writers and jock sports editors still don't appreciate any kind of fishing *as a sport*, although they do have more respect for competitive fishing because there's a box score, and they condescend to print local-area fishing reports because there's advertising support for them and because the reports at least show tangible *results*, even if usually exaggerated by the sources.

In fact, sports editors at most major newspapers today are less inclined to run articles about angling for pure fun or relaxation because they view fishing as a consumptive activity (many of them choke on the word *sport*) that should be in the lifestyle section of the paper. Meanwhile, the lifestyle editor thinks that fishing is a hook-and-bullet outdoor hobby that should be in the sports section, if indeed it should be anywhere in his or her (usually her) paper.

Most of the "generalist media" that have covered the Bassmaster Classic or major bass fishing tournaments in recent times, rather than focusing on the activity of fishing, have reported on it as (a) a business story by virtue of marketing associations and regional economic benefits; (b) a NASCAR wannabe; (c) a quirky, cultlike activity bringing fame and fortune to a few; (d) an interesting, gee-whiz, whitebread social phenomenon; or (e) all of the foregoing.

Some generalist media reported on the Bassmaster Classic, in fact, long before McNeilly and ESPN entered the scene. Sports-generalist magazine *Sports Illustrated* was represented at the Classic in 1971, 1973, and again in April 1976 when it was held in Currituck Sound, North Carolina. Roy Blount attended the 1976 Classic and in his article "5,760 Casts a Day: Now That's Plugging" commented that the angler's boat "looks like you ought to drive it to the country club dance" and presciently noted, "These pros would like to get network exposure and expect to when prize money increases."

No less a generalist publication than the *New Yorker* reported on the southern bass fishing tournament phenomenon and the Bassmaster Classic, when Calvin Trillin wrote his "U.S. Journal" column from Wheeler Lake in Alabama, for the December 2, 1974, issue. "What Scott is selling to bass fishermen," wrote Trillin, "is partly the same thing that encyclopedia salesmen are selling to families in small Southern towns—a ticket to the middle class."

No less a generalist television show than ABC's *20/20* reported on the Bassmaster Classic in New York in 1980. And the *New York Times Magazine* wrote about the phenomenon as well in "Fishing for Bass and Big Bucks," which appeared in July 1985. Author Nick Taylor profiled the big-money tournament scene, hitting the nail squarely with this observation, "So far, the hullabaloo of its professional competition hasn't lured a mass audience. But BASS is working hard to give bass fishing broad television appeal."

Evidently, the now seven-member communications staff at BASS has diversified media attendance at the Bassmaster Classic. I shared a taxi in Pittsburgh with a business correspondent for *Time*, who, in October 2005, wrote about the fight in cable TV land over professional bass fishing and repeated the BASS mantra about the Classic being like the Super Bowl (he actually said, "of rod-and-reel events," taking in the entire universe of sportfishing).

Yet while the BASS communications staff says that some three hundred members of the media were at the 2005 Classic, I have my doubts. At the final-day press conference, there couldn't have been more than three dozen people in the room—some of them BASS staff. At no time did I encounter more than several dozen people, most of them media, in the press room at the Mellon Center during the weigh-ins. Ditto at the Steelhead Lounge on Media Day. Sure, there were numerous writers from Pittsburgh newspapers and crews from the local TV stations (usually, at least three to a crew), and the like, but given the propensity for hyperbole that I've witnessed—400 people at the launch multiplying into 2,000; 5,000 fans at the weigh-in turning into a full house; and so on—I'm skeptical about the 300 figure and all of that "generalist" media in attendance.

Of course, there were a lot of writers, producers, analysts, commentators, cheerleaders, photographers, and cameramen there on the BASS-ESPN payroll, although they were allegedly not counted among the three hundred.

Whether the number is a hundred or three hundred or does or does not include their own people, the exact count really doesn't matter. Whatever the generalist and outdoor print media do is essentially reinforcement publicity these days. Now, the Bassmaster Classic is all about television.

With few exceptions, members of the generalist media know very little about fishing. In fact, if you ask most people from the generalist media—or from major advertising agencies or in the executive conference rooms of major corporations—about the vast and diversified subject of recreational fishing, they are most likely to associate it with fly fishing, having seen *A River Runs Through It* and perhaps vaguely being aware that some deep-pocketed Gen X yuppie colleague or relative makes an annual pilgrimage to a ranch in Montana where he goes fly fishing for trout.

Thus, members of the generalist media cannot evaluate the state of the fishing at a given Classic or the efforts and the technical nuances of the competing anglers, which is what really drives the bassheads. Without whose television viewership, there would be no phenomenon. Without whose attendance at the Outdoors Expo and the weigh-in—both free, by the way, which makes you wonder if they would come *if they had to pay*—there would be no pageantry.

The generalist media, in fact, generally mirror the generalist sports fans and the generalist public. When *Wall Street Journal* reporters in 1996 and 1997 wrote about the booming world of professional bass fishing, they got lost in promoters' smoke screens. The generalist media don't get it because they have not spent time in the trenches, on the water, fishing. If you don't have the passion for fishing, you don't understand the attraction of it to other people. That's exactly how I feel about car racing.

Oddly enough, even other fishermen don't get all of the bass tournament madness.

There are loads of saltwater-only anglers who look at the bass pros they see on TV—catching bait-sized fish and whooping and being rewarded with money and notoriety—and they snicker. Guys who fish for tarpon and bonefish and big red drum and sharks and tuna and billfish all know, to a man, that there is not a bass alive that can outsmart or outfight even the smallest of those other species. They watch Gerald Swindle skip a 14-ounce 12-inch-long bass across the surface and derrick it into the boat in two seconds flat and then point his finger at the camera and scream, "You're in my house, baby!" and they think (a) what a jerk, (b) what kind of sport is this?, and (c) what is wrong with the world for making heroes out of this?

And the stream trout fly fisherman, the guy who drives a Beemer and drinks Simi cabernet, who treats fly fishing for trout like a religion and reads books that equate fly fishing for trout as a life metaphor, he does not get the bass thing *at all*. He can spew the Latin names of little bugs, for crissakes, and he thinks that the closest thing that a bass fisherman can quote in Latin is Skoal and Copenhagen.

Even ESPN may not get the divergence within the whole fishing community. It's unclear whether its producers realize that they are really playing to a small piece—the people who fish for bass in tournaments—of the 34-million-angler pie.

And there's the rub. Many of the outdoor media who used to attend the Classic—who may have been *had* by BASS but who also *got* the *whole* fishing thing—are absent today. Dozens who used to go to the Classic no longer bother. Many of them speak unfavorably about the mass changes that have occurred at the Classic, with BASS and ESPN, with *Bassmaster* magazine, and with people who handle media relations. They realized a long time ago that the Classic was becoming more about producing entertainment than about showcasing bass fishing. Now it's become something they barely recognize.

Nevertheless, members of the non-BASS outdoor media who helped to grow Bass Anglers Sportsman Society and the stature of the Bassmaster Classic, and who, starting in 2000, were not being comped for their expenses, recognized that Chicago was going to be a disaster from the perspective of the fishing and the fans' attendance.

Which it was.

Piloting their flat-water 70 mph bass boats on the rough seas of Lake Michigan, the anglers pounded their vertebrae and labored through unimpressive fishing. The BASS media guide calls it "one of the most challenging Classics ever staged."

Weigh-ins were held at Soldier Field. Said one writer, "I went over there, stood on the fifty-yard line, closed my eyes, and could hear the roar of many great football games. I thought to myself, 'What the hell am I doing here for a bass fishing contest?' The weigh-in was lost in the cavernous infield of Soldier Field. At the Outdoors Expo, you could fire a cannon down the aisles and not hit anybody. It was a total failure."

For all of the other outdoor media attendees, fishing and boating product manufacturers, bass fishing fans, and the sportfishing industry in general—everybody except the $100,000 winner, Woo Daves—the Chicago Classic was a disaster.

You could analyze this a dozen ways and always conclude that Chicago is not a hotbed of bass fishing. Which it is not. But Chicago has a number of very successful outdoor consumer shows each year. Check that, each winter. Not in the third week of July when people who like to fish are out fishing. There are a lot of outdoor enthusiasts in greater Chicagoland, and they have a potpourri of species to fish for in Lake Michigan, as well as the bountiful waters of Illinois and bordering states. Black bass are just one of a dozen great freshwater gamefish there, unlike in Oklahoma or Alabama.

How many of the generalist media got that part?

Disaster or not, and coincidentally or not, the following year BASS was acquired by ESPN and took the Classic back to New Orleans, where jambalaya and crawfish etouffe, plus a lot of bassheads at the Superdome weigh-ins and the Outdoors Expo, helped to wipe the taste of Chicago out of their mouths.

THIRTEEN

More Money

You guys didn't get a hundred million dollars because you were
worth it. You got it because you were just born later.
—FORMER BASKETBALL STAR CHARLES BARKLEY,
ON CURRENT NBA SALARIES

Notwithstanding the contributions to the growth of professional bass fishing by Ray Scott, BASS, the early bass pros, and the media, it was a corporate raider from the heart of walleye-fishing country, Irwin L. Jacobs, who muddied the waters of professional bass fishing, sent a tidal bore through the brain trust of BASS, and reconfigured the tournament landscape. Through his chutzpah, salesmanship, and hyperbolic promotion, professional bass fishing took a quantum leap forward, as extraordinary amounts of money were offered in premier bass fishing tournaments.

Gasoline cost about 40 cents a gallon when BASS offered $10,000 to the winner of the first BASS Masters Classic. Ten grand was then more money than many people earned for a whole year of working a normal job, which they may have hated. Surely, there were people in 1971 who thought ten grand was a preposterous reward for three days of catching bass on Lake Mead—a lake artificially created for the purpose of powering slot machines, watering desert golf courses, and eventually filling a Treasure Island Hotel moat that would be used to stage nightly productions of *Pirates of the Caribbean* (which was first a Disney theme ride).

A large amount of prize money did in 1971 what a large amount of prize money does in 2006: attract attention. Attention from people who want to win it. Attention from media people who cover the story of those trying to win it. Attention from businesses that want to market to the people trying to win it or to those watching the people trying to win it.

On February 26, 2006, the winner of the Citgo Bassmaster Classic will receive a check for half a million dollars. Even with gas averaging $2.50 a gallon, and even though the ceremonial check presentation will occur in the shadow of the Magic Kingdom, where Disney probably rakes in half a mil before ten o'clock each morning, that's a lot of George Washingtons.

No matter what or where the catch is, a half-million-dollar fishing payday gets a lot of attention. So does a total payout to the fifty-one competitors of $1,201,900. The last-place fisherman in the 2006 Classic—even if he falls flat on his keister and has nothing to weigh in, even if he gets DQ'd for speeding through a no-wake zone or kicking his observer out of the boat for dropping a smidgeon of mustard on his plastic worms—will get as much money as Bobby Murray did for winning in 1971.

And yet, $1.2 mil is *not* the richest bass fishing purse. You'd think that the Super Bowl of bass fishing, owned and televised by the Worldwide Leader in Sports, would provide the highest reward to all of the superbassheads who fish in it, no? In fact, the $1.2 million purse is eclipsed by the total payout in another 2006 bass fishing tournament and is totally blown away by one planned for 2007, neither of which belong to BASS.

It was 1976 when Roy Blount wrote in *Sports Illustrated* that the pros expected to get network exposure once prize money increased. Two decades later, the foundation was laid for that to happen, but it wasn't laid by BASS.

In 1996, Ray Scott was nearing the end of his spokesman role with Helen Sevier and her investment partners. A competing bass tournament circuit, the seven-year-old Red Man Tournament Trail, was gaining momentum. Title-sponsored by the chewing tobacco company and geared originally to provide working bassheads with weekend contests, Red Man had grown out of a tournament-organizing company called Operation Bass, Inc., originally formed in 1989.

In 1996, Red Man held 132 regular-season bass tournaments around the United States, plus 6 regional championships, culminating in a national championship event called the Red Man All-American that offered a $368,000 purse and a $100,000 first-place prize. The event was held on the Arkansas River and was won by Stephen Browning of Hot Springs, Arkansas.

George Cochran, also from Hot Springs, won the Bassmaster Classic that August in Alabama, banking $100,000 out of the total purse of $301,500.

One hundred grand for three or four days of fishing was a big prize in 1996. And still is. But professional bass fishing in 1996 needed to attract nonendemic sponsors who would pony up big bucks for marketing sponsorships, which would help to provide eye-bulging prize money and get the attention of television outlets that could supply a mass audience.

On July 24, three weeks before the 1996 Bassmaster Classic, Minneapolis businessman Irwin L. Jacobs purchased Operation Bass and the Red Man Tournament Trail. In short order, he signed Wal-Mart to be the title sponsor of that trail, which he renamed FLW, an acronym for Forrest L. Wood, who has a bombproof reputation as the founder of Ranger Boats, a premier bass boat manufacturer acquired by Jacobs.

In 1997, the Wal-Mart FLW Tour debuted with the sponsorship of such nonendemic and heretofore non-involved-with-bass-fishing-tournament sponsors as Coca-Cola, Land O'Lakes, Northwest Airlines, and Fujifilm, plus outdoor advertising veterans Chevy Trucks, Citgo, Evinrude, and Ranger Boats.

The October 4, 1996, edition of the *Minneapolis/St.Paul Business Journal* reported on the vision that Jacobs had, which had not come to him while being rained out of fishing and while watching a golf tournament on television in his hotel room but still nonetheless contained parallels to professional golf.

"Minneapolis financier Irwin Jacobs has a vision," said the article. "He sees professional fishing elevated to the high-profile status of golf and tennis. He sees professional anglers as the new heroes of the sports world, garnering $100,000 first-place prizes and fat contracts for being corporate spokesmen. He sees sport fishing as a way for advertisers to reach millions of loyal customers. He sees the FLW Tour."

Ironically, the article also quoted Dave Barton, the director of operations for Outdoor Entertainment Inc., the Nashville Network's (TNN) outdoor programming subsidiary, which then broadcast BASS tournaments, as saying, "Mr. Jacobs is not going to lose money doing a major tournament trail."

Jacobs had already purchased time from ESPN2 to run FLW programming. And he had arranged for that programming to be videotaped and produced by Jerry McKinnis's company, JM Associates, which was then coordinating most of the outdoor block programming on ESPN and ESPN2, as well as producing some of its shows. The taped broadcast of the 1996 Red Man All-American was televised in October on three-year-old ESPN2, a sister sports cable network of ESPN where, in theory at least, it could be exposed to a wide sports audience. ESPN2 then reached 37 million households.

A taped broadcast of the 1996 Bassmaster Classic was televised on TNN, which then had the largest block of outdoor programming of any network and was broadcast to 65 million households. Appearing on TNN, however, was like preaching to the choir and its predominantly britches-and-bubba base, much like BASS did when it was primarily attuned to outdoor print media.

From the start, the one-hour ESPN2 shows about the FLW Tour were different, not only from a production standpoint but because of the format of their events. The four-day FLW bass tournaments started with hundreds of participants but reduced the field to twenty anglers on the third day, and to five on the final day. JM Associates put cameras on each finalist's boat, as well as on roving camera boats. On the last day Tommy Sanders was the anchor, and McKinnis was the analyst, with McKinnis able, via live audio hookup, to hold on-water conversations with the fishermen. It was a new way of televising an activity that is notoriously spectator-unfriendly.

Said TNN's Dave Barton in the *Journal* article about Irwin Jacobs, "I don't think it's got anybody shaking in their boots."

But they should have been concerned.

When Jacobs upped the ante by pumping more money into the

top prize and paying large cash prizes deeper into the field of contestants, much as in professional golf, it brought some of the top names in the BASS tournament sphere into FLW events. As Jacobs did this, as he continued to forge alliances with major nonendemic sponsors, as FLW's way of televising bass tournaments got more attention, and as press releases about raising the stakes in professional bass fishing flew out FLW's door, BASS was forced to react, especially by showing the pros more prize money and by trying to find ways to bring excitement into its rather dramaless events.

Still, BASS was usually a step, or two or three, behind "Irv the Operator," as *Forbes* called him in 2004. On Sunday afternoon, November 7, 1999, Jacobs fired a nuclear missile across BASS's bow when Fox broadcast live the final day of the Ranger M1 Millennium tournament, which offered a $600,000 first prize. Fox publicized it heavily on the air and on its Web site—I had written several articles about bass tackle and bass fishing for foxsports.com prior to this event—and FLW claimed that two million households tuned in.

Fox sports announcers Joe Buck and Bob Brenly seemed like ducks on a highway during the broadcast, which looked like a dud but made a bold statement that was in tune with Jacobs's 1997 comment to a *USA Today* reporter that he would "bring the stakes up to the biggest single payoff in any sport."

If Irwin L. Jacobs has a fire in his belly to fish for bass or any other species, it isn't readily apparent in the extensive press releases and corporate information of his various companies, although he is described as an "avid fishing and boating enthusiast." Perhaps not spending a lot of time on the water is wise for someone who has such an appetite for acquiring, fixing, dissembling, reorganizing, selling, and managing businesses that, according to the *Wall Street Journal*, in the early 1980s he was known in corporate boardrooms as "Irv the Liquidator."

A *Journal* article stated, "Mr. Jacobs made big profits in that junk-bond era by making hostile runs at such big companies as Walt Disney Co., Avon Products Inc., ITT Corp., and BorgWarner Corp. He frequently bought minority stakes in companies, agitated for changes, and then agreed to sell his stake for a profit—either to the target company or another, more-determined investor."

Jacobs owns, partially owns, or has owned a labyrinth of companies across a checkerboard of industries and interests. These include the Minnesota Vikings, Bekins Moving & Storage, CVN (the company that led to the QVC shopping network), Hatteras Yachts, and AMF. His profile on the FLW Outdoors Web site says that he "has been involved with such industries as television shopping, professional football, various sports product companies, banking, oil and gas. He currently owns businesses involved with boating, direct marketing, closeout and return merchandising, and professional fishing tournaments."

One of Jacobs's investments was the bankrupt Larson Industries in 1977, which made Larson boats. Another, in 1981, was Arctic Enterprises, which owned Lund Boat Company. Another was a company called Minstar, later renamed Genmar Holdings, which is now privately held but was once publicly traded.

According to *Forbes*, Jacobs is a 40 percent stakeholder in, and chairman of the board of directors of, Genmar, which has seen a lot of acquisitions, dispositions, and slicing and dicing over the years.

In 2001, for example, Genmar bought all of the U.S.-based boat and trailer manufacturing assets of the bankrupt Outboard Marine Corporation. Genmar then became the manufacturer of eighteen brands of fiberglass and aluminum boats, including newly acquired Four Winns, Lowe, Seaswirl, and Stratus/Javelin, plus previously owned Aquasport, Carver, Crestliner, Glastron, Hatteras, Larson, Logic, Lund, Nova, Ranger, Trojan, and Wellcraft. A company media release stated that with the acquisition of OMC's aluminum boat businesses, Genmar was then "the world's largest boat builder."

In 2004, Genmar sold all of its aluminum boat-manufacturing businesses to Brunswick, the parent company of Mercury, the outboard motor manufacturer that currently sponsors the Bassmaster Classic.

At the end of 2005, Genmar had five thousand employees and more than a thousand dealers. Its twelve boat brands, manufactured in nine locations, generated $1 billion in sales and accounted for approximately 15 percent of all fiberglass boats sold in the United States. Of these, Ranger was the big dog in bass boats.

When competitive bass fishing started, there was no such thing as a *bass boat*. The term grew out of competitive bass fishing from the people who were modifying their boats to accommodate developing needs—safety and speed, live-fish retention, foot-controlled manueverability while casting, and so on. The term quickly came to refer to a type of boat that is popular for largemouth and smallmouth bass angling; it is simply a good fishing boat that is particularly functional where a lot of casting is required and where presentation and boat positioning are especially important. Today's top-end fiberglass bass boats are super fast (up to 80 mph), super sleek, macho high-performance machines.

Ranger Boats, which primarily makes high-end bass boats, is an icon in this genre. It was an icon long before Jacobs and Genmar acquired it in 1991 from the family that then controlled 7-Eleven. It was arguably the best bass boat manufacturer, and certainly the most well-known bass boat brand, at that time in the country. And it was the brainchild of a former fishing guide, a former professional bass tournament fisherman, a two-time contestant in the Bassmaster Classic, and one of the finest men in the fishing and boating universe, Forrest L. Wood.

Wood started Ranger Boats in 1968. He had been a fishing guide for fourteen years on Bull Shoals Lake, the White River, Buffalo

Forrest Wood (in white cowboy hat) greets visitors at his Outdoor Sports Gallery in Flippin, Arkansas.

River, and Crooked Creek in the Ozark Mountains of north-central Arkansas and had been mentioned or featured in several outdoor magazine articles.

In fact, a minor league baseball player for the Kansas City A's, Jerry McKinnis, read the April 1956 issue of *Outdoor Life* and clipped out an article written by Charles Elliott about float fishing in the Ozarks. The following year McKinnis went to the White River boat dock of G. O. Tilley, who had been featured in Elliott's article. When McKinnis walked down the ramp, the fellow at the end said, "Hi, my name is Forrest Wood. I'm gonna be your guide today." Says McKinnis, "That was the turning point in my life. That's where it all started for me."

The two became friends, and Wood later talked McKinnis into moving there and becoming a guide. He met and fished many times with Harold Ensley, an outdoor television show pioneer, before moving to Little Rock and guiding out of a boat dock on Lake Maumelle; he started his own regional television show in 1964.

Forrest Wood's guiding business prospered enough that he had to hire others to work for him. To keep good guides available for the fishing season, he needed to find them off-season work, so he became a contractor and built houses. When he was temporarily weathered out in the construction business, he looked for something to do indoors.

He had been thinking of getting into plastics manufacturing. McKinnis remembers Wood thinking about building plastic telephone booths. Instead, Wood decided to build a "lake boat" called Ranger, out of respect for the rock-solid Texas lawmen.

Wood built six Rangers in 1968 and that same year fished a tournament at Greers Ferry Lake in Arkansas with several friends, one of whom was McKinnis. In 1969, at the suggestion of a friend, he went to a BASS tournament at Smith Lake, Alabama. There he met Ray Scott for the first time, as well as many of the early bass tournament fishermen, and found a couple of men who were interested in buying a boat. It was the beginning of several decades of varied participation in competitive bass fishing.

While Wood enjoyed competing in bass tournaments, his objective was always to sell more boats. His participation in BASS tournaments and the Bassmaster Classic, and his company's sponsorship and

Originally belonging to Jerry McKinnis, this is one of the earliest Ranger bass boats ever built. It's on display in the Forrest L. Wood Outdoor Sports Gallery.

support of BASS as well as many other tournament circuits, helped to sell boats by growing the market.

"It was very valuable in selling boats," says Wood of his association with BASS and the Classic, "and it helped us grow rapidly. In the early days the bass boat business was just a small part of a boat dealer's business. Today the bass boat business is a big business. Then we had to talk the dealer into taking the boat and talk the buyer into buying one. When people realized that bass fishing was here to stay, it got easier to sign up dealers. After we got more [bass boat building] competition, that became tougher. Now we're back to where you not only have to promote the sport of professional bass fishing, but you have to promote your product. And the key, as we've proved, is to build the best product that we can, one that will stand the test of time."

Although the number of bass boat manufacturers grew and then diminished through attrition and acquisition, today there are half a dozen companies that make very good fiberglass bass boats, the chariot of choice for anyone who is serious about fishing in major bass fishing competitions. None of these manufacturers is more highly regarded than Ranger.

It is likely that Ranger bass boats would have been used in the first Bassmaster Classic, but on May 4, 1971, Wood's entire boat-building operation, uninsured, burned to the ground. Ranger was the official Bassmaster Classic boat in 1972 and remained so through 2001, even as the company was acquired by the owners of Southland Corporation in 1987 and four years later by Genmar.

However, in 1999, BASS got into the boat-racing business via an affiliate called World Championship Fishing, which conducted events that included bass boat performance trials. BASS sanctioned the organization's highly publicized Illinois Bass Quest '99. The event, which merged bass boat racing with fishing competition, was promoted heavily and televised on Fox Sports Network (FSN) on Thanksgiving Day. Ranger wanted nothing to do with it.

"We had spent all those years promoting safety and conservation," says Wood today, "and we just didn't need to be part of that kind of thing. It wasn't the right thing to do then, and it's still not the right thing to do. Nothing against boat racing, but we didn't need to be in the boat-racing business."

The bass boat–racing business didn't last long, but it left a bad taste with Ranger and with Wood, who was by then a spokesman and no longer running the company. It didn't help that as of 2000, Ray Scott was endorsing Triton, a competitor owned by former world powerboat racing champion Earl Bentz.

Wood wasn't pleased to see his old friend Ray Scott appearing in advertisements and proclaiming that Triton made "the finest bass boats ever built." And although Wood is as amiable, honest, helpful, and loyal as they come, these events cooled his, and Ranger's, relationship with Scott and BASS.

Today Forrest Wood stands as square and confident as a Texas lawman when he says, "With all due modesty, Ranger did more than anybody else to promote the sport of competitive fishing. We happened to be in a position where we could. And we didn't turn down very many people if we thought they were going to do something worthwhile. We still do a lot of that today."

What he means is that Ranger supported more bass fishing tournament organizations, more charity fund-raising events, more bass fishing pros, more members of the media, and more people associated with the sport of bass fishing and bass fishing competitions than any other company, big or small.

Coincidentally, one of the tournament trails that Ranger sponsored from its very beginning was Red Man, which was merged into FLW by Irwin Jacobs.

At one point, Ranger sponsored a large majority of the bass pros who were fishing in BASS events. Many of them would not have had an opportunity to prove themselves—and sustain a career—if it hadn't been for Ranger (and especially Wood and his wife, Nina).

Moreover, Ranger was well known for providing memo-billed boats within the sportfishing industry, which, though not technically sponsorship, is a form of subsidization. These were boats (and trailers) that were loaned to individuals for a year, after which they were purchased, usually at less than dealer cost. Most people sold the boats at the end of the year at no loss to themselves (in some cases, with a small profit) and got another brand-new memo-billed model. This arrangement still continues with Ranger and other bass boat companies.

Ranger did not sponsor the Bassmaster Classic after 2001, instead concentrating its promotional efforts on the tournament trails being run by FLW Outdoors. Triton Boats became a sponsor of the Classic in 2002.

Perhaps not coincidentally, the FLW tourneys soon afterward began showing entry preference and offering large incentive awards to participants who were using Ranger brand boats. Then FLW required that final-day contestants—the ones who would be shown on television—fish out of Ranger boats wrapped in the colors and the logos of FLW's sponsoring companies. This created, and continues to create, problems for many of the bass pros, some of whom have relationships with other boat companies as well as with other sponsors, who help pay expenses and, they claim, are looking for television exposure for their products.

Meanwhile, the Bassmaster Classic and the major BASS tournaments moved to ESPN2 in 2000 when the roof started leaking at TNN, which changed its programming tastes and was renamed Spike TV. Today Spike TV has no outdoor-topic programming, and ESPN2, which has lots of it, reaches 89 million households.

When BASS's tournament coverage moved to ESPN2, FLW took its programming briefly to the PAX cable network, which was akin to being televised on Mars, before landing on FSN. JM Associates didn't go with FLW, which bitterly hired a new production company.

"When FLW left ESPN," says Jerry McKinnis, "they left me, too. Irwin Jacobs will hate me till the end of the world because I didn't go with him, but I worked for ESPN when FLW came along, and when they left, I continued to work for ESPN."

"FLW didn't have to leave ESPN," McKinnis says. "They left because they didn't want to share television time with BASS."

A year after FLW's departure, ESPN acquired BASS. Then JM Associates—which today bills itself as the "Worldwide Leader in Outdoor Television"—began producing the televised BASS tournaments and working on the Bassmaster Classic, elevating the coverage each year.

Irwin Jacobs, who had once battled Disney in his junk bond days, was now in a different battle with its subsidiary, ABC-ESPN. There were moves and countermoves to be made, not all of them having to do with prize money.

In early 2005, for example, Ranger Boats dropped its affiliation with Byron Velvick, suddenly a marquee personality because of his just-concluded appearances on *The Bachelor*, after he began working for ESPN's highly promoted *BassCenter*, which debuted on January 1, 2005. Jacobs undoubtedly had a lot to do with the disassociation, as well as with rescinding Velvick's invitation to fish in FLW's top-tier bass tournaments. Perhaps he thought that Velvick had in some way gone over to the enemy. Triton Boats wasted no time expanding its pro team to include Velvick, who has rewarded them, plus Mercury and his other sponsors, by getting them into *BassCenter* footage on countless occasions.

That's piddling stuff, however, in the big scheme of things. While Jacobs has been upping the ante in prize money and sponsorships, ESPN has been upping the ante in sheer hours of television coverage. Their moves have gotten attention. As Jeffrey Ressner noted in his *Time* article, headlined "Will Disney Out-Fox the Competition in Its Bass Battle?" and published in October 2005, "Cable networks are battling over bass, with three of the industry's major players trolling for profits."

The third, he speculated, was Outdoor Life Network (OLN),

owned by cable-giant Comcast, although OLN—which was renamed Versus as of September 2006—has shown no inclination to become a goliath in the bass fishing tournament ring. And it isn't exactly ESPN against Fox any more than it's Iger versus Murdoch. It's BASS/ESPN/Disney/Citgo against Jacobs/FLW/Wal-Mart/Fox.

So, in the continuing thrust-and-parry battle being waged, while the August 2005 Bassmaster Classic presented by Citgo awarded a $200,000 first prize and a $671,000 total purse, the July 2005 Forrest L. Wood Championship presented by Castrol awarded a $500,000 first prize and a $1.5 million purse (more than double the Classic).

And although the February 2006 Citgo Bassmaster Classic will award a $500,000 first prize and a $1.2 million purse (double the previous year), the July 2006 Forrest L. Wood Championship will award a $500,000 first prize and a still-greater $1.5 million purse.

Just when it looked like BASS was closing the prize-money gap, a month prior to the 2006 Citgo Bassmaster Classic, FLW announced that its new 2007 Forrest L. Wood Cup would be "the most lucrative championship in bass fishing history," offering a total purse of $2 million and a first-place prize of $1 million if the winning angler uses a Ranger Boat (half of that if he uses another boat). The event will be held on Lake Ouachita in Hot Springs, Arkansas, hosted by the Hot Springs Advertising and Promotion Commission, the Arkansas Game & Fish Commission, and the Arkansas Department of Parks and Tourism.

So it looks like part of FLW's battle plan is adapted from the United States versus Soviet Union Cold War ploy: outspend them into submission or implosion. And it looks like part of ESPN's battle plan is to pump up the television coverage, even if, as reported, it lost money on televising the 2005 Classic in Pittsburgh—a "loss leader," one ESPN executive called it. Some observers think all of ESPN's exposure of professional bass fishing will make both the sport and BASS explode. With such an explosion will come willing advertisers, and thus profits for ESPN.

Today ESPN is seen in 89 million households. Fox Sports Network reaches 81 million. Both companies play these numbers up, but no advertiser buys on household reach. The more households, the better the potential for viewers, but it's not a guarantee of viewership.

It's the number of homes that are tuned into a given program (often called eyeballs) that advertisers pay for.

ESPN's final weigh-in show for the 2005 Citgo Bassmaster Classic in Pittsburgh had a 0.6 household rating and was seen in 526,000 homes. That number was reportedly a 9 percent increase over 2004, yet it's far short of the 34 million people who are actually counted as anglers in the United States and well below the 3.2 million cable homes that were watching *Raw Zone*, a wrestling program that was broadcast the same week. It also pales next to TV poker shows, which *Media Post* reported two weeks before the Pittsburgh Classic was "a surging programming area." Insiders say that ESPN will have to at least double its Classic viewership to show that this is the big deal that everyone says it is, and that it might have a NASCAR-like future.

As of January 2006, FLW Outdoors was administering a total of 235 fishing tournaments via its Wal-Mart Bass Fishing League, Wal-Mart FLW Tour, Wal-Mart FLW Series, Stren Series, Wal-Mart Texas Tournament Trail, Stratos Owners' Tournament Trail, Wal-Mart FLW Walleye Tour, Wal-Mart FLW Walleye League, Wal-Mart FLW Kingfish Tour, Wal-Mart FLW Kingfish Series, and Wal-Mart FLW Redfish Series. The combined purses for these events exceeded $36.5 million.

Professional bass anglers say that all of the increased prize money is good for the sport. Translation: my bank account. And FLW and BASS repeatedly deny that there's a death battle going on, although many of their actions contradict this. "This will help grow the sport" is the official mantra from both FLW and BASS when new directions or events are announced.

Can two major bass fishing leagues offering outrageous monies continue? Many of the bass pros think so, which may be wishful thinking. Ray Scott agrees.

"Sure, there's room for both," says Scott. "There would have been room twenty-five years ago. I'd have probably been better off and the Federation better off if I'd had somebody punching me up. A little competition is what makes America. If Henry Ford or the Wright Brothers had been the only games in town, we wouldn't have progressed very far."

Many insiders are split on the question, noting that both organizations have different business models, FLW's bottom line being to sell more high-priced boats, and BASS's being to grow more television viewers and sell more advertising.

Jay Kumar, cohost of the discontinued *Loudmouth Bass* and CEO of bassfan.com, a successful upstart company that has out-bassed BASS with its broad, intelligent, and objective coverage of all things important to probass worshipers, is on the fence.

"I think they can both survive, but not necessarily in the directions one or both are going," says Kumar, who notes that there are sixty or more regional or local tournament organizations of some size that are doing fine, signaling that there is a good demand for bass tournaments.

"You cannot claim that you have the best tour in the world and the best championship in the world when half the best guys are not fishing your tour, which is the case for both. Neither one of them is really doing the greatest tour."

Many people who are close to the tournament bass fishing scene don't think two leagues can survive, although they won't say it publicly. Even the levelheaded McKinnis, one of the constants in this saga, doesn't think there's room for both.

"It would be wonderful if we had some of their assets and they had some of our assets," he says. "And we were one going in the same direction. But right now we're competing against them, and we're going in different directions. There's not enough room for that. Some day that's going to change. Some day they are going to come together, or one of them's going to go away."

And if neither happens, you might wonder, is there some tectonic occurrence that might make this irrationally exuberant high-dollar bass tournament madness explode like an atom bomb? Gasoline going to $5 a gallon, perhaps, so that the boat and truck industries plunge down the toilet? A clever techno-cheating scandal that causes widespread suspicion? A new, cheaper next big thing (curling maybe?) for the television cameras to shoot? A serious lack of eighteen- to thirty-four-year-old eyeballs watching or, just as important, buying?

And where is the non-ESPN, non-FSN outdoor media in all of this? The ones who should be asking what this is doing for the at-large sport of fishing?

While FLW has been winning the prize money battle and may be winning the sponsorship battle, it does not appear to be winning the media battle. If it was, then its top event would be the Super Bowl of bass fishing. The FLW Championship would be covered by all of the beat reporters at the major papers, as happens at major golf tournaments. The bassheads watching TV would be counted in the millions, not hundreds of thousands.

Notwithstanding FLW's repeated press-release references to its history-making purses, media attention from around the world, and entry into 81 million FSN households, there are virtually no endemic and few generalist media at its biggest event. Mark Taylor, a writer for the *Roanoke Times*, attended the 2003 FLW Championship and counted six members of the media, not including the folks doing the TV work or writing for FLW's publications. An exhibitor at the 2005 FLW Championship estimated media attendance at "a few," which included two regional television shows, and said he did not meet one writer. A media attendee at that same event said that the most people in the FLW media room at any one time might have been ten. A January 2006 Google search under "FLW Championship" drew 550 results, and one under "Bassmaster Classic" drew 145,000 results. That's unscientific, of course, maybe meaningless, but you have to wonder.

Whatever the number of media attendees is at either the Bassmaster Classic or the FLW Championship, the Classic certainly has exponentially more, although most of the outdoor media are essentially writing just about the who-won and how-they-caught-'em details. And then there's all of that coverage of the Classic on ESPN and ESPN2, which has enormous self-promotional value. Could *ESPN the Magazine* have been so successful so quickly (versus *Sports Illustrated*, which was in the red for many years upon its start-up) if it had not been for the incessant cross-promotional television advantages that it had?

ESPN can cover and promote the Bassmaster Classic and its other major tournaments mercilessly, not to mention that it can leverage many tie-ins with its parent, the entertainment king Disney. Since it does not own Genmar, Ranger, or FLW, does Fox's commitment to bass fishing tournaments run any deeper than the willingness of Irwin Jacobs, big-league advertisers, or both to pay for the programming?

FOURTEEN

Growing the Sport

*You can't touch Iaconelli for at least $75K a year. That's
a blink of the eye in our world. What these guys do and
the exposure you get, it's not take the money and run.
That's a great value. My fear is that if ratings go up and
they get more exposure, that may not last long.*

—ROB FUNK, DIRECTOR OF EVENT MARKETING FOR TOYOTA

So many bass fishing pros, BASS and FLW spokesmen, and ESPN
brass talk about "growing the sport" that it begs the question:
which sport?

Often the answer from these individuals is that they hope to get
more people involved in fishing, especially bass fishing.

The best single measure of fishing participation in the United
States is the U.S. Fish and Wildlife Service's (FWS) National Survey
of Fishing, Hunting, and Wildlife-Associated Recreation, which has
been conducted every five years since 1955. The last survey, in 2001,
determined that 34.1 million people age sixteen and older fished in
the United States. That number was 3 percent less than the total
number of anglers in 1996 and 4 percent less than 1991. The survey
noted that from 1991 to 2001, "saltwater fishing increased 2 percent
(not significant), but freshwater fishing declined by 8 percent."

Results of the next FWS survey will not be available until late
2006 or early 2007. It is unlikely that there will be a statistically significant increase, if indeed there is any increase, although there was a

slight uptick in the number of fishing licenses sold nationally in 2005 over 2004.

While the 2001 FWS survey is the best known study of the number of Americans who fish, it has its flaws, since it accounts for all people in all states who purchase licenses. For example, someone who buys a license in two states is counted two times, even though he or she is just one person. A bass pro, who might buy a license in twelve states during the course of a year, would be counted twelve times.

On the other hand, some people are not required to have a fishing license. Some states do not have a license provision for saltwater anglers, some states don't require them of people over or under a certain age, and others don't require them for fishing on private waters. Those people are not counted in the FWS national survey.

So, what's the real number of American anglers? The American Sportfishing Association (ASA) says that there are 44 million anglers over the age of six who fish at least once annually, which means they are adding 11 million anglers from the ages of six to fifteen from the FWS survey. Not exactly your major marketing targets.

No matter how you look at it, the number of anglers in the United States has been trending slightly downward for a couple of decades. Rob Southwick, a numbers-crunching consultant for the ASA, refuses to use the *down* word and says that it's statistically flat but notes that thanks to new product innovation, television exposure, and industry promotions, anglers are spending more on their sport per capita. This, he says, is a good thing for manufacturers. But what it means is that they're pressing more juice out of the apple.

As to the number of bass anglers, it is known that more people fish for black bass species than for any other single species or group of species. The 2001 FWS survey indicated as much and put the number of bass anglers at 10.7 million, or 38 percent of freshwater anglers.

Here, too, the actual number of bass anglers is hard to pinpoint. Across the United States, anglers don't purchase a license specifically to fish for bass. People who indicate that they fish for bass include the person who fishes for bass once in a given year (and fishes for trout a dozen times and catfish a dozen times), as well as those who fish 150 times a year for bass alone.

What is certain is that the number of anglers as a percentage of the U.S. population has been decreasing. That population in 1991 was 252 million. By January 2006, it had risen to almost 298 million. From 1991 through 2005, the number of Americans increased by 46 million, or 18 percent, a number that exceeds the entire universe of American anglers. So, the U.S. population increased significantly, yet the number of people fishing for recreation declined.

In 2004, the National Sporting Goods Association (NSGA) placed fishing sixth in its 2004 ranking of annual sports participation by people aged seven and over. Though once it was second in the NSGA rankings, fishing came in behind exercise walking, camping, swimming, exercising with equipment, and bowling. Among the top ten activities, fishing was the only one with a decrease from the previous year, listed as a 3.6 percent decline by NSGA. The 2005 rankings were not available when this was written.

The ASA, which contains more than six hundred members who market to all members of the sport fishing community, has been concerned for more than a decade about growing the numbers of people who fish. Its president and CEO, Mike Nussman, wrote in his organization's June 2005 newsletter, "There is no way that we can ignore the fact that fishing participation in the United States is not growing. No matter which way you interpret the numbers, or whose numbers you use, that is the reality. So why aren't people out on the water? Richard Louv, the author of *Last Child in the Woods*, struck a nerve in all of us with his description of 'nature deficit disorder' depicting a nation of children tied to their computers and video games and disconnected from the natural world, to their detriment. His message of fishing as a great way to connect with the outdoors is one we can all support."

True enough, but what does it say if people eventually spend more time watching the entertainment of a bass fishing tournament on television instead of going out and actually fishing for bass?

What about growing the membership of BASS, which in 1995 was an organization with 660,000 members, 160 employees, federations in forty-six states plus Asia and Africa, and its own zip code? All of the television attention—ESPN runs commercials for the organization regularly with its programming—should at least be growing or sustaining the society that Ray Scott founded.

The numbers tell a different story, however. In January 2001, Bass Anglers Sportsman Society was owned by B.A.S.S. Inc. of Montgomery, Alabama. Its magazine, *Bassmaster*, had a paid circulation of 598,016, which is equivalent to the number of members, since every member gets a subscription with his or her dues. Membership dues were then $20, of which $19 was attributed to a year-long subscription to the magazine.

In January 2002, the company had become B.A.S.S. of Montgomery, Alabama, and was owned by ESPN Inc. of Bristol, Connecticut, a subsidiary of ABC and Disney. *Bassmaster* then had a paid circulation of 593,757. Membership dues were still $20, of which $19 was for the magazine subscription.

As of December 2005, the company had become BASS, LLC, of Lake Buena Vista, Florida (it had moved near Walt Disney World earlier that year), and was owned by ESPN Inc. The paid circulation of *Bassmaster* was 504,792. Membership dues were $25, of which $24 was for the magazine subscription.

In just under five years, BASS lost 93,224 members, or 15.6 percent. That is hardly growing a sport. Perhaps some of that loss can be attributed to raising the cost of membership 25 percent, as dues or subscription increases are often followed by a decline in members or subscribers. Perhaps not.

Notably, press releases issued by BASS in November 2005 and January 2006 claimed that the organization had 550,000 members. In February 2006, a spokesman for BASS said that there were 535,000 members but could not reconcile that with the December membership figure reported in its magazine.

Perhaps what everyone means about growing the sport is growing the number of people fishing in bass tournaments. Indeed, ASA president Mike Nussman noted in the same June 2005 article referenced earlier that "tournament fishing is one of the fastest growing sports in the United States." That may or may not be true and is mainly speculative—likely fueled by pronouncements from FLW and BASS—since there is no individual body that collects information about all fishing tournaments for all species in all locations of the country.

Perhaps eye-popping prize money and expansive television exposure is getting more people who already fish to find their competitive side and take a run at winning a big prize—again squeezing more juice out of the apple—or at the very least making enough to offset the costs of the equipment and traveling that they might likely incur anyway just to pursue a hobby. If they can make enough to show a profit every few years, they have a deductible business venture, and, who knows, they might hit the jackpot once or twice.

The super bassheads who do this would be mostly XY-chromosome anglers chasing the same dream that Ray Scott and Bobby Murray had in the late 1960s, when the game was more about bragging rights and making a living by fishing than about being a television personality and making a fortune by bass fishing. If so, that's merely drawing from the same pool.

Certainly, the money that is now offered in premier events has substantially increased, as have the sponsorship affiliations with the events themselves. Evidently, both are aimed at the people who participate in bass fishing tournaments. In early 2005, BASS claimed that approximately 50 percent of its members fished in tournaments. That is highly doubtful, but using its end-of-2005 membership as a guide, that would be 252,396 people. That's just 2.4 percent of the number of bass anglers identified by the FWS survey. More people than this watch BASS tournament coverage on ESPN. And only a tiny fraction of BASS members compete in top-tier events.

It may well be worth marketing to this highly dedicated and gear-purchasing subgroup of the U.S. angling marketplace, but there isn't statistical evidence to indicate that the sport of fishing, or the sport of bass fishing, is growing.

Marketing to bass anglers is growing, however, because 10.7 million bass anglers is a sizable group of customers for boats, lures, motor oil, trucks, margarine, and prostate or erectile dysfunction drugs.

Sponsorship Marketing

It was obvious after the first Classic that professional bass fishing tournaments could not prosper solely on the backs of sponsors from within the fishing tackle manufacturing industry, which is a fragmented group of many small businesses, some family owned and run, and most with little or no advertising and marketing budgets. Nor could it prosper with just the support of a small cluster of bass boat and outboard motor manufacturers.

Over the years, BASS did manage to involve some nonendemic or quasi-endemic companies as first- or second-tier sponsors for a few years, but most of them changed or dropped their affiliation with either the Classic or the major BASS tournaments. For a long time, BASS gave sponsors a three-year deal with a year free, but many of them did not re-up, often because key personnel at sponsoring companies had changed, and marketing needs or focus had also changed.

Although not often mentioned, the Bassmaster Classic in 1973 and 1974 was known as the Miller High Life Classic. BASS's championship event went a long time without a title sponsor until Citgo Petroleum Corporation took over in August 2001. The person in charge of that annual seven-figure deal at the time for Citgo, then brand manager Don Rucks, today is vice president and general manager of BASS, and there are some in the bass fishing industry who note how coincidental it was that Rucks brokered the deal with BASS for what would be his own secure-until-retirement job, the Citgo title sponsor contract lasting to the year 2009.

Irwin Jacobs has shown that major bass tournaments can be marketed to nonendemic, large-company sponsors, without whose involvement upper-level bass tournament competitors would still be fishing entirely for their own money.

Pre-Irwin Jacobs, the purses were mostly derived from the pool collected by all of the entry fees. In other words, if 250 anglers paid $600 apiece to enter an event, BASS collected $150,000 and offered perhaps $35,000 for first place and decreasing amounts for second through fortieth or fiftieth place. Anglers on the lower end of the payout scale virtually got the amount of their entry fee back in "winnings." Often, the total payout didn't equal the total of entry fees collected.

Sometimes larger prizes included the retail value of a boat or other merchandise, which the winner wound up selling for less than the "value" of the prize. That was good for BASS, which got the boat for a deal, valued the prize at retail level, and pocketed the difference, but it was not so good for the angler, who nearly always pocketed less than the "value" when he sold the merchandise but had to account for more to the IRS. Furthermore, this evaluation doesn't take into account whatever subsidies BASS received for each event from sponsors, the site host, and others.

The pre-Jacobs BASS tournament scene looked a lot like a bunch of guys sitting around a poker table. When the game ended at a designated time, there was one big winner, a few small winners, and a lot of losers. This is still the situation today in many premier and most nonpremier bass tournaments.

To draw more players and especially to attract television, it was necessary to significantly increase purses and have only cash prizes. This began with Jacobs and FLW in the late 1990s. There was, and is, just so much you can ask the competitors to pay to compete (although the top-tier BASS events today, the Elite Series, cost $5,000 to enter). So Jacobs put up more of his money, which BASS had been unwilling to do, and he convinced large nonendemic companies to sponsor events, teams of anglers, and television programming. Now, payouts exceed the total of entry fees collected, but not by a great deal, and all of the newer sponsorships have done nothing to lower or eliminate entry fees in all but a few elite events. So anglers are fishing for larger purses but also paying more.

What do Wal-Mart, Citgo, Castrol, Purolator, Toyota, Chevy, Cialis, Busch, Unilever, Johnson & Johnson, Land O'Lakes, Ranger, Triton, Mercury, Yamaha, Lowrance, Shimano, Berkley, et al., get out of their sponsorship and association?

It depends on whether they are endemic or nonendemic to the fishing and boating businesses. For endemic companies, which market to anglers in general, and perhaps to bass anglers in particular, it's mostly about sales and partly about brand affinity. For nonendemic companies, which market to the world-at-large, or predominantly to males-at-large, it's mostly about brand affinity and partly about sales.

For boat and outboard motor companies, it's greatly about selling product. "Tournament fishing definitely drives sales," says Steve Smith, the marketing manager for Ranger Boats. "Our average owner cares very much about the incentive and performance programs that we have because they do fish tournaments, all kinds of tournaments."

Ranger and some other boat and motor companies have elaborate incentive programs to reward owners of their boats for using them in tournaments and placing well. And although the bass boat market peaked around 1998 and has since been flat or declining, depending on who you talk to, Ranger had a very good 2005, as reflected by the fact that in midsummer of 2005 it was producing the maximum number of boats that was possible for its facility and eight hundred employees, running three shifts per day five days a week.

Smith likens the presence of his company's logo on boats in fishing tournaments, especially those on television, to the auto-racing scene, which has similar fan demographics and where logos on the cars are a constant brand reminder that helps drive sales. The difference is that while auto makers are appealing to NASCAR fans who drive street cars, his company makes boats for anglers who fish in tournaments.

The twenty- and twenty-one-foot fiberglass bass boats used by the pros need big muscular outboard powerhouses to move them like bullets down the lake, electric motors to position them for casting, and electronic devices to help navigate and decipher the underwater world. Some of the companies that manufacture these products are represented in sponsorships for much the same reason as Ranger, not to mention that being a major sponsor keeps its competitors at bay in that arena.

Mercury Marine, for example, a company known for aggressive product launches, is a major sponsor of the Citgo Bassmaster Classic and other BASS tournaments. It pays big dollars for this, over $5 million for its full involvement, according to a source, which is why its motors and pros are plastered everywhere, always featuring very large and very expensive 225 horsepower V6 motors that can propel bass boats at speeds between 70 and 80 miles per hour. When a television viewer watches the fishermen in the Citgo Bassmaster Classic, there's a slim chance that he will get a close view of a boat that is not a Triton or a motor that is not a Mercury.

The cost of these powerhouse motors is in the neighborhood of $18,000. The boats used by professional bass anglers—as well as by wannabe professionals working their way to the top rungs of competitive bass fishing—fully rigged with motors and other boating paraphernalia, including trailers, cost $50,000 to $55,000.

In spite of there being 10.7 million bass anglers in the United States, the market for such a package is not very big, according to Larry Vandiver, the marketing director for American Suzuki Motor Corporation, which focuses on grass-roots promotion efforts and selling lower-horsepower motors (often on aluminum boats) to bass anglers.

Vandiver, a fisherman who hails from Texas, where bass tournaments are as common as barbecue joints, knows the bass scene well. He points out that Suzuki has had a profit for fifty-eight consecutive years and is a profit-oriented company. And yet Suzuki does not sponsor a major bass tournament or a tournament trail, preferring to furnish cash rewards (incentives) to owners who do well in tournaments and to provide support services at various event sites, as determined by Suzuki dealers.

"Fifty-thousand-dollar bass boats are not within reach of the average working guy who dreams he could be a bass pro," says Vandiver. "That's why the bass boat market has been on a decline. Think of what the payments are on such a boat. Three to five hundred a month is tough."

Vandiver thinks that some bass boat manufacturers want to build fewer boats at a higher cost, thus making more money.

"I understand that the bass pro wants a big boat and wants to go fast," he says. "But how are you going to grow bass fishing if everybody has to buy a $50,000 boat? Not to mention a pretty substantial vehicle to tow it with?"

But there's more to his company's lack of involvement in sponsoring tournaments. He adds, "Consultants and other experts say that when the word *sponsorship* comes up in a business discussion, run away as fast as you can. Because it's probably not a good thing for you."

Boats and motors are high-ticket items, but what about selling the less costly rods, reels, lines, and lures that are used by the pros in these events? Pure Fishing, one of the largest fishing tackle companies in the world with some of the most well-known brand names in fishing (Stren, Berkley, Garcia, Fenwick) is a major sponsor of both FLW and BASS tournaments, yet its most prominent competitor, Normark (which owns Rapala, Storm, Luhr Jensen, and other well-known tackle brands), is not a sponsor of any major bass tournament or series of tournaments. And not because Normark can't afford it.

"We have never found a return on our investment when we've been involved in tournaments," says Tom Mackin, the president of Normark. "At the last Classic in New Orleans, we bought billboards around town and got much more exposure for $10,000 than did the $150,000 sponsors."

Unlike some companies, which sponsor (to varying degrees) individual bass pros, Normark is very light in this activity, preferring, according to Mackin, to be associated with fewer pros who are really good and who provide Normark with relevant product feedback.

Speaking of trucks, as Vandiver did earlier, although a truck or an SUV is not by definition endemic to angling, as a fishing rod or reel is, you do have to get to the bass lake with all of that gear and the boat. So truck and SUV manufacturers, as well as petroleum companies like Citgo and parts or accessory companies like Purolator and Advance Auto Parts, straddle the endemic/nonendemic line. And a bass fisherman without an extended-cab pickup or Chevy Suburban is like a duck without feathers.

Toyota assumed tow-vehicle sponsorship of the Citgo Bassmaster Classic in 2004 when Chevy bailed out, only to reappear later as a sponsor of FLW. Its involvement in this arena, a first for Toyota, presents an interesting dynamic, given that bass fishing is apple-pie American and Toyota is part of the foreign juggernaut that is kicking Detroit's butt.

(In a similar vein, the Houston-headquartered Citgo is owned by PDV America, Inc., which the company describes as "an indirect, wholly owned subsidiary of Petróleos de Venezuela, S.A., the national oil company of the Bolivarian Republic of Venezuela." That puts it under the aegis of the Venezuelan Ministry of Energy and Petroleum and thus the influence of Venezuelan president Cesar Chavez, a vocal socialist critic of the United States, which he calls an imperialist empire.

Venezuela is the fourth-leading oil supplier to the United States and is viewed by the U.S. government as an unstable country. The State Department's travel advisory for all of Venezuela is ominous, noting the high incidence of robberies, kidnappings, and murder, as well as strong anti-American sentiment. It is, at the very least, ironic that BASS, which has been patriotic to the extreme and whose core audience is solidly pro-Bush, pro-military, pro-flag, should be reaping the benefits of association with Citgo, a company that has been making record revenue on petroleum products and is owned by a country with profound social and human rights problems and an outwardly anti-U.S. position.)

Like Citgo, Toyota has money to spend on sponsoring affinity events and maintaining other associations. It is also the official truck and SUV of Bass Pro Shops and its Tracker Marine division and a large sponsor of NASCAR. It recently became the sponsor of the halftime shows on *Sunday Night Football* on NBC and *Monday Night Football* on ESPN.

While its Classic involvement is costly in gross dollars—around $1 million for BASS Classic sponsorship and more than $1 million for related promotions and advertising in 2005—it's just one piece of Toyota's large event-marketing portfolio, which, although the company is deep-pocketed in comparison to most endemic companies, is much less than what Chevy and Ford have in the past allocated to major events and promotions. Nevertheless, like Citgo, Toyota's sponsor participation allows it to have a bigger impact in this arena than similar dollars do in more marketing-cluttered arenas (like NASCAR). Like other nonendemic companies, Toyota believes that bassheads associate brands with their sport in a big way.

Rob Funk, the director of event marketing for Toyota, sees association with BASS as part of the company's heartland truck-marketing initiative. Toyota is intent on familiarizing the truck buyers of Texas (the truck capital of the world), other Gulf States, and a swath of the "heartland" from Kansas City through Cincinnati and Chicago with the Toyota brand. Eventually, Toyota hopes to increase sales of its trucks and SUVs there. Research has shown that its full-size vehicles are less widely known in the "heartland," and that brand loyalty to its competitors is high.

"In the full-size truck market," says Funk, "there is such brand loyalty. A lot of this is a generational thing, so associating with BASS is perfect for us in the future. Our big growth in the heartland has to come in full-size trucks over the next five years, so the current BASS demographics fit us perfectly. We know we're not going to lose those guys. They're gonna grow."

Toyota fishing team member Mike Iaconelli fishes out of his wrapped Ranger boat in February 2006.

Developing affinity in the heartland region and among the bass fishing demographic should be helped by the fact that the next generation of Toyota Tundras will be built in a San Antonio plant that was completed in 2006. Coincidentally, the San Antonio area is very high on the priority wish list for locations where BASS would like to hold a future Bassmaster Classic.

But there's more to Toyota's sponsorship than making inroads among bass anglers. "With a powerhouse like ESPN behind this," says Funk, "we feel that nonanglers and nonoutdoorsmen will get interested as well."

Like Toyota, Wal-Mart straddles the endemic/nonendemic line. Wal-Mart sells a large percentage of the fishing tackle sold each year in the United States, so aligning with professional bass fishing is partly about selling fishing equipment to bassheads and partly about selling anything, since it has an especially strong retail presence in Central and Southern states where bass fishing is particularly prominent. Ditto for Bass Pro Shops, a major retail, mail order, and Internet supplier of all things outdoors. In fact, Bass Pro Shops' ascension to major retailer sprang from the early days of BASS tournaments.

After participating in his first BASS tournament in 1970 at Table Rock Lake, Bass Pro Shops founder Johnny Morris went home to Springfield, Missouri, where he tried to get the manager of the local Gibson store (an early-day Wal-Mart) to carry a lot of the lures that he discovered at that event.

"I thought there was a great opportunity for this new bass gear," says Morris.

But the manager couldn't get permission from the home office to carry them. Morris's father owned a Brown Derby liquor store on the way to Table Rock lake and allowed him to put some of the lures on a rack in the store. That eight-square feet of space in 1971 led to a history-making American success story.

As of February 2006, Bass Pro Shops operated thirty-three retail stores (most of them megastores) across North America. It experienced more than 78 million annual visitors and was scheduled to open seven new stores in 2006 (including one in San Antonio). The Springfield headquarters store of Bass Pro Shops—which sits on the site of the old Gibson store that Morris frequented—is now and has long been the number-one tourist attraction in Missouri. The company prints a gazillion mail order catalogs each year, and its boating division, Tracker Marine, is one of the largest fiberglass and aluminum boat-manufacturing companies in the world.

It was Morris's involvement in tournament bass fishing—he competed for five years and participated in five Bassmaster Classics from 1972 through 1976—that helped him build a company that was recently named the "number one outdoor retailer" by *Sporting Goods Business*.

"We were right there," says Morris, "and Ray Scott's tournaments were having a great impact on the demand for fishing tackle. . . . By involving the press, he was promoting the sport and building heroes, like golf tournaments. Without golf tournaments, and heroes being made through the media, it wouldn't impact sales or influence equipment."

It was definitely the breeding ground of product development. Being right there, I could see what was happening better than a buyer in the home office of one of the manufacturers."

Morris feels strongly that his company's association with the Bass-master Classic and other BASS tournaments, as well as sponsorship of individual bass pros, most of whom he says are "super quality people," is important to his customers. "It definitely influences sales. I feel even stronger about investing in the personalities than in the events themselves. There are varying views on that, but I think it's a good thing for our business and for our customers to actually meet these people."

FIFTEEN

Anglers, Gambling, Women, Locations

It's probably the cleanest competitive sport that we have in this country today. Iaconelli may scream and Reese may dance, but not one of these guys has a parole officer he's got to report to.

—TWO-TIME BASSMASTER CLASSIC WINNER BOBBY MURRAY

The Road to the Classic

Ever since Ray Scott held his first bass fishing tournament, the definition of a professional bass fisherman has been anyone with the money to pay an entry fee. That is arguably still true, although many people would argue that an individual whose primary job is fishing in bass tournaments, working for sponsoring companies, and not deriving a living from another job is a professional bass fisherman. However you define it, you can't just pay to play in the top BASS tournaments, hoping to do well enough to earn a free trip to the Classic, as was once the case. You have to qualify through other events.

BASS has a byzantine array of tournaments today and has changed its event names, formats, and Classic-qualifying schemes virtually every year since ESPN acquired it. Most of the anglers in the Classic qualified through their season-long performance in previous BASS-sponsored events.

Bassmaster Classic participants each year also include six anglers who come from the so-called "amateur" ranks, qualifying through Bass Federation tournaments. These anglers are not full-time professional bass fishermen. Since some of them have minor local sponsor arrangements and many have fished in events in which they've won money or merchandise, they might be considered semi-pro anglers. Many of them aspire to be full-time pros and use their participation in the Classic as a springboard for attempting such a career, with or without a regular nonfishing job.

The presence of these "amateurs," however, underscores the fact that the Super Bowl of bass fishing, the so-called World Championship, is a tournament in which *only* members of BASS are eligible to compete and which features some amateurs competing against full-time touring pros.

Furthermore, all of the full-time pros in the Classic are not necessarily the best bass anglers in the world, as BASS claims, since there are highly accomplished and long-established professional bass anglers who fish only in FLW tournaments and are ineligible to participate in the Bassmaster Classic.

So, technically, it is inaccurate for BASS to claim, as it does every year, that the world's best bass anglers are fishing in the Bassmaster Classic. What it has in the Classic are the top-performing anglers who are members of BASS and who qualify for this event through their achievements in other BASS tournaments during the previous season.

BASS has a longer history—and a greater media following—for its championship event than FLW does. But that does not necessarily make the Bassmaster Classic a "world" championship or one composed of the "best" bass fishermen in North America, let alone the world.

In fact, the FLW Championship, which will be held for the eleventh time in 2006, has been fished by many of the top pros who have competed in BASS events. Roland Martin fished in the very first one in 1996. Gary Klein and Rick Clunn fished in the second one. All three of them fished in the third one, as did two-time Bassmaster Classic winner George Cochran. In 2005, the FLW Championship was won by Cochran, who will fish only FLW tournaments after the 2006 Classic. In 2004, the FLW Championship was won by Luke Clausen, then twenty-five years old and a 2002 Classic qualifier. Like Cochran, Clausen plans to fish only FLW events after he participates in the

2006 Bassmaster Classic; he finished twenty-sixth in the 2005 Classic.

Both Cochran and Clausen received half a million dollars for their FLW Championship victories, which was more than double what their counterpart Classic winners received in the same years, lest anyone think that the largest amount of money goes to the "best."

BASS says that it sanctions some twenty thousand bass fishing contests every year, which seems a stretch but at the very least includes many thousands of club events at local levels across North America through its Federation, as well as numerous events in recently created weekend-angler events dubbed the Bassmaster Series or, technically, the ESPN Outdoors Bassmaster Series presented by Advance Auto Parts.

The Bass Federation, currently in upheaval, once had 100,000 members but was down to about 45,000 in July 2005, and 20,000 the following March. A few months after many state chapters voted to disassociate from BASS and join arms with FLW, BASS reorganized its chapters to bring them under stricter BASS management and control, renaming its affiliates the Federation Nation. They continue to offer weekend wannabe bass pros a chance, however slim, to get into the Classic through Federation events and the Bassmaster Series.

An amateur member of BASS who woke up one day and decided he wanted to fish in the Bassmaster Classic would have to qualify through local, state, and regional Federation or Bassmaster Series events, coming out tops in either to earn a berth in the Classic. One angler from the Bassmaster Series and six from the Federation's tournaments qualify to fish in the Bassmaster Classic. According to BASS, fifteen thousand anglers competing in the Bassmaster Series will be reduced to one Classic qualifier, and a greater number will compete through the Federation for its six slots. Together, these form the base of the steep BASS pro fishing dream pyramid, and some participants have risen from the very wide bottom to the very narrow top. A number of anglers—Mike Iaconelli among them—have emerged from the most grass-roots level of the Federation to enjoy professional bass fishing tournament success.

. . .

Only one person, however, achieved the ultimate dream by winning the Bassmaster Classic as a Federation "amateur." Bryan Kerchal of Newtown, Connecticut, qualified as the Northeast Federation representative in 1993 when the Classic was held at Lake Logan Martin in Alabama. He finished last, in forty-first place. The following year, he fished six regular-season BASS events, which arguably made him a professional at that point, and he did not do well enough in that series to qualify for the Classic. But he did qualify again as the Northeast Federation representative for the Classic, which was conducted at High Rock Lake in North Carolina.

The twenty-three-year-old Kerchal, who worked as a cook at a Ground Round restaurant, collected autographs of the other competitors on a cap that he kept in his boat and blew a lucky fish whistle each time that he caught a keeper. He beat thirty-nine other anglers in 1994, winning by 4 ounces, and collected the $50,000 first prize, which was to launch him on a career as a professional bass angler.

According to BASS, after winning he told the weigh-in crowd, "If this is your dream, kids, don't ever let anybody tell you that you can't do it because it's definitely possible for anybody in this crowd or anywhere to do what I have done. I think that's what I proved by winning the Classic this year. That it can be done. Always work as hard as you can and put as much as you can into it, and don't give up."

The only "amateur" to win the big event (two others have placed second) and the only person to go from last one year to first the next, Kerchal is still the inspiration for many workingman wannabe bass pros. On track to be a role model and a bass fishing superstar, Kerchal was killed on December 13 of that year in a commuter plane crash in North Carolina.

Bryan Kerchal was also the first Classic winner who didn't hail from a Southern state, helping to debunk the myth that only good ole boys can be accomplished bass anglers.

"Two bubbas in a boat. That's what a lot of people think about these guys," said Jerry McKinnis on camera during the 2005 Citgo Bassmaster Classic.

Replied host Ron Franklin, "There are a lot of people who stereotype [them] and say that's what it's about, but it's so far from that."

The 2004 Citgo Bassmaster Classic winner, Takahiro Omori, talks with emcee Keith Alan one morning in Pittsburgh.

However you define "bubba" or distinguish that characterization from "good ole boy," the fact is that professional bass fishing has been predominantly the domain of anglers from Southern states. Through the first three decades, the top performers and an overwhelming majority of the Classic competitors showed a special affinity for country music, grits, and hush puppies.

That continued after Bryan Kerchal's win through the year 2000. With 2001 through 2005 winners being Michigan's Kevin VanDam (twice), Japan's Takahiro Omori, New Jersey's Mike Iaconelli, and Texas's Jay Yelas (a transplant from Oregon and California), plus two second-place finishes by Californian Aaron Martens (recently transplanted to Alabama), the Citgo Bassmaster Classic winner's podium and television coverage has lately looked and sounded much more diverse, which could not have been scripted any better for the likes and wants of ESPN.

The 2002 Citgo Bassmaster Classic winner, Jay Yelas, considers himself an athlete and doesn't view competitive bass fishing as gambling.

.   .   .

In fact, many of the bass pros who compete at the top level, and especially those in the Bassmaster Classic, are far removed in look and sound from their counterparts of three decades ago or even one decade ago. Most are fit and bodily trim. Few have tire-tube bellies, chew tobacco in public, or look in any way like beer-swigging, baggy-panted, real-work-avoiding bubbas (BASS forbids them to wear jeans at the Classic). Many of them do regular physical workouts and pay close attention to how they look and to the appearance they project.

That's not to say that there are not still a lot of good ole boys in the bass fishing tournament game. But overtly good ole boys who have just taken a fling on a career in tournament bass fishing as a way to avoid a real job are giving way to self-promoting anglers who have studied marketing, communications, or both; have prepared a business plan for a professional bass fishing career; and, when attired in a suit and tie, could easily be mistaken for career businessmen.

On the water and at consumer shows wearing their ball caps and cluttered sponsorwear, bass pros look exactly like NASCAR drivers. Which is to say, walking and driving billboards. They also look a lot like athletes, especially the younger participants.

The subject of athleticism, in fact, is a sore one with many bass pros. As far back as the early 1970s, Bob Cobb was calling bass pros, especially Classic contenders, athletes, noting the stamina and the endurance it took to do well and to be consistent. Some people scoffed. After all, one of the things that distinguishes fishing from other sports is that anyone can do it, since no special strengths or physical attributes are necessary, and the fish have no idea who is at the other end of the line.

Nevertheless, it does take a lot to cast all day for many days on end, including practice—almost always standing up (often on one leg while the other leg is perched on the electric motor), enduring the elements, cold and wind in particular—while also driving a boat at high speeds and often for long distances on rough water. And then the anglers have to take care of boat and tackle issues each night. Like people who participate in recognized athletic events, bass pros experience injuries (as do others who fish a great deal), particularly having back, neck, shoulder, elbow, and wrist problems.

But if you consider an athlete to be someone who runs a fast 440 or plays a game with a ball or a puck, the bass pro doesn't fit the bill. A lot of people who view an angler as someone who sits idly on the shore or in a boat waiting for a fish to bite think this way, too, and likely wouldn't consider race car drivers, golfers, or poker-tournament players athletes, either. (If you think it doesn't take some endurance to win a poker tournament, ask thirty-nine-year-old Joseph Sachem; he won $7.5 million in the 2005 World Series of Poker Championship after what was described as a "grueling 13-hour and 56-minute final round table.")

To a man, bass pros consider themselves athletes. Yet the top pros are so nearly equal in fishing skill that athleticism—in the sense of being able to cast farther or more accurately or have some superior physical characteristic—is not a factor in their performance, although stamina and occasional injuries, most notably for older anglers, can be factors.

At the premier events, superior fishing performance often comes down to mental attitude. To fish successfully on a top competitive level requires a clear mind and total devotion to the fishing tasks at hand. Thinking about business, bills, or an argument with the wife can cause an angler to miss a strike. And that one strike could mean missing a check or losing a winning fish. So the ability to achieve total concentration is important, especially to attain consistency over a career.

This is one of the reasons why four-time Classic winner Rick Clunn has excelled, especially in big events. Some bassheads in the past have disparaged Clunn as a "damn Buddhist" because *Bassmaster* and others reported on his varied efforts to relax, focus, and concentrate and because of his well-known penchant for staying in campgrounds while at tournaments so he can be more attuned with nature. Indeed, emcee Keith Alan frequently refers to Clunn at tournaments as the "Zen Master." But Clunn proved that being consistent as a bass pro was very much a mental game, requiring tremendous focus and mental toughness.

Clunn and others paved the way for big money to come into professional bass fishing. Ironically, in so doing they attracted newer players who today are proving that they can make a good living as bass pros, even without having nearly the success or the dominance that Clunn did, by being fairly consistent and by being charismatic businessmen. Or, in many cases, having a spouse who is a good businesswoman.

Gerald Swindle of Alabama exemplifies the well-hyped bass star with a modest accomplishment portfolio. As of the 2006 Classic, the brash, hip-talking thirty-six-year-old Swindle, who is almost as widely quoted and promoted by ESPN as Mike Iaconelli, had fished in ninety-seven BASS events and won $480,000. He had won no BASS tournaments, was Angler of the Year once, and had been in the Classic six times.

By contrast, the subdued forty-nine-year-old Ron Shuffield of Arkansas had fished in 196 BASS events and won $1,080,821. He had won 7 BASS tournaments and had been in the Classic 14 times.

Swindle has been termed one of the ESPN "brat pack" by bassfan.com writers and is all over the place in ESPN coverage and in advertisements and commercials for BASS sponsors. But you have to look extremely hard to find Shuffield, an older and nonflamboyant success.

Byron Velvick, incidentally, is almost as golden as Swindle, despite being far less accomplished in BASS events. As of February 2006, the forty-one-year-old pro angler and TV celebrity from Nevada had fished in seventy-seven BASS events and won a total of just $48,365, more than half of which had been in merchandise. He won one BASS event and has yet to qualify for the Classic. But thanks to his analyst role at ESPN and his stardom on ABC's *The Bachelor*, he is now prominent in Triton, Mercury, Berkley, Coca Cola, and other promotions.

Swindle, Velvick, and the other anglers who will fish in the top BASS pro series in 2006, the eleven-event Elite division, have narrowed odds for getting into the 2007 Classic. Thirty-six out of 106 pros fishing in the Elite Series will qualify for entry in the Classic, based on their total performance over the season. This means that inevitably a certain core group will sustain a career, provided that BASS doesn't change the rules dramatically, if these anglers merely average being in the top third of the class at the end of each year. It's a lot easier to do that in a small field than in a field with two hundred to three hundred anglers, which is how it used to be for most of the older pros, who have sustained long careers by out-fishing many more anglers.

But the cost to fish the Elite Series is steep. BASS is charging $5,000 in entry fees per angler per Elite event and mandating that anglers fish in each of them. Thus, entry fees alone cost $55,000. Up front. Add on travel and miscellaneous expenses, and the nut for just these tournaments is probably $80,000, with the odds being three to one that you make it to the Classic. If you fish the three other BASS Tour events in 2006, which have lower entry fees, you're probably looking at up to $100,000 just to fish as a pro for the year, in the hope of making it to the entry-fee-less Classic. And that's without paying the bills and the expenses at home, obtaining various types of insurance, maintaining your tow vehicle, and so forth.

Elite Series pro Terry Segraves, who placed fourteenth in the very first FLW Championship and who will fish seventeen events between BASS and FLW in 2006, says that he'll spend at least $120,000 in entry fees and expenses to compete at the highest levels for one season.

"There's not many top sports where you have to pay to play," says Segraves, a Floridian who echoes the sentiments of many other pros who feel that they are essentially fishing for their own money. Says Kansas pro Brent Chapman, "I have to pay to go to work, and there's no guarantee I'll get my money back."

Segraves had about 80 percent of his costs for the 2006 season covered by various sponsors and has calculated the odds of winning money in these tournaments, based on the number of anglers in the respective events, how far down into the field each offers a paycheck, and what they pay. According to him, the odds of making money—placing fiftieth or better and getting a minimum check of $10,000—are two to one in the BASS events and four to one in FLW events.

Many of the bass pros who do not have top-level sponsor arrangements—which is most of the field—are making a major financial commitment with the hope of solidifying a career and earning a good living. Some of them are likely to take a big financial hit or be wiped out if they don't have a high level of success in just one season. Others, who have achieved enough success in the past to be able to make this commitment—and perhaps don't have family-support issues—may be on the verge of making a fine career out of professional bass fishing.

Thirty-seven-year-old Terry Scroggins of Florida, who was an auto body painter for twenty years, had the good fortune to win two big tournaments in 2003 and 2004 that garnered him a total of $150,000 while he was still holding down his painting job. He saved the winnings, which allowed him to quit painting in January 2005 to fish bass tournaments full time. Thirteen months later, he was named to the Toyota national fishing team and had enough sponsors to cover his BASS costs for at least 2006. If Scroggins wins a good amount of money in 2006, it will be counted as profit, not payback against loans.

Ditto for Marty Stone, another "brat packer" and an articulate, outgoing North Carolinian who, like Gerald Swindle, is a prominent member of the Citgo national fishing team.

"I had a blueprint and I knew what I needed to do," says the forty-year-old Stone, who wanted to fish for a living after high school but went to college at the insistence of his parents. He graduated from college in 1991 and worked until 1996 framing houses, fishing in tournaments part time and with the support of a wife who had a good job. He made the BASS Tour in 1997 and has not looked back. In 1999, his wife, who had a college degree in communications and a minor in marketing, quit her job and became his full-time manager.

"She has really helped move my career forward," says Stone, who fished FLW tournaments for six years but now fishes only BASS because it "makes good business sense." That may be pro-speak for "my sponsors made me choose," but Stone says, "with BASS I am allowed to promote freely and am able to get my sponsors exposure on TV. And I get paid a premium for that. With BASS, I've made my money before I ever show up [for a tournament]."

Most of the top-level pros have personal stories that entail sacrifice, taking chances, the support of a family (and in many cases a divorce), and at some point having just enough money to get to or from an event. This is how it has been since the beginning, in fact.

Forty-eight-year-old tournament stalwart Gary Klein, for example, has been a competitive bass angler since he was fifteen, placing third in the year-end standings for a major Western circuit that he fished at sixteen when he still lived in his native California. His parents put up his entry fees in the early years of his tournament fishing, with the understanding that he would pay them back with his winnings. Klein failed to do that only twice in six years through forty tournaments, although from time to time he lived in his bed-equipped van when he didn't have enough money to afford a motel room. His breakthrough came when he won $10,598 and a Ranger boat in a 1979 BASS event. As of 2006, he has qualified for the Bassmaster Classic twenty-four times (fourth most), placing second in 2003, and his BASS winnings alone placed him sixth on the all-time BASS winnings list, with more than $1.3 million.

There are a hundred tales of anglers who worked hard and sacrificed, and there has been almost since Ray Scott started BASS. Lately, professional bass anglers from Japan—a country that is trying to eradicate imported bass because they have harmed native species, but where avid freshwater anglers are crazy about American bass fishing—have taken sacrifice, persistence, and perseverance to an even greater extreme.

To prepare for a January 2006 FLW event on Florida's Lake Okeechobee, Shinike Fukae went to that lake in December 2005 and practiced on the water for eighteen days straight prior to the practice cutoff time. Said Fukae later, "No Christmas. No New Year's. Just fishing." He won the tournament.

Nothing takes the grit-and-determination award, however, more than the saga of 2004 Citgo Bassmaster Classic champion Takahiro Omori, who now hails from Texas, living near the renowned bass factory of Lake Fork, but who came to the United States virtually penniless and without speaking English, expressly to achieve his dream of being a professional bass fisherman and winning the Bassmaster Classic.

Now thirty-five, Omori grew up near Tokyo and had fished as a youngster with his father, read Japanese bass fishing magazines, and idolized Rick Clunn. To the dissatisfaction of his father, he worked various jobs instead of going to college, saved up $2,000, and flew to the United States in 1992. Here, he rented a Ford Escort, which he lived out of, and he competed in two tournaments, finishing 304th out of 325 anglers in the first, and 256th out of 326 in the second.

He returned to the United States the following year as a boat hauler for another Japanese angler, living out of a 1965 Chevy Suburban for the next three years. In 1996, he won a BASS event that garnered him a bass boat and $14,000, and in 1997, he bought a camper van and a trailer at Lake Fork. In 2001, he qualified for the Citgo Bassmaster Classic and along the way made enough money to buy a home, which he is rarely in, near Lake Fork, spending an additional $25,000 to install a swimming pool, which he does not swim in but uses only to test lures.

Staying in campgrounds while fishing tournaments, eating rice with chopsticks in his RV, and often being the first person on the water and the last one off it during practice days, the single and hobbyless Omori is probably the most dedicated, focused, and obsessive of all professional bass fishermen.

At the 2004 Bassmaster Classic, Omori was in second place after two days. On the third and final day, he caught three keepers in the final forty-five minutes, the last of which came with just five minutes to spare. When named the $200,000 winner, he raised his fists in the air, then sunk to his knees and pounded the stage. Afterward, the jubilant-tearful-relieved look on Omori's face said everything that his limited English could not.

Business or Gambling Addiction?

Omori, like all of the bass pros and many of the wannabe bass pros, is extremely competitive and believes fiercely in himself. Because of that belief, he was willing to take what many people viewed as a foolish gamble to invest his talents, energy, and passion in pursuing his dream of forging a career in tournament bass fishing. In some ways, and given the fact that anglers have to ante up to participate in most bass tournaments, it seems like there could be an analogy to gambling. After all, Texas-Hold-'Em Poker tournaments have been the rage for nearly a decade, with the Worldwide Leader in Sports as well as other cable networks making poker tournaments a major part of their programming.

Which begs two questions about competing in bass fishing tournaments that have cash and merchandise payouts: Is this gambling? Is it addictive?

"Oh, yeah," says Terry Segraves, "It's pretty addictive. You're always gambling that the next one's gonna be 'it.'"

Rick Schair, a Georgia businessman and a former avid bass tournament angler who is very involved in the bass fishing industry as president of Wet-A-Line Tours, a company that takes anglers to premier upscale destinations in Mexico and Brazil, has a salient take on this subject.

At a BASS tournament in South Carolina one time, I was eating dinner with a bunch of fellow competitors before the last day of the tournament. One guy said, "If I don't get a check in this, I won't have enough gas to get home or enough money to make my rent payment."

I told him, "That has to be the dumbest thing I ever heard in my life. You should be home flipping burgers and feeding your family rather than here gambling away your last few dollars!"

Tournament fishing is an absolute gambling addiction. A lot of people don't realize it, but on the local and national level it's like playing cards or shooting craps. It's a compulsive gambler's habit. Not to mention the money that is spent to facilitate it. In today's environment, you can spend $100 a day in boat gas and oil alone in a tournament on a big lake. Every time you come off the water, you have something that's broken or needs replacing. And all of us are compulsive tackle junkies. Each of us has enough tackle in his boat to fish for a hundred years. None of us can pass up more tackle. We can't buy one red crankbait. We have to get two, just in case. What if we lose the first one?

At some point I came to the realization that unless you have the time to devote to practicing and putting in the hours on the water, you're just donating money. The compulsive gamblers never come to this realization. They have forgotten why they started fishing in the first place, which was to have fun and enjoy a day on the lake. Tournament fishing is not fun. It is a long, hard day of running and gunning, fishing too fast, and then regretting taking off work and spending all that money when you don't win.

And there are many guys whose only fishing is done in tournaments, so they compete in order to try to win money. I drew a partner in a tournament once who said to me, "Why would you want to go fish for fun when you have a shot at winning some money?" When you reach that state, you're addicted.

Most of the top bass pros, and especially those in the Citgo Bassmaster Classic, do not feel that they are addicted to fishing competition or that they are gambling. BASS issued a media release in March 2006 touting anglers in its Elite Series and quoted the following from Brooks Rogers, a thirty-year-old Texas guide who could not find enough sponsors to cover his $55,000 entry fees and other costs, so he invested in himself by taking out a bank loan—without hesitation, according to BASS. One can only imagine that the loan officer must have been a tournament angler.

"I'm looking at it like any other business opportunity," said Rogers. "If you're fixing to buy a restaurant, you've got to come up with the money, and hopefully you do well enough to pay it off. And that's how I'm approaching this."

Rogers must have been talking with Jay Yelas, the 2002 Classic champion and fifth all-time BASS money winner, who considers a career in professional bass fishing no different from taking a chance on a start-up business.

"Tournament fishing is like an obsession or a passion for a lot of guys. It can be like gambling, but I don't think it is," says Yelas. "It's like any small business owner starting up a new business. You have to spend a lot of money in investment to get it going, and the early stages are the growth part. All our expenses are tax-deductible, and a gambler's are not. Any new business would be a gamble, whether it's a donut shop or a software company or whatever. That's what fishing is for these guys, it's just a small business."

The business, of course, is part catching bass and part being a walking-driving-casting pitchman for fishing tackle, boats and motors, trucks, petrol, and assorted other products—not to mention tourism, at least tangentially.

It's interesting that both Rogers and Yelas make comparisons to opening up a food business. Twenty-six percent of all independent start-up restaurants fail within the first year and 60 percent fail within three years, with initial investment costs averaging between $250,000 and $500,000.

And neither bass pro mentioned that most of the money he expects to win will come out of the pockets of fellow competitors. That sounds like a poker game.

Speaking of gambling, there is no formal betting on professional bass fishing tournaments, at least not in Las Vegas, the home of the first Bassmaster Classic. I was in the Sports Book at the Las Vegas Hilton two weeks before the 2005 Classic and sat in its large room watching eleven different professional baseball games at one time, with other large screens switching to the latest horse race from Santa Anita, Pimlico, Aqueduct, or wherever.

Odds were posted for upcoming baseball games, the 2006 Super Bowl, assorted boxing matches, a hundred horse racing events, NASCAR races, the World Series, the Indy Racing League, golf tournaments, the Gold Cup in soccer, WNBA games, Formula 1 Grand Prix racing, and a slew of other sporting contests. The Bassmaster Classic, just two weeks away, wasn't noted.

So I went to the betting window and asked whether I could place a bet on the Bassmaster Classic.

"The what?" said Gerry, a teller in black pants and a white dress shirt.

"It's a major bass fishing tournament being held in two weeks."

"Nah," he said. "We don't do fishing."

"Does anyone?"

He shook his head. "Maybe someone, but I couldn't tell you where to go."

Evidently, there is also little or no informal betting on the Bassmaster Classic or other major bass fishing tournaments, including calcuttas. At least, not that I learned about.

Calcuttas are auctionlike pooled wagering systems (using computer software, in some cases, to calculate odds) outside of a tournament's awards and payback structure in which individuals, including and especially competitors, bet on who will win. The money collected goes into one pot, most of which goes to the winning bettor(s).

Calcuttas are common in golf tournaments and big-game saltwater fishing tournaments; in the latter, where teams of well-heeled anglers fish out of million-dollar-plus sportfishing boats, it is common for calcutta pools to exceed the total tournament purse and reach into the hundreds of thousands of dollars. One of the richest such saltwater events is the Mid-Atlantic $500,000 held annually in Cape May, New Jersey. In the August 2005 Mid-Atlantic, in which teams on 169 boats participated, the total calcutta payout was nearly $1.2 million dollars, more than twice the total purse.

There is no mention of calcuttas, gambling, wagering, or prohibitions thereof in the 2006 BASS rules. But it seems like there's an

opportunity for someone, probably bassfan.com, if not to run a calcutta, then at least to create a system for setting odds on the pros and
generating some buzz. Bassfan.com sort of has that in its proprietary
world rankings of bass pros, which does not discriminate based on
whose tour a pro fishes, although its calculations do not incorporate
odds-making on upcoming events.

Women and BASS

While it was previously noted that most bass pros are Wonderbread-
white and that there is little ethnic diversity among them—there
seems to be more Asian bass fishing pros, in fact, than black or His-
panic pros put together—it bears mentioning that women are, and
have been, remarkably absent as participants in BASS tournaments.
But not because none of them wanted to compete.

When Roland Martin competed in the first Classic, he was not
allowed to bring along his fiancée, Mary Ann—whom he was introduced to at a bass tournament by Bill Dance—because they were not
married. That was Ray Scott's dictum. The year was 1971, and Mary
Ann was then a good-enough bass angler to probably have bettered
many of those who fished at Lake Mead. In fact, she was the first
woman to fish an otherwise all-male bass tournament, doing so in
1970 at a non-BASS event at Millwood Lake in Arkansas.

In 1973, at a BASS tournament at Ross Barnett Lake in Mississippi, then as Mrs. Roland Martin, she walked up to Ray Scott in front
of a bunch of people and handed him a personal check.

"What's this for?" said Scott.

Martin replied, "It's for an entry fee for me to fish a Bassmasters
tournament."

"You gonna fish one of my tournaments?" exclaimed Scott. "It'll
be a cold day in hell before a woman ever fishes one of my tournaments." Then he tore up the check.

"He was upset at me for trodding on sacred ground, I guess," says
Martin. "It kinda hurt my feelings and embarrassed me. And I think
Roland was embarrassed."

Not so embarrassed that he didn't win that tournament. And
although upset, Mary Ann and Roland named their son, born two

years later, after the founder of BASS. She remains friendly with Ray Scott to this day, and her son, Scott Martin, is a major competitor in FLW tournaments, which also have very few female competitors.

"I dropped it and got involved with Bass 'N Gal," says Martin.

Bass 'N Gal was a national women's bass fishing tournament organization that was started in 1972 by Sugar Ferris, now in the Texas Freshwater Fishing Hall of Fame. It prospered in the 1970s and 1980s but eventually went out of business. Nevertheless, in ten years of competing on that circuit, Mary Ann Martin was perennially one of the top Bass 'N Gal competitors and won the year-end Bass 'N Gal Classic in 1978.

When queried by the media in the early years about not allowing women to participate in BASS tournaments, Ray Scott always raised the awkward "potty issue" and professed to be concerned about the feelings of the spouses of his "hairy-legged" male anglers, who would be worried about their men spending an entire day alone in a boat with another woman. But the fact is that he considered participation in his tournaments to be by invitation, and, male or female, if he didn't want you or didn't approve of you for any reason, you weren't invited. And no women were.

It would not be until 1991, when Ray Scott no longer owned BASS, that a woman—Vojai Reed—would fish in one of its events. Reed fished in seven BASS tournaments in total, with little success.

Despite there being no great movement for women becoming involved in fishing and no significant groundswell of sponsor support, BASS announced a women's professional bass fishing trail in 2005, with most of the events taking place in 2006 and being sponsored by Triton and Mercury. Coincidentally, a woman named Martin—Pam Martin-Wells—won the first event of the new Women's Bassmaster Tour, which, like the very first Bass 'N Gal event, was held in Texas.

Location, Location

Oddly, only one of the thirty-six Bassmaster Classics has been held in Texas. Actually, half in Texas.

While it is true that bass fishing is popular across the United States, the diversification of recent Classic winners belies the fact that bass fishing tournament participation is still strongest in number of events and number of participants in the South.

Texas in particular likely has more bass fishing tournaments, BASS-sanctioned or not, than most other states put together. In 1993, the Inland Fisheries Division of Texas Parks and Wildlife estimated that there were fifty-five hundred black bass tournaments in that state. No updates on that number have been done since, and there is no permitting or regulation process for tournaments in Texas (tournament anglers opposed and defeated a bill several years ago for a no-fee permit that fisheries managers requested).

However, it is not a coincidence that many of the players and the events that have shaped the course of professional bass fishing have a connection to Texas, Alabama, Missouri, and Arkansas, where bass fishing is well rooted socially and culturally.

On an angler-per-capita basis, there are more people who fish avidly for bass and who fish in bass fishing tournaments in the swath of the United States that stretches from Virginia to Florida and west to Texas and Oklahoma than anywhere else. In other words, the constituency is very much still Southern. And while many current professional bass fishing stars may not be good ole boys, a lot of bassheads are. There's a striking similarity in this respect to NASCAR racers and its fans.

Although BASS has held professional regular-season tournaments in many places, including Texas, there is much repetition to the states and the sites where their regular-season and Classic events have been held in the past. With respect to the Classic, this is mostly due to which localities had deep pockets and less out of a need to appeal to where the core membership is or was located.

The Classic has been held nine times in Alabama, the former home of BASS and the state where Ray Scott was the chairman of George H. W. Bush's presidential campaign in 1980. According to the U.S. Fish & Wildlife Service survey of 2001, Alabama ranked nineteenth in total number of anglers.

Five times the Classic has been in North Carolina (ranked eighth in anglers). Three times it has been in Virginia and Louisiana (respectively ranked thirteenth and fourteenth), and always at the same location in those states.

The Bassmaster Classic has never been held in California, which ranks second in numbers of anglers. BASS has held very few regular-season professional events in California or elsewhere "out West" in nearly forty years of competition, and the region has been under-represented in major fishing tournament sites and stars. A number of top California bass anglers moved eastward (Klein, Martens, Rojas, and Yelas, to name some notables) in order to be closer to the places where the major tournament action, and money, was.

Texas ranks third in total anglers, just a short count behind California. Only in 1979 did BASS hold the Bassmaster Classic there, or half there. That year, the location was Lake Texoma, which straddles the Texas-Oklahoma border and is a notable striped bass factory but an unremarkable black bass fishery. None of the twenty-five anglers in that event registered a single limit of black bass.

Through 2005, the Bassmaster Classic was held only once in Florida, a state that ranks first in the country in total number of anglers and first in total number of boat registrations, and where the largemouth bass is hands-down the king of freshwater species. The 2006 Classic will be the second one held in Florida—ironically, at the same venue where it was previously held in 1977.

And Florida could not have laid out the welcome mat more.

Only a year earlier, a consortium of economic development interests in the Sunshine State had provided incentives for BASS to move its headquarters and personnel from Montgomery to Buena Vista in Osceola County, smack in the middle of the fantasy world of its corporate parent, Disney.

One of the agencies responsible for bringing BASS to central Florida was the Metro Orlando Economic Development Commission, whose chairman, Al Weiss, was at the same time president of Walt Disney World Resort, which operates four of the top five most visited theme parks in North America (the other one is Disneyland in California). Another player was Florida governor Jeb Bush, an occasional fisherman, the brother of a president who fishes for bass on his Texas ranch, and the son of a former vice president and president who once told the national press corps that *Bassmaster* was his favorite magazine.

The relocation was accomplished in April 2005, and it came as little surprise two months later when BASS announced live on

BassCenter that it was bringing the Classic "home" and holding it on Lake Tohopekaliga. Said general manager Don Rucks, "It just makes sense for us to take advantage of our new location this time and bring bass fishing's biggest event to an area that offers some of the very best bass fishing in the world."

To bring the Classic to Lake Toho, the Kissimmee Convention & Visitors Bureau (CVB) and the Central Florida Sports Commission paid about one-third of what Pittsburgh did, although that amount doesn't take into account the assistance that was offered in BASS's relocation, with the evidently implicit understanding that the Classic would be held locally in the near future.

John Saboor, the executive director of the Central Florida Sports Commission, a nonprofit sports-related economic development agency, said that locally, there would be a direct $20 million benefit because of the 2006 Classic. That in itself is significant, because several hundred thousand dollars of that will likely be collected by Osceola County in resort taxes, offsetting some or all of its contribution to host the Classic and contributing to the $40 million in taxes it takes in annually.

But securing central Florida's position as a leading sports destination was also one of the primary motivators for welcoming BASS, the Bassmaster Classic, and any other tournaments or events that the company will conduct in the area. Saboor says that with all of the attractions that go on at Disney's Wide World of Sports complex (where ESPN routinely broadcasts), with NASCAR's signature Daytona 500 race nearby, with the Orlando Magic here, with professional baseball teams conducting spring training annually, and now with BASS planting a firm foot in the ground, the region has diversified itself as a sports-destination brand.

"In many respects, television coverage is as, if not more, important, than economic development," says Saboor, noting how valuable it is to be able to communicate to a national audience in February, especially to people who are sitting at home in subzero temperatures.

"The branding exposure that isn't generated through commercial spots," says Saboor, "that is actually generated in the body of the program in the form of vignettes and interstitials and billboards in and out—what a wonderful bully pulpit."

Saboor also notes that since the "experience around the experience issue" is very strong in Osceola County and Orlando, they expect to get incrementally more people during the Classic because of what the area offers besides fishing.

Of course, the biggest thing the area offers is Walt Disney World, and Tim Hemphill, the executive director of the Kissimmee Convention & Visitors Bureau, says that Kissimmee as a brand has been so aligned with Disney over the years that it's a challenge to overcome this.

Evidently, they are overcoming. Or simply coming. Having been to the area in the past, but not for some time, I was surprised to see how strip mall–developed the major highway, Route 192, had become virtually from I-4 all the way to Kissimmee. Out on the water, especially on the west side of Lake Toho, you could not go anywhere on a weekday afternoon without hearing heavy machinery at work. The area is booming, and real estate has virtually doubled in a few years.

"Osceola County is big," says Hemphill, "yet only about a third of it is developed. The demographers' prediction about this entire area is that it will be a super city in twenty-five years. We can't stop it. But having this event here allows us a platform to remind everybody how important the protection of our resources is. So, as growth occurs around the lake, our leadership is more and more reticent to approve those developments without any thought. And that has happened."

Kissimmee, in fact, would seem to be an ideal place to host all aspects of the Classic, instead of having people go from the lake all the way to the outdoor show and the weigh-in at the Orlando Convention Center, which is a forty-five-minute drive for those mortals who do not have a sheriff's escort and aren't held up by the incessant traffic on Route 192 and I-4. But Kissimmee lacks a 250,000-square-foot facility for the weigh-in and the outdoor show, and its arena will hold "only" eight thousand people.

"We'd like to have the whole thing in our county sometime," says Hemphill. "Maybe in 2009."

That is when he and Saboor expect the Classic to return to their area. Indeed, Saboor has negotiated the right to host the event that year, if not in 2008—if the Convention Center dates, usually booked many years in advance, can be worked out.

"I think it makes sense for BASS to plan ahead," says Saboor. "Look at what that does for sponsorships and marketing. If you can approach that in three- or four-year increments, look what that would do for sponsors, BASS, and us."

The fact that BASS changed the timing of the Classic—it was held in the fall from 1971 through 1982 and in the summer from 1983 through 2005—to late winter for the first time meant that BASS had to shorten one season, bring many anglers into two Classics on the strength of their showings in one season and the previous Classic, and drastically reduce the number of venues where BASS could hold the event.

The new target time for the Classic is to hold it in the last week of February or early in March, and the amount of money that a locality offers will be only part of the consideration, with infrastructure and good fishing being the others.

"It has to be before college basketball and after Daytona," says Don Rucks, alluding to television's dead sports zone. He would like to partner with three or four locations for rotational visits. He's keen on holding the future Classics in Texas, especially San Antonio, Houston, or Dallas; New Orleans, when the infrastructure is reestablished; California, "which only leaves the Delta outside Sacramento"; Nevada, where "Lake Mead would be good"; and Florida, including Kissimmee and Jacksonville.

Says Rucks, "I made it a priority for 2006 to hold the Classic in Florida so that we could set a standard for a big catch. The anglers like to catch fish, and nothing's more important than that the anglers are jazzed."

With ample pre-event predictions that Bassmaster Classic records will fall—for heaviest winning weight, largest single-day weight, and biggest bass—as the Bassmaster Classic gets underway in late February, there is a buzz in central Florida that is distinctly different than it was last summer in Pittsburgh.

SIXTEEN

Sporting Issues

Bass fishing is hot. Bass tournaments are on television. But then
there is no Save the Bass constituency. Bass aren't cute
like deer. Walt Disney never drew a baby bass.

—SPORTSWRITER AND NPR COMMENTATOR FRANK DEFORD

For the first time in thirty-six years, the Bassmaster Classic, which the 2006 BASS record book calls "bass fishing's world championship," is being held in the winter. There will be three competition days from Friday through Sunday, February 24–26. That's three weeks after the real Super Bowl, won for the fifth time by the Pittsburgh Steelers, and one week after the Daytona 500, which a local tourism rep refers to as "the Super Bowl of NASCAR."

The oddity of this event is that the fishing takes place south of Kissimmee, but the Outdoors Expo and the weigh-ins are a long haul away in Orlando, making the fishing seem almost incidental, like an activity taking place on a distant galaxy. It's all central Florida, of course, which has gotten crowded enough to use more than 768 million gallons of water per day and clog the major roadways nearly all the time.

The Classic venue is the Upper Kissimmee Chain of Lakes. This includes four major lakes starting at the launch site in downtown Kissimmee with 18,810-acre Lake Tohopekaliga and ending at the mouth of the Kissimmee River with 34,918-acre Lake Kissimmee. In between are smallish Lakes Cypress and Hatchineha.

Professional bass angler Terry Segraves holds an 8-pound largemouth bass caught in Lake Tohopekaliga near Kissimmee, Florida, in February 2006.

Tohopekaliga meant "fort site" in the Seminole language and was so named because the lake's many islands provided refuge to the Seminoles from the U.S. Army in the 1800s. Kissimmee is said to have meant "long water" in the language of the Ais Caloosas Indians.

The town of Kissimmee had grass streets in the early 1900s and was nicknamed "Cow Town" because cows were allowed by local authorities to graze in the streets. Electricity arrived in 1901, the same year that Walt Disney was born, and Kissimmee's first automobile tourists arrived in 1916 along the new Dixie Highway, free-roaming cows being the major road hazard.

Nonstop visitation ensued, especially during the winter, and this year is no different. In fact, although it's still winter, according to the calendar, to this Yankee it hardly feels like winter. Winter is what's going on at home, where the lakes are frozen and each morning the temperature is in high-single or low-double digits, about the same number as will be recorded in pounds for some of the bass expected to be caught here.

Although it was frigid here two weeks earlier, the recent weather has been consistent and stable, which is exactly what a bass fisherman wants to hear. A cold front is forecast for the weekend, however, which is exactly what he doesn't want to hear, because in these shallow waters, Florida's bass are notorious for getting lockjaw when the barometer and the thermometer plummet. If you can catch a bass in central or southern Florida after a severe cold front, which is usually followed by blue skies and a strong wind, brother, you have earned it.

Weather is something that neither anglers nor BASS can control. By scheduling this event forevermore at this time, BASS is flirting with Mother Nature and the chance that northerly winds and cold temperatures will put fishing in a tailspin, producing a less-than-stellar catch. Of course, two decades of mid-summer championships have shown that hot weather and warm water can take a toll on fishing productivity, too, although the generally mediocre results of past summer Classics have been caused more by the fishing quality of the venues than by the weather.

The upside to holding the Classic in the winter is that in those southerly venues where it may be held, the bass are likely to be hefty, shallow, and visible. And these competitors know how to catch bass when they are shallow, especially when they can see them.

The reason why they can see them is what I am anticipating might become an issue, or at least a subject of some discussion: many of the bass, or at least some, will be in love mode. Make that a procreating mode, since "love" has an anthropomorphic connotation that we don't want to ascribe to animals, even though the creator of the company that owns BASS did so with mice (Mickey and Minnie), ducks (Donald), dogs (Goofy), deer (Bambi), and other critters, and his successors have likewise done so with some fish, most notably a clownfish termed Nemo (created by now-Disney-owned Pixar).

From the moment that it was announced that the 2006 Bassmaster Classic was going to be held in Florida in late February, I wondered whether anyone would address the propriety of stalking bass that are vulnerable because they're spawning, bass that will be striking lures not for predatory reasons but for protective reasons. Does anyone have a problem with that?

I do.

Largemouth bass, which are the target here at Kissimmee, are territorial nest spawners. They spawn when the water temperature rises and stays above sixty degrees. A male bass, which is usually in the 1- to 3- or 4-pound class, finds an appropriate nesting location and uses his fins to sweep a tire-size area free of debris. This is the nest, called a bed by most bass anglers. The male stays on or around the nest, waiting for a ready female, at some point nudging a female bass to the nest site, where she deposits her eggs, which he fertilizes. The female leaves the nest and the male then guards the eggs, which hatch in a few days, and he guards the young fry for a short period.

Seldom do all of the bass in a given body of water spawn at once. Usually, they do so in stages, which in Florida can occur over a month or even two, depending on weather and water conditions.

Many nests are made near shorelines and in water that is one to four feet deep. Some are deeper. The average depth in Lake Toho is just 5 feet, so all of its nesting bass are shallow. If the water is clear, fresh beds are usually very visible to anglers who stand in a boat and wear wide-brimmed hats and polarized sunglasses. A bass that is on or near the nest is also usually visible. Looking for these beds and spotting bedded fish, as well as deliberately casting to them, is known in tournament bass fishing parlance as bed-fishing and sight-fishing. Clear water, sunlight, and lack of wind enhance visibility and fishing for bedded bass.

A lure either is cast into the nest and allowed to rest there or is slowly wiggled in place. Sometimes it takes many presentations before a bass strikes the lure, doing so not to eat the intruder but to remove this potential threat to the eggs or the fry from the nest site. The bass moves immediately away from the nest and expels the lure. In places with a lot of fishing pressure, where bass have seen many lures, it may take a long time, perhaps hours, before a fish is irritated into striking the lure.

The real target of sight-fishing is the female bass, because she is almost always larger. In Florida, and at Kissimmee, female bass are commonly caught in the 7- to 9-pound class, which is big by most standards, and occasionally in the 10-pound or larger size. In Florida, 10 pounds is the magic "trophy" number.

When sight-fishing, anglers take their boats into likely areas where beds may be located, put their electric motor on high speed, and move quickly to cover a lot of ground looking for beds, stopping to fish only those active beds where fish are present. Some anglers are especially skillful at fishing for bedding bass, having had a lot of experience at doing so with a variety of lures.

In a tournament, once the female is caught, it is placed in an aerated livewell in the fisherman's boat for the remainder of the day, transported later to the weigh-in site (which here is in Orlando), weighed and held up for photographs, then placed in a chemically treated and aerated holding tank. It is later returned to the tournament waters, although not to the same location or necessarily to the same lake where it was caught.

Professional bass anglers and fisheries managers maintain that the removal of bass from their beds and subsequent relocation, while likely causing individual fish to avoid spawning, does little if any harm to the overall population, and that anglers encounter few of the spawning bass in any given population, since not all of them spawn shallow or at a time or in a place where they are visible. The killing of these and other bass by nontournament anglers for food or taxidermy purposes, as well as habitat alteration and water-level fluctuation, are often cited as actions that have far more potential to harm the bass resource at a given lake than does fishing for bedded bass.

Decades ago, the practice of bed-fishing would have been a hot topic in the sporting press. But today, so ingrained has this become that hardly anyone openly questions whether it is a "sporting" thing to do, and especially whether it is a sporting thing to do when fishing in a bass tournament, which essentially is a commercial enterprise in which tournament organizers, sponsors, and participants use a public resource for private gain.

In their annual fishing regulations booklets, many states address the legal manner of taking gamefish and note that they must be taken in a sporting manner, although there is little or no specificity to the definition of *sporting*. Many states, including Florida, do not even mention that fish must be taken in a sporting manner, perhaps because it is so difficult to achieve consensus on what that means.

With the exception of a reference to sporting goods stores, the word *sporting* does not appear in the regulations booklet distributed with freshwater fishing licenses by the Florida Fish and Wildlife

Conservation Commission (FWC). Under "Methods of Taking Freshwater Fish," that booklet merely says that fish may be taken with pole and line or rod and reel but not with free-floating or unattached devices or "by use of firearms, explosives, electricity, spear gun, poison or other chemicals."

Incidentally, that same section of the Florida freshwater fishing regulations booklet also specifies that "it is unlawful to sell, offer for sale or transport out of the state any freshwater game fish unless specifically permitted by the FWC, except that licensed anglers may transport two days' bag limit of legally harvested game fish."

Ironically, no less a figure than the Bass Boss himself, Ray Scott, ran afoul of the transport provision of Florida's freshwater fishing regulations almost twenty years to the day before the 2006 Citgo Bassmaster Classic.

On February 19, 1986, Scott shipped 366 live bass from the Bassmasters Florida Invitational tournament at Lake Okeechobee to his own private lake near Montgomery, Alabama, for research to test a lake-aerating pump. On the night of February 21, 1986, he shipped another 400 bass from that three-day tournament, which had just concluded. The second transport was ended near the lake when the driver was arrested by Florida officials; the fish were released back into Lake Okeechobee.

Scott did not have a permit for such transport but had secured the signatures, the addresses, and the fishing license numbers of twenty Bassmaster Florida Invitational fishermen, which he believed allowed him to transport the bass. He also had the belated verbal blessing of the executive director of the now-defunct Bass Research Foundation, an organization that he helped create and whose founding directors included Bob Cobb.

A March 8, 1986, *Montgomery Journal-Advertiser* article about the incident quoted Scott as saying, "My national fishing programs give Florida a million dollars a year, and now they're trying to do this to me."

It also quoted Jim Doering, a director of the Florida Bass Federation, who said, "I am ashamed of being a member and supporter of BASS. If he wants bass, he could have taken them from Alabama. The man has plenty of money."

According to a later article in the *Orlando Sentinel*, investigators found no wrongdoing by Scott, although he and BASS received complaints from local bass anglers. Scott admitted to impatience and bad judgment and said that the matter was "just another attempt to help improve fishing."Alabama officials expressed no concern about the 366 Florida bass that had already been deposited in Scott's lake.

About Scott's research lake, Roland Martin said in a May 2004 interview, "His lake is the best in the country. In the Eagles of Angling tournament, out of twenty pros that fished his lake, fourteen of them caught the largest bass of their life."

Twenty years to the week after this episode, as part of its pre-Classic hype, BASS and ESPN have repeatedly harped on the fact that the all-time record weight for a five-fish limit in a BASS tournament was set in Kissimmee on Lake Tohopekaliga in January 2001. At the time, there had been a prolonged cold spell that was broken by an eight-day warming period prior to the first competition day of that tournament.

On that day, Dean Rojas fished an area of the west shore of Lake Toho where huge spawning bass stacked up, registering the heaviest one-day BASS tournament record of 45 pounds 2 ounces. That catch exceeded the previous record by more than 10½ pounds and averaged an extraordinary 9 pounds per fish. Rojas won the four-day event with a record-setting total of 108 pounds 12 ounces. This achievement has been promoted by BASS and others ad nauseam and has made Rojas a household name among bassheads.

A pre-Classic BASS media release stated that "anglers and fans call it the most phenomenal big-bass bonanza in the history of tournament fishing." Not mentioned, but evidently taken for granted, was that Rojas (and other top finishers) was sight-fishing for bedding bass.

Sight-fishing for bedding bass has become a constant in the professional bass fishing world now that tournaments are routinely scheduled to take place during the spawning season, and the only stipulation of the tournament managers or the state laws is that the fish have to be hooked in the mouth and cannot be kept if they are foul-hooked, that is, snagged with one or more lure hooks on the side or elsewhere on the body. The latter stipulation is to avoid the deliberate, intentional foul-hooking of fish, which is deemed to be unsportsmanlike. If you are observed deliberately doing this by a wildlife law enforcement officer, you will be issued a summons.

Fishing for bass on their beds is legal in Florida and almost everywhere else. But the issue is whether this activity is fair, ethical, and sportsmanlike.

In my opinion, it is not. And as the 2006 Citgo Bassmaster Classic is about to get underway, I'm wondering about the propriety of fishing for bedded bass in this event, showing it repeatedly on TV to thousands of viewers, and exhorting the catches made by this method.

In fact, I had asked Jerry McKinnis about bed-fishing, especially in the Kissimmee Classic, many months earlier.

"I told ESPN that there could be some backlash over this," said McKinnis in May 2005. "I don't like the actual catching-the-fish-off-the-bed-deal, although we're told it doesn't hurt anything. But I just don't like it. Maybe that's because I'm not good at it. But a lot of our anglers feel that way, Rick Clunn being one of them. At an E-50 in Alabama the fish were bedding, and he went into it realizing that the fish were bedding and was going to try to figure out how to do that. He had never done that before. Can you imagine? But he dedicated the whole week in the tournament to trying to learn how to do that because he knew that he had better join the crowd, because it's not going away. . . . I'm just hoping that [in the Classic] there are other ways to catch fish where it's not just solid guys catching fish on beds. Because if we are making [the Classic] our showcase event, that's a little scary to me. The PR that could come out of that could be pretty dangerous."

On Wednesday, the fifty-one Classic anglers had a one-day opportunity to go onto Lake Toho and the other lakes. That night BASS distributed a media release about their day on the water and the good things it portended for the first day of Classic competition.

"The pros reported seeing a bevy of big females up shallow and accessible on spawning flats in Lake Tohopekaliga and the rest of the Kissimmee Chain of Lakes," said the news release. "'I think, at least the first day, the fishing's going to be awesome,' reported Preston Clark, one of two Floridians in the Classic field. 'Everybody's doing the same thing—just standing on the trolling motor and looking at them.'"

What a difference from Pittsburgh. Here we've got lots of fish, and big ones just like Don Rucks wanted for the "wow" factor, as well as a full-frontal display of an ethically dubious method of fishing for them.

The day before the Classic started, Toyota held a conference and luncheon to announce its new national fishing team of Greg Hackney, Mike Iaconelli, Terry Scroggins, and Dave Wolak. Their boats and trucks for future tournaments will be decked out in spiffy new red-and-gray wrapping. And they've been issued new color- and design-matching sponsorwear shirts and hats. Suddenly it hits me: the bass pros are "wrapped," too. They're shirtwrapped.

Afterward, all of the pros have a mandatory session with the media at the ESPN Club restaurant and bar on the Boardwalk in Downtown Disney. This begins inauspiciously when the new BASS Boss, Don Rucks, is introduced and loudly tells the entire crowd that they are to be quiet while he is speaking. The abrupt and impolitic way that he did this causes many members of the media to comment unfavorably about it among themselves later on.

Several dozen media representatives attend the two-hour session billed as Media Day, where each pro sits at a table with his name placard in front of him. All of them are wearing their shirtwraps, and I notice that Aaron Martens, who last year was sponsored by Ranger but who showed up at a Triton-hosted party, is now wearing a Triton shirtwrap.

I'm wondering how some of the pros feel about sight-fishing for bedded bass. I can't get to speak to all of them, but here's a sample of their comments.

Marty Stone: "It's a very specific technique, a skill. . . . Some guys who have learned this technique are light years ahead of everybody else. . . . We have little impact. . . . We're taking very good care of these fish and recycling them. . . . A low water level is more devastating than angling pressure."

Greg Hackney: "If we never have another tournament where there's sight-fishing, that wouldn't bother me. . . . I'll do it, but if I think I can catch a big bag doing something else, I will. I can find 'em without looking at 'em on the beds. . . . If I can find 'em on the beds, chances are somebody else can find 'em, too, so I'll do something everybody else isn't doing. . . . A lot of these guys are a lot more aggressive on bedding fish than I am."

Gary Klein: "I absolutely love sight-fishing for bedding bass. . . . It's truly an art form and a tremendous challenge. . . . A lot of fish at this time of year are caught by weekend anglers who don't know how to bed-fish or can't find 'em. . . . If there's a strong bed bite, it wouldn't surprise me if anglers are only able to see less than a tenth of what is actually going on. . . . Where they can, bass will spawn deep. . . . Some of the best sight-fishing for bass is in the fall."

Edwin Evers: "It's all part of the process of catching bass. . . . I don't believe it's a detriment, by any means, to the fishing. . . . I don't think it will be the main deal here."

Stacey King: "Some guys are good at it. There is a skill to sight-fishing. . . . I'm not an advocate of sight-fishing. I don't see 'em well, that might be part of it. . . . I was never taught to do that when I was a kid. . . . It's always been kind of like shooting quail on the ground to me. It's more sporting to shoot quail when they're flying."

Terry Scroggins: "This time of year, sight-fishing comes into play. . . . Some of the best sight fishermen come from my area. . . . I would just as soon see everybody not do it, but when you're in a tournament, if you don't do it, they're gonna beat you. . . . For every fish you catch, there's thousands that you never see, so overall, I don't think it hurts the population. . . . I think sight-fishing will play a major role here the first day."

The bottom line for some is, no harm, no foul. For others, it's not right, but everyone's doing it.

Scroggins, who lives about a hundred miles up the road in Palatka, is looking very confident. Perhaps he and fellow Palatkan Preston Clark are the guys to watch. They've fished this venue many times, they are accomplished at sight-fishing, they know Florida bass and conditions very well, and they know how these fish react when the weather changes. And weather will probably be a factor.

It's forecast to be mostly cloudy tomorrow, high in the mid-seventies, with winds out of the east-northeast. Clouds and wind will hurt most of the sight fishermen, and the first half of the day may be especially important, since that's when there's likely to be the most sun and the least wind. Historically, the first day of the Classic is the best fish-catching day, with results tapering off each succeeding day.

SEVENTEEN

Records, Star Angler, Melt

Florida imported dreamers and exported oranges.
—GARY MORMINO, FROM HIS BOOK *LAND OF SUNSHINE, STATE OF DREAMS*

Friday, February 24, 2006

It is damp, cloudy, and still dark on Friday morning before the 2006 Bassmaster Classic officially starts. About three hundred people line the seawall along the small confines of Big Toho Marina, adjacent to the launching ramp at Lakefront Park, which the Osceola County sheriffs have blocked to the public.

Thirty feet behind the spectators is a black-and-red eighteen-wheeler called the Johnsonville Big Taste Grill. It has a domed barbecue grilllike top where two men cook bratwurst—up to 750 at a time—which are supplied free on rolls with condiments to all passersby. The sixty-five-foot-long grill and its staff appeared at Daytona last weekend and are headed to Bass Pro Shops in Orlando.

After a breakfast brat, I head out to the dock, where Keith Alan is talking with Dean Rojas, milking the record Toho bass haul from 2001. Then he's talking to Skeet Reese, who says he's not nervous but is sure that a couple of the guys are making trips to the bathroom right now. With five hundred grand on the line, says Alan, there's a lot of reasons to be nervous.

"It ain't about the money," says Reese, "It's about the trophy. You're all invited to a major party on Sunday if I win."

Behind the marina and away from the spotlight I chat up Bob Kostrzewa, who is a runner for the TV crews, shuttling tape to and from pickup locations. He's also president of the Florida Bass Federation and responsible for obtaining the nearly one hundred volunteers necessary to assist BASS and ESPN throughout the tournament, especially at the lake.

Getting the volunteers was a tough job, he says, since the Florida Bass Federation disassociated itself recently from BASS, and its member bass clubs are unhappy with BASS. In fact, says Kostrzewa, a lot of other state Federations helped to supply volunteers, and he's assisting only because he made a commitment to do so long before the divorce.

"Florida is breaking away," says Kostrzewa, "We like to do things with youth and conservation. . . . If ESPN's direction was clear, maybe things would be different. But it's not. . . . Many states have their own sponsors that have supported them for a long time. BASS asked us to back off from them and to advertise their sponsors. Demands are being made. . . . Their new Federation will be more submissive. . . . It should be called the Triton Federation Nation. . . . When BASS doesn't own you, they can't tell you what to do."

In short order, I've gotten an earful about the internal membership struggles of BASS. There's more to be said, but the National Anthem is announced.

"Call me if you want to know more," Kostrzewa says.

A hush comes over the crowd, and while the anthem is playing, I'm thinking that I don't need to know more because I've been hearing about this from many others, and several things seem clear. One, there's a lot of dissension surrounding BASS. Two, BASS and ESPN are now one and the same to the rank-and-file. And three, BASS used to be like family for media, pros, and Federation members, but not any more.

A bunch of $18,000 Opti-Max engines roar to life, and Alan introduces the competitors as they point their boats southward.

As the show winds down, I realize that the launch crowd is much less vociferous than it was in Pittsburgh. Older, too. There's very few kids or teenagers here. Most of the cheering for individual anglers seems to come from their families and friends.

And where was Yamaha? A bass boat with a Mercury banner on it patrolled the marina, and onshore there were plenty of Mercury and Purolator hats being given out. But no Yamaha presence. I'm disappointed.

During the day, the partly cloudy forecast turns to darkly cloudy and the wind picks up, occasionally gusting over 15 miles per hour. When all is settled late Friday afternoon at the Orange County Convention Center—after an interminably long and excessively drawn-out weigh-in production—many of the pregame predictions came true.

It was a haul.

Fifty of the fifty-one anglers weighed in a five-fish limit. Four anglers topped Ricky Green's twenty-year-old record for biggest bass (one did it twice, in fact), and four broke Paul Elias's thirteen-year-old Bassmaster Classic record for the heaviest single-day five-fish catch.

The first angler to weigh in a record limit was Kentuckian Kevin Wirth, a former jockey who once raced in the Kentucky Derby. He temporarily takes the lead with 22 pounds 5 ounces and gets a terrific ovation from a half-full arena, also decidedly light on youngsters and older on average than in Pittsburgh.

It's only day 1, but already my sense is that the notion that families would come to the Classic because of the timing or because of this particular location is wrong. The kids are in school. And if families don't come here, where they can also enjoy forty-seven square miles of Disney entertainment and recreation—the experience around the experience—are they going to go to Texas or New Orleans or anywhere else at the end of February?

Mark Tucker of Missouri gets a big ovation for the large bass that he hoists out of the well, and then more applause and hollering when Alan excitedly announces that at 9 pounds 12 ounces, it is the new Purolator big bass record for the Citgo Bassmaster Classic.

"I caught it on the last cast of the day," says Tucker. "I just had eight minutes left."

When Oklahoma's Edwin Evers comes up a little later, he needs two hands to hold his big fish, but it turns out to be 8 pounds 15 ounces, smaller than Tucker's big bass but also bigger than the old record. However, Evers temporarily jumps into the tournament lead with a new record-setting limit of 23 pounds 10 ounces. This draws a big ovation.

Thirty-three anglers have weighed in when the first of the two Florida representatives, Preston Clark, is wheeled into the arena. When Alan, peering into the boat, shouts, "That is a toad!" the crowd is expectant and Preston delivers, lifting up the biggest bass that has come to the stage so far, an 11-pound 10-ounce beauty. The crowd, which evidently includes many full- or part-time Floridians, roars.

Clark has more beauties to go with that one, including a 9-pounder, which means that he's caught two fish larger than the old Classic record. He struggles to fit them into Trip Weldon's plastic weigh-in box.

"Hey, Trip," says Alan, "if we're gonna keep catching fish like this, we may need a larger tub."

Clark ups the ante with a 29-pound 1-ounce catch that draws prolonged applause and puts a sustained buzz into the crowd. For the time being, he's got both the big-fish and the single-day records—in

ESPN host Ron Franklin awaits his cue on the floor of the convention center while anglers weigh in behind him.

front of a home crowd, to boot. No angler has won the Classic in his home state, but Clark is well on the way. And the forty-one-year-old former insurance salesman has a feel-good story to go with his success today; he just found out that his wife is expecting triplets.

Clark's total means nearly a 6-pound average. Plus, he has a fish that would be the bass of a lifetime for many in the audience. One for the wall.

"Last year," says Alan to Clark, "you said you were just happy to be here. What do you say now?"

"I was so nervous after I caught that big fish, I had to sit down for fifteen minutes."

Many people in the crowd chuckle, perhaps because they'd feel the same way, perhaps because they're glad to see a top pro show how excited such an accomplishment gets him.

Clark, who was using a pushpole to silently move his boat along in bedding areas, says that he was sight-fishing. But, he adds ominously—or as a psychological tease for his competitors—that tactic dried up by midday.

Clark is followed by Missourian Rick Clunn, at fifty-nine the oldest angler in the Classic, who shows off a 10-pound 10-ounce largemouth that is now the second-largest bass ever caught in the Bassmaster Classic. But he doesn't get nearly the applause that was generated by Clark.

The bass is the largest that Clunn has ever caught on a spinner-bait, and he says it was between beds. The big-screen footage of him shows that like Preston Clark, he was excited after he caught that giant, his right hand visibly shaking.

Clunn's comments infer that he was predominantly sight-fishing, as he was moving between beds and casting a lure that he would not have used for bedded bass when the big female struck. "That was a surprise," he'd say later. It was on Lake Toho in the 1977 Classic that Clunn found a good spot by accident on the first morning in the fog and immediately was surprised by a big bass that wound up making the difference in his victory. Could there be a repeat brewing for the thirty-time qualifier?

Soon it's weigh-in time for Terry Scroggins, who won a tournament on Kissimmee a few months earlier. Big expectations for this

Floridian go unrealized when he weighs in less than 11 pounds and admits to making bad decisions and doing too much running. Scroggins says that his sight-fishing fell apart today—luck of the draw made him the next-to-last angler to leave the launch, and every place he stopped was already covered by another angler. So Alan asks him about Saturday.

"A lot of sight fish are gone," replies Scroggins. "You're not gonna be able to catch them tomorrow."

Scroggins is followed by Virginian Rick Morris, whose 18 pounds and 7 ounces would be remarkable almost any other time, but it gets just polite applause. Morris's biggest fish, a 7-pounder, draws hardly any love from the crowd, and it occurs to me that the attention for such a fish in Pittsburgh would have caused the building to shake. The crowd is getting used to seeing some big toads, as they are now called, not many using the old terms *lunker, hawg, pig,* or *gorilla* these days. Or maybe they're getting bored. There's been eight "commercial" breaks so far, and we're almost two hours into the show-and-tell parade.

A few minutes later, the basseheads are still pretty mute when Washington State angler Luke Clausen takes over the lead with 29 pounds 6 ounces. His biggest bass weighs 7 pounds 9 ounces and gets virtually no applause when it is weighed, but this shows that he hasn't just gotten one lucky monster but a bunch of really good fish.

At twenty-seven, Clausen is the youngest angler in this Classic and the only one in a shirtwrap that has a black background. This is his third Classic appearance, and he looks pleased but calm, neither overwhelmed by the big stage he's on nor giddy. Alan prods for some details about the day.

"I couldn't go wrong," says Clausen. "Everywhere I went, I caught a big one. I caught a limit pretty quick and then just kept going throughout the day. . . . I was just out fishing."

"Just out fishing," says Alan. "Dude, you're gonna have to do better than that. You're leading the 2006 Citgo Bassmaster Classic, a tournament that is worth half a million dollars. Day number 1 you have put almost 30 pounds on the scales. You have shattered the five- and seven-fish Classic records. Did you know that this was going to be your day?"

The kid's unfazed. "I wasn't really sure what I was going to do today," he answers. "I had a couple of things to go on. . . . I caught more big fish than I thought I was going to catch."

Twenty minutes later, the weigh-in is near conclusion, and there's two more pros left, one of whom a bunch of ready-to-leave fans want to see. The next-to-last angler is ushered into the arena in his boat with the let's-get-ready-to-rumble-voiced announcer urging the bassheads, "Let's go Ike for Michael Iaconelli!"

This is Iaconelli's first big platform since he was included as athlete number six in a January article in *GQ* titled "The Ten Most Hated Athletes." The author called Iaconelli "America's biggest basshole," and fellow anglers, among them ESPN's analyst at this event Denny Brauer, described his behavioral crimes against the fishing world.

There is plenty of cheering and clapping as Iaconelli exits his boat with a black bag of fish in one hand and a strategically placed bottle of Mountain Dew, label to the camera, in the other. But Iaconelli hasn't done very well, and from the moment his visage at the weigh-in podium appears on the big screen, you can sense something's amiss.

He's subdued. Decidedly not pumped. Two of his five fish are dead, so 10 ounces is deducted from his weight for a mandatory fish care penalty, which brings his total to 11 pounds 9 ounces.

Alan explains fish care penalties and says, "This is a tournament where you really need every ounce and every pound. What happened today?"

I'm expecting Iaconelli to say something less than favorable about his boat's livewell, perhaps not using Triton by name but somehow alluding to his own boat sponsor, Ranger, and the fact that he's fishing out of an unfamiliar brand and model of boat. Last year he took this opportunity to thank Ranger and Yamaha for making such great products.

Like a politician, however, he ignores Alan's question.

"I had a tough day," says Iaconelli. "I caught a ton of fish. This is an amazing lake. I fished hard. Just never got the big bite. But this is Florida, and you can make it up real quick. . . . Some of those guys proved what you can do here, and I could very easily go out and do

Preston Clark, left, and Luke Clausen at a media conference after the first day of the 2006 Citgo Bassmaster Classic.

that tomorrow. That's my motivation, to go out and fish hard and maybe catch thirty pounds tomorrow."

"Were you frustrated today?" quizzes Alan.

"Absolutely."

With everyone accounted for, it's Clausen by 5 ounces over Clark, with Evers third, Wirth fourth, and Clunn fifth. Seven anglers have turned in catches exceeding 20 pounds, and eighteen exceed 16 pounds. Twenty-eight anglers have a one-day catch that exceeds Kevin VanDam's three-day winning weight in Pittsburgh of 12 pounds 15 ounces. One of them is VanDam himself, who had 14 pounds 2 ounces today yet is disappointed.

Skeet Reese is nineteenth, nearly 14 pounds back, and he's going to have to turn it on to throw the party that he wants. Davy Hite is sixth, Mark Menendez fourteenth, Aaron Martens twenty-first, George Cochran twenty-second, Kevin VanDam twenty-fifth, Iaconelli thirty-fifth, Scroggins thirty-eighth, and Gerald Swindle forty-sixth. Only one of the competitors failed to catch his five-bass limit, and 5 of the 252 bass weighed in were dead.

This is the kind of water where someone who is well down after the first day could have a monster catch the next and get back in contention, just as Iaconelli said. But if the leaders keep up the pace they've set, very few will have a chance to catch them.

Later, Scroggins tells the media that a 30-pound bag isn't out of the question for him tomorrow. Clunn says that one big fish could neutralize the lead. I wonder if these comments reflect the inner gambler. *If I draw a full house next hand, I'll be back in the poker game.*

Nearly all of the leaders are sight-fishing or doing a combination of sight-fishing for bedded bass and blind-casting in areas where there are beds. All of the top seven anglers have been fishing along the east shore of either Toho or Kissimmee, which was protected today from the easterly wind. Many anglers who are behind the leaders complain that it was hard to sight-fish because it was generally overcast and dark, with developing wind; they were in areas where the wind roiled the water.

A lot of anglers talk about having to swing for the fences. Almost none acknowledge, this being Florida and this lake having a lot of big bass, that they are out of it. But the field will be cut to the top twenty-five anglers tomorrow night, so many of them are hoping just to make the cut. Still others are aiming to be in the top six or seven after tomorrow to have a good chance of winning.

As all of these fishermen know, they can't win it the first day, but they can lose it the first day. Realistically, some already have lost it. Without a miracle catch, probably the bottom third of the field is already out of it.

Speaking of losing it, a bizarre turn of events unfolds about the time that the daily newspaper writers are polishing their stories and putting their cursors on the send buttons. Many others have left the convention center.

A small number of media assembled in the conference area of the media room at the request of George McNeilly, who then ushered in tournament director Trip Weldon.

"First of all," said Weldon, "Mike Iaconelli's catch for this day has been disqualified."

"These anglers, in our briefing and everything we've sent, have been told that we're fishing under 2005 Citgo Bassmaster Tour and Elite 50 rules. I'll read you rule number five, sportsmanship.

"'Competitors in BASS tournaments are expected to follow high standards of sportsmanship, courtesy, safety, and conservation. Any infraction of these fundamental sporting principles may be deemed cause for disqualification.'

"We have a videotape of an incident today with Mike, and it's our opinion, our ruling, that he broke our sportsmanship rule. He destroyed some safety equipment, so his catch for today has been disqualified."

Asked how long it took to reach this decision, Weldon, who is holding a printed rule book in his hand, said, "We had to get him off the stage and check the scoring, so there was a lot to be done. I wanted to review the tape. Our folks in our TV truck were on the air, so there was a delay there. But once we saw the videotape, it took maybe three or four minutes."

Asked to explain what occurred to cause the disqualification, Weldon said, "He used some very profane language in front of a lot of spectators. He removed the running light, part of the safety equipment of these boats, and destroyed that running light."

Asked about whether Iaconelli released a dead fish, Weldon said, "We were not there to confirm that the fish was dead or alive. We did talk to game wardens, and if the fish moves one time, according to them you can still release it. So, from what we know, the fish did move. I was not there, so I don't know."

Asked about whether desecration of the flag attached to the running light entered into the decision, Weldon said, "No, it didn't enter into the decision. There was a flag there. We live in the greatest country in the world, and people have the right to do what they want to do. But we have to protect our sport. From [the] sportsmanship [rule], the destruction of a safety device on the boat is what made us come to our decision."

McNeilly then ended the conference. When asked where Ike was, he answered, "Michael Iaconelli has left the building."

After a pause, someone said, "With Elvis?"

. . .

In my hotel room later, I turned the television to ESPN, where a box in the lower-right corner of the screen said: BASS—Iaconelli DQ'd. My e-mail soon contained a BASS media release for the day that mentioned the disqualification. And bassmaster.com shortly had the news on its front page.

"Iaconelli said he was upset because of what he thought was a livewell malfunction," the release stated. "Tournament officials later determined the livewell was functioning properly. 'I disagree with the decision that was made today,' he said. . . . 'I'm trying to figure out if I have any recourse for appealing the decision.'"

At bassmaster.com, which had been running live updates and leader board reports, there was an "exclusive" transcript of Iaconelli's reaction. This raises a little red flag because Iaconelli had left the building as far as most of the media knew, yet he had been accessed by the BASS and ESPN media behind the stage after the weigh-in.

From the Web site interview, it's obvious that Iaconelli was mad and frustrated after his disqualification. He says he's going to stand up for himself. He says a lot. And he makes some good points. Like, the sportsmanship rule is broad. Like, has anyone ever been DQ'd for cursing before? Like, his anger was directed at an inanimate object, so no one was harmed. Like, no one's safety was jeopardized. Like, it's not an offense worthy of disqualifying his catch.

I'm perplexed and a little annoyed. I've asked BASS communications personnel whether I could see a printed copy of the official rules for the Citgo Bassmaster Classic at least five times. Once before Pittsburgh. Once in Pittsburgh. Once between the two Classics. And twice here, the first time being when I picked up my credentials several days ago. They can't produce a copy. Nobody's got one. Once, I'm told that these can't be let out to the general public. Twice, I'm told that they'll get a copy for me or send it to me, which never happens. Twice, I'm told I can find them at bassmaster.com.

I don't know what the secret is or why this is such a hassle, but it strikes me that the rules should be out in the open in an unalterable printed form for everyone to see and digest. Including the media. Hiding the rules leads to suspicion. How can an independent observer evaluate whether the players are playing by the rules if he or she doesn't have the rule book? Maybe that's the point.

Speaking of observers—the ones who are the de facto referees in the boat with the pros—a media member who has been an observer in numerous recent Classics, including the 2006 event, and who requested anonymity, told me in Kissimmee that although there is a meeting with observers prior to the Classic, he has not once been given by BASS staff a copy of the rules that the anglers must abide by. Probably the cameramen haven't, either. He pointed out several issues with regard to the rules, particularly with respect to culling fish, that were problematic, and he noted how different it is in professional golf.

"A USGA official is available to give a ruling on the spot in a professional golf tournament," he said. "They're not even remotely close to that in professional bass fishing. In the Classic, the observers are the ones who are supposed to know and enforce the rules, but probably none of them have the rule book or know what the rules are, other than that they are not allowed to assist the angler."

I did not want to see the rules that are on the Internet. I wanted an official printed copy, the same as the one provided to the anglers, which I know cannot be amended or changed the way an article on the Internet can be changed at whim.

Sorry, I'm just a suspicious sort.

But I found the rules at bassmaster.com, and Rule 5, regarding sportsmanship, is exactly as Trip Weldon earlier read it.

Which is pitifully, piously, and perhaps purposefully, vague.

"Competitors . . . are expected to follow high standards of sportsmanship, courtesy, safety, and conservation. Any infraction of these fundamental sporting principles may be deemed cause for disqualification."

Could we be a *little* more specific?

Could we have some definitions?

Let's start with *sportsmanship*. We all know this one without looking it up. It means to act like a sportsman, which, according to *Webster's* definition 1 is a man who takes part in sports, especially hunting and fishing. According to definition 2, a sportsman is a person who "can take loss or defeat without complaint, or victory without gloating, and who treats his opponents with fairness, generosity, courtesy, etc."

I'm wondering if Jimmy Mize thought that it was sportsmanlike when George Cochran encroached on him last year on the Monongahela River. Or as so many others have done in bass fishing tournaments, especially when held during the spawning period. Probably every bass pro could cite five examples of unsportsmanlike things that have happened to him at the hands of another competitor in BASS tournaments.

In early 2005, in fact, there was an incident that was covered well on *BassCenter* and *Loudmouth Bass*, in which a competitor during practice deliberately hooked and landed fish in one area (shallow spawners, in fact) that he knew other competitors would try to catch during the tournament. His purpose was to keep others from catching those fish, and he called it defensive fishing. An exasperated Roland Martin, on camera, called it a dumb thing to do.

BASS said it was not against its rules. But how can this be considered good sportsmanship? Or courteous behavior? How about Rule 5 (ii): "Any act of a competitor which reflects unfavorably upon efforts to promote fisheries conservation, clean waters and courtesy, shall be reason for disqualification."

Of course, the original meaning of *sportsman* pertained to hunting and fishing and to the ethics of the chase. "Fair chase" was the guiding principle. And the opponent was never another person but the game or the fish that was being sought.

So, you could say that the opponents at Kissimmee are the bass and that every angler who drags fish onto Trip Weldon's scales and then holds them up for pictures should be tagged with unsportsmanlike conduct for gloating.

And who determined that it was okay to harass female bass that are in the act of doing what nature has involuntarily caused them to do to perpetuate their species? (Sorry to go PETA here, but this can reasonably be interpreted as *harassment*; look the word up.) Does a *sportsman* deliberately take fish off their nests, even if they are hooked in the mouth? Is pestering a spawning fish until it strikes a lure—not to eat it but to remove it from its bed—the act of a sportsman?

Here's what Rule 6 for this Classic says: "All bass must be caught live and in a conventional sporting manner. Anyone guilty of snatching or snagging visible fish will have his or her catch disqualified. When visually fishing for bedding bass, to be counted as a legal fish all bass must be hooked inside the mouth and must be verified by your partner before being unhooked."

It's ironic that BASS invokes the "sportsmanship rule" against Mike Iaconelli for profanity and equipment destruction but thinks there's nothing unsportsmanlike about "defensive fishing" and completely condones the harassment of female bass on spawning beds.

Indeed, BASS encourages and facilitates it, because Don Rucks and BASS deliberately scheduled the 2006 Classic on the Kissimmee Chain of Lakes in February so that big spawning bass would be virtually assured. Who is going to slap an unsportsmanlike conduct penalty on BASS? Certainly not the state of Florida.

On a broader scale, professional bass fishing cannot be considered a top-tier sport unless it has rules that are open, reasonable, unambiguous, and applied equally by someone who is a disinterested party. It needs independent sources to monitor what happens. It needs an independent arbiter of disputes and an enforcer of rules. It needs a commissioner and a team of referees.

And by the way, who actually made the complaint about Iaconelli's behavior that caused his disqualification? Must have been the cameraman, because—and this seems unusual—it was the first day of the event and Iaconelli did not have an observer in the boat. The cameraman was his observer. Or the camera. Exactly who or what was checking to see that the fish he caught—or that anyone who was bed fishing and did not have an attentive real-person observer with him caught— were not snagged?

In fact, I have noticed many times that anglers have been shown on television setting the hook and not connecting, which can happen when fishing for bedding bass because they often do not have the lure very long in their mouths since they are not taking it to eat it, but which also can happen when an angler is trying to snag a fish. In decades of fishing, I've watched loads of anglers attempt to snag fish—trout, salmon, and striped bass, in particular—and it looks exactly the same.

So, another pro a hundred yards away could have had a profanity-laced blowup and taken his frustrations out on the light pole or some other piece of equipment, and, sans videotape, it would be unlikely that his real-person observer would make a complaint. Yet because Iaconelli has a camera with him, he's caught in a moment of irrational fury, rather than in a moment of irrational exuberance. Either way, it's theater.

One of the reasons why I had been looking for the rules was that in the last Classic, Iaconelli ran his boat aground and was unable to get it free by himself. The cameras showed him trying to motor, then shove, it free. Iaconelli grabbed some tackle and jumped into a nearby camera boat and used it for the rest of the afternoon. Which struck me as unfair to the other competitors. What would happen to a different competitor, who similarly got stuck by his lonesome but had no camera boat to rescue him? Iaconelli could have caught the tournament-winning fish in the borrowed boat, and the other guy could have had the tournament-winning fish that never got to the weigh-in because he had no help.

There is nothing in the BASS rules about this, although I had been told by BASS officials that it was allowed. But here's what Rule 13 says (caps belonging to BASS): "COMPETITORS MUST REMAIN IN BOAT: During the competition days, competitors must not depart the boat to land fish or to make the boat more accessible to fishing waters. Boats must remain in tournament waters during tournament days. Competitors must leave from and return to official checkpoints by boat. Both competitors must remain in the boat at all times except in case of dire emergency. In such an emergency, competitors may be removed from their boat to either A BOAT OPERATED BY OTHER COMPETITORS OR A RESCUE BOAT DESIGNATED BY THE TOURNAMENT DIRECTOR."

Is running aground due to your own carelessness an emergency? I think not. My sense is that he should not have been given another boat as a convenience simply because ESPN had a camera boat shadowing him all day. Chalk one up for Mike.

But media attention is a two-edged sword, as Iaconelli now knows.

He created the monster that ESPN wants to film all the time so he's caught on film going postal on the stern running light.

Now that "going Ike" has taken on a new meaning, what's the charge against him?

He lost his cool. He swore. He busted a light pole. There's no charge about dead fish, which maybe there should be, but that's another deficiency in the rules and with the camera-as-observer program. And there's no charge about the flag. At least, none that's admitted.

Mike, say three Hail Marys and go to your room.

BASS should have given him a reasonable fine for bad behavior and made him pay for the equipment he damaged. It was unnecessary and excessive to make such a big fuss about a meltdown in which Ike hurt only Ike.

End of story.

But that will not be the end of the story. I'm sure we'll get much more on this tomorrow.

EIGHTEEN

Turbulence

*It's one of the reasons athletes become assholes;
they're overexposed constantly.*

—OLYMPIC SKIER BODE MILLER

Saturday, February 25, 2006

The new scorecard provided by BASS shows that the results from
yesterday have been amended due to Iaconelli's late disqualification.
The number of limits has been reduced to forty-nine. The number of
dead fish weighed in has been reduced to three. Iaconelli is now in
last place, with no fish, no weight, no chance of winning, and virtually
no chance to make the cut.

And the day starts as an Iaconelli bashfest.

ESPN shows and discusses the whole sorry episode to lead off
BassCenter, including some obscenity-bleeped passages. Then they
rerun the whole thing again later. From the footage shown, it appears
that Iaconelli's aerators were not on, that he ripped the light pole out
of its socket and threw it over the gunwale and into the water, and that
he worked hard to resuscitate his fish.

Later, Denny Brauer, an icon in professional bass fishing, a previous Classic winner, and an analyst at this event for ESPN2, twice calls
Iaconelli a jerk for his behavior. I guess he's never exploded in his boat
before or used profanity. "It's horrible," says Brauer.

Everyone who works for BASS-ESPN, plus a couple of the pros interviewed, are in agreement with the BASS catch disqualification. I have to wonder if this piling-on commentary and coverage isn't meant to be sensational and also to bolster BASS's decision.

What I'm not seeing is a "There but for the grace of God go I" sensibility. Or a "people who live in glass houses shouldn't throw stones" sort of humility.

No one has expounded upon the vagueness of the rules and the lack of definition. Nor has anyone addressed the question whether Iaconelli's behavior rose to the level of a DQ. Maybe that's because none of them really knows what does and what doesn't rise to such level, except perhaps the tournament director, whose attitude is probably like Supreme Court justice Stewart Potter, who in 1964, while trying to define obscenity, famously said, "I know it when I see it."

That no one is questioning the rules at all is terribly obvious.

As a result, the whole reportage of this matter appears biased or, at least, unbalanced. The television, BASS, and bassmaster.com media work for the company that is broadcasting this event and that also owns the event and sets the rules. Therefore, to criticize in public the company that you work for could be tantamount to writing your discharge papers. Furthermore, access to the person charged with unsportsmanlike conduct was limited by BASS-ESPN, which also provided the only available documentation and explanation of the incident.

Elsewhere, at the entrance to the media room, someone has scribbled in the name "Ike" on a BASS poster for the 2006 Elite Series next to the words, "Gentlemen, start your aerators."

And now there's scattered babbling about desecration of the flag. People singing this tune probably hated Iaconelli before his explosion anyway.

Then there's the theory that Iaconelli is once again grabbing attention when he's doing poorly. In the 2004 Classic, his catch on the second day was disqualified for his fishing in an off-limits area. Iaconelli was doing poorly in that event, and some people believe that he intentionally fished in an off-limits area to get disqualified and become a media focus.

Then there's people speculating about what this may do to his relationship with his sponsors. Toyota's event marketing staff members have counseled him and won't say what they told him other than that Iaconelli, who has gotten to where he is so far on his own hustle and merits, now has advisers who can help him deal with an image crisis.

Meanwhile, another Iaconelli and BASS sponsor, Berkley, has released an official printed statement that praises Iaconelli's spirit and assistance with its brands and supports him.

"Mike clearly had a bad day yesterday," says the statement. "However, we are confident he will put it behind him and get back to meeting the high standards we set for the company and all of our brands. We look forward to continuing our partnership with Mike as a valued member of the Berkley pro staff for years to come."

It's a sensible statement. Would that everyone else took such a level-headed tone.

Enough already. Now that Ike has been voted off the island, can we focus on bass fishing?

Or is this a harbinger of what the sport of professional bass fishing is going to be like when it reaches its NASCAR-like zenith? Is this incident symbolic of what fishing for a $500,000 payday can cause?

Iaconelli is out on the water, where the weather may be an increasing factor. The forecast is for a mostly cloudy and breezy day, with winds from the south-southeast, gusting to 20 mph, and the barometer falling. A front is coming tonight or tomorrow morning, which makes today pivotal.

While the pros are fishing and a few bassheads are hanging around the cameras at Big Toho Marina, I'm catching up on ESPN's television coverage of the Classic from last night and watching it live this morning.

Last night's coverage from the convention center, announced by Ron Franklin as being live but not, was uneven and disappointing, with major gaffes.

It's annoying that the commentators are again cheerleading. They lob or field sponge-ball questions, providing shallow analysis for diehard bassheads. Grigsby, a Floridian, and Velvick, a Nevadan by way of California, are locked into a sophomoric West Coast-East

Coast thing, as if it's news anymore that anglers from Western states can compete in this arena. That's not a story line unless you're prepared to explain how few BASS events are held out West and how much harder it is for Western anglers to travel, learn the primary Eastern tournament waters, and so on.

The producers get a D-minus grade for which anglers they include and exclude from the weigh-in show and the amount of time devoted to some of them. Edwin Evers winds up in third place with a spectacular catch but is given brief "live" TV time. Gerald Swindle gets championlike prime TV time, despite laying an egg and winding up in forty-sixth place. I have to think this is because he has a big logo on his shirtwrap that says Citgo.

Do we need to hear him tell about his "butt whipping" and whine about being one of the few people who doesn't get any help? In fact, the latter comment raises a red flag. What was Swindle referring to? Do others get help (the answer is yes), and if so, what help and when and from whom and is that in the rules? That might be a story.

What's puzzling is that all day the producers have been tracking who caught fish and what everyone's estimated weight is. So why focus on a fisherman who has bombed and has no real story to tell onstage? Unless it's that Citgo title-sponsor thing.

And why leave out the two guys who have blown open the contest, set new records, and are leading the event?

Unbelievably, inexcusably, ESPN skipped over the weigh-ins of Preston Clark and Luke Clausen. Combined, the two of them get fourteen seconds of screen time near the end of the program, with a voice-over comment about their record-setting achievements. Why weren't their full weigh-ins at the podium shown, along with the tremendous applause that they received, especially Clark?

But Mike Iaconelli was on-screen for two minutes and thirty seconds for his five small fish, after which the producers returned to Byron Velvick and Shaw Grigsby doing analysis with Jay Crawford. Obviously, they've been alerted to Iaconelli's aeration issue and temper tantrum because they show footage of him discovering the suffocating fish, frantically trying to revive them, jumping to the rear deck and abusing the running light, then talking on the phone to Trip Weldon, asking, "Can you cull dead fish, or a dying fish?"

Weldon's answer is inaudible. Iaconelli checks on the fish that appear to be dying, then dumps one overboard without any attempt to revive it or check on it.

Analyzing this, Grigsby drops the ball. A BASS pro who lives in Florida, Grigsby says that culling a dead fish is not against BASS rules but *could* be against state law. Hasn't he fished in enough BASS tournaments, and especially in bass fishing tournaments in Florida, to know the answer to both? Rule 5 (iii) for this BASS event says, "All competitors are bound by the prevailing statutes and regulations of the various states within which they fish." The Florida Freshwater Regulations booklet that is supposed to be handed out with all licenses, but often isn't, makes no mention of culling fish, dead or alive.

And what about the main problem itself: the aerators not being on? Velvick says that Iaconelli didn't turn the aerators on. Velvick is sponsored by Triton. So is Grigsby. Neither of them asks how come Iaconelli had a problem with the aerators. No one brings up the fact that in the Bassmaster Classic, the Super Bowl of bass fishing, the competitors must fish out of boats that belong to the tournament boat sponsor—in this case, Triton—and that some of them may not be familiar with the features of a boat that they are not accustomed to using (the same can be said for the electric motor, the electronics, and the outboard). In fact, some competitors in the past have had trouble with some of the boats, particularly the electronics, because they were used to other brands of equipment. This would be a good time to address the topic of why the "world's best bass fishermen" can't use their own boats. Why they must use the boats provided by BASS-ESPN, which is like forcing Tiger Woods to use unfamiliar clubs for the Masters.

But the analysts can't or won't go down that road. And, of course, no one asks Iaconelli whether it was his fault or the equipment's fault because no one wants to hear what his answer might be.

Instead, Crawford asks, "Are there any sportsmanship issues?"

"It's questionable," fudges Grigsby.

"Anger management issues," says Velvick.

Another disappointment is how this trio addressed the subject of sight-fishing. Crawford asks why the bass are so shallow. Velvick, whose profile on bassfan.com notes that sight-fishing is his biggest strength, says it's because they are up making beds to spawn, which makes them more accessible to anglers. Then he talks about the single-day record that Rojas set on this lake, while the producers show a clip that looks to me like a reenactment.

Rojas is shown setting the hook while his partner is poised to jump forward with the net in hand. He sets the hook on a fish that is just a few feet away, and it's in the net in seconds. It looks fake, staged.

Afterward, they show an illustration of a bass on a bed taking a lure.

"It's cool," says Grigsby about sight-fishing for bedded bass, a technique that he specializes in. "This is kind of a neat deal. What's really special is that all of the biologists say no impact whatsoever."

"It's not gonna hurt the fish," adds Velvick. "It's a proven fact this does not hurt fisheries."

Maybe. But does that make it right?

Perhaps in looking for balanced reporting and a higher level of integrity I'm asking too much. Sportscasting today is rambunctious, and television in general is full of shrieking heads. With its own property, BASS, ESPN's goal is to entertain, not to provide independent journalism.

The best thing that can be said about Saturday morning's *BassCenter* is that once Mark Zona, Trey Reid, and Velvick stop piling on Iaconelli, the cameramen and the producers have to keep the Yamaha guerrillas out of the frame.

On the water near the shore and behind the set where John Kernan and Byron Velvick are seated, there's a huge saltwater boat jockeying for position with the—tiny by comparison—Triton boat carrying a Mercury banner. It says "Yamaha" in big letters along each side, and there's about a dozen people onboard. Eight or ten of them are in the bow, and they must be talking by cell phone to someone sitting in front of a television, because at one point the bow of the boat comes into the tight shot of a teleprompter-reading Kernan, and everyone on the boat starts waving and bouncing.

That was entertaining.

On the live morning coverage that follows, Tommy Sanders is

excellent as usual because he keeps things moving with just the right tone, puts fairly good questions to guests, knows enough about the game and its players to make questions and comments relevant, and has a well-honed instinct for juggling the anchor's responsibilities. Denny Brauer, who will soon be competing in the new BASS Elite Series, has good insight from his vast tournament experience but lacks the perspective of how nonbass pros see things and seldom takes analysis far enough. And it's so annoying to hear him repeatedly use backwoods grammar; "them fish" and "them anglers" come up too frequently. Funny, I've never heard Iaconelli say "them fish."

The short reports by Jerry McKinnis and the live on-the-water reports by Kim Bain, Robbie Floyd, and Mark May are good elements of the program, although there's just so much that these reporters can learn without getting so close as to interfere with the anglers. In fact, the system ESPN has created for relaying information from the water to the production centers is as impressive as some of the fish that they're getting video of.

It is not easy to adequately cover a sporting event that has fifty-one participants scattered over a 107-square-mile playing field. The Kissimmee chain requires going through a lock to get to the lower lakes. It's a long way, nearly forty miles, from the south end of Lake Kissimmee to the north end of Lake Tohopekaliga. So ESPN uses a number of boats that have radio frequency–equipped cameras. These point a signal to repeater boats, which send the signal to one of four cranes situated at each lake. A crane sends the signal to the radio frequency truck at Lake Cypress, which sends the signal to an uplink at Lake Cypress, which sends it to a satellite. Production centers (adjacent to Big Toho Marina or at the Orange County Convention Center) receive the signal from the satellite and prepare it for use on the various programs and as weigh-in vignettes that recap same-day activity. In addition, a network of shuttle boats is used to periodically obtain tapes from cameramen out on the water, then bring them to distribution points where a helicopter ferries them to the production centers.

ESPN has more than 250 people on site working on this event. At least 14 of them are crammed into the back of one production trailer at Lake Toho, where panels of monitors and rows of technical equipment form just one part of the production jigsaw puzzle. This is more effort than anyone has ever gone to before to show competitors catching bass in or close to real time, as well as to have footage of the day's action ready to show at the weigh-in and during the evening broadcast. It's an awesome technical production feat.

At the end of the day, the youngest angler in the field has widened his lead. Not with a huge catch but with enough of a catch. Luke Clausen continued what he was doing the previous day and had 1 ounce shy of 15 pounds to show for his effort, with a two-day total of 44 pounds 5 ounces. Preston Clark's sight fish evaporated, as he feared, and his 10-pound limit dropped him three places to fifth.

Edwin Evers had half the weight of the previous day and fell from third to seventh place. Kevin Wirth caught more weight than Evers but dropped two places to sixth. Rick Clunn caught just three small fish and fell from fifth to eighteenth.

Fans cheer Ron Shuffield's 8½-pound bass, as Keith Alan announces the weight and a cameraman films the proceedings.

There were three big movers, however. Rick Morris had the third-best limit of the day, with 18 pounds 14 ounces, and ascended from twelfth to fifth place. Ron Shuffield had the second-best limit with 21 pounds, anchored by an 8½-pounder, and leaped from tenth to second. And Terry Scroggins vaulted from thirty-eighth to third with a 28-pound 6-ounce catch that included the largest bass of the day, which weighed 9 pounds 5 ounces and also set a record for the largest bass caught on the second day of the Classic.

Clausen's lead is less than 4½ pounds over Shuffield, who is fishing in his fifteenth Bassmaster Classic, and just 5 pounds over Scroggins and Clark. Shuffield and Scroggins are both brimming with confidence, and Scroggins in particular is a threat, being from Florida. He's the only one with a huge second-day catch, and he's shown that anyone might do the same on Sunday and steal this tournament.

It's not exactly a shabby field behind the leaders. Six of the seven prior Classic winners fishing in this contest have made the top-twenty-five cut. George Cochran is eighth, Larry Nixon eleventh, Kevin VanDam twelfth, Davy Hite and Jay Yelas are tied for fourteenth, and Clunn is eighteenth. The only previous Classic winner not in the final round is Iaconelli, whose five-bass limit—all alive today— weighed just 8 pounds 13 ounces and kept him in last place. Gary Klein, Mark Menendez, and Marty Stone are among the twenty-six anglers who can go to Disney World tomorrow.

The catch was down on the second day, as it usually is, and the wow factor wasn't at the weigh-in as it had been the day before, when the stands were about two-thirds full. The weigh-in show went noticeably quicker, too, with Luke Clausen the first angler to come to the podium, followed one angler later by Terry Scroggins, who showed both irrational exuberance and a bit too much ego when he said, "I know Luke's probably over there listening. He'd better watch out tomorrow."

Edwin Evers, who struggled today, refers to it being a "war out there," a term overused by the pros and TV analysts, totally out of context for a fishing contest, and more likely to be spoken about a wrestling match.

When his fish flop wildly in the tub at the weigh-in podium, Kevin

Wirth gets a plug in for the good aerators on the Triton boat, Triton being one of his sponsors, and makes a notable comment when asked whether he was sight-fishing, "The fish are bedding, you just can't see 'em."

Davy Hite is shown on the big screen putting a bass in his livewell and saying to his cameraman, "That Triton livewell will keep 'em alive just fine if you turn it on." Of course, he's wearing a Triton shirt and maybe was just trying to be funny instead of sending a message or sucking up to a sponsor.

Mark Menendez, who is sick with the flu and slurping Pepto Bismol out of the bottle, misses the cut but is genuinely happy just to stand on the Classic stage, considering that a year earlier he was hospitalized with viral meningitis. Affable and humble, Menendez provides the most touching feel-good moment of the weigh-in when he thanks his "main sponsors": his wife, his daughter, and his dog.

Ron Shuffield gets a good ovation when his weight moves him into second place. Yet in a gaffe similar to yesterday, ESPN shows exactly four seconds of him on its later televised weigh-in show. ESPN had to have known that he had a good catch and would move up, but it chose not to feature the angler in second place with the second-best limit of the day and the second-largest fish of the day (8½ pounds).

At the media conference immediately after the weigh-in, Scroggins shows some more cockiness when, in answer to a question about tomorrow's rugged weather forecast, he says, "I think I have a little bit more experience than some of these guys when it gets like this. That's what I'm counting on anyway. The bite's gonna be a little tough."

And Shuffield is very buoyed by his success today, especially by his afternoon efforts. He pulls a Joe Namath, predicting, "I'm gonna win this Classic."

It is possible that both Shuffield and Scroggins are trying to mess with Clausen's head, but Clausen appears unfazed, predicting nothing and promising only to go back to where he's been catching bass and keep casting a Mann's HardNose worm. It's tempting to dub him "Cool Hand Luke" because he seems poised, relaxed, and confident.

Perhaps that's because he's been in a similar situation before— leading a championship going into the final round. He won that one, the four-day 2004 FLW Championship, and pocketed $500,000 for it at the age of twenty-five.

Watching Clausen and Shuffield sitting side by side at the media conference table in front of a BASS-Bassmaster Classic curtain, I realize that these are probably two of the last people whom BASS and ESPN would like to see win this event. Neither is fishing any more BASS tournaments after tomorrow. Both have aligned themselves with FLW and will be fishing only FLW tournaments. Which means two of the best bass fishing pros in the world are choosing another league.

Clausen, in fact, is wearing a NASCAR-like shirtwrap with the word "Chevy" and with Chevy's gold logo prominently on his chest. His upper-left shoulder boasts Ranger, and the upper right boasts Yamaha. That ought to sit well with Triton, Mercury, and Toyota.

Shuffield is wrapped in a Triton shirt with Mercury and MotorGuide displayed on his left shoulder, but as soon as the Classic is over, he won't be wearing it anymore, since he's going to be a Ranger Boats pro.

In fact, there are seven notable bass pros in this Bassmaster Classic who are forsaking BASS tournaments entirely the day after tomorrow: George Cochran, Stacey King, Jay Yelas, Larry Nixon, and David Walker, plus Shuffield and Clausen. All but Clausen have had long, distinguished careers with BASS. Four of them are on the top-ten BASS money-winning list.

When asked about this big change in their professional fishing paths, most of them say that it has to do with their sponsors lining up more with FLW, but the reality is that they are very unhappy with the direction of BASS under ESPN's ownership and about how they, and other anglers, are being treated.

At media day, Stacey King of Missouri, who is fifty-seven years old and has fished BASS for twenty years, explained his attitude. "This will be my last BASS event," said King, who has been in twelve Bassmaster Classics. "In general, I don't agree with the direction that BASS and ESPN are taking the sport. They're trying to build a TV show on adversity and a bad boy image. Maybe I'm from the old generation, but that just doesn't sit well with me."

It took King awhile to make his decision, but it was a load off his mind when he did. Another factor was the latest schedule change that BASS instituted—and mandated participation in. "When I saw that their schedule for this year had fourteen events, plus the Classic," said King, "that would have required me to fish fifteen events, and I don't want to be away from home for eight months."

The forty-one-year-old Jay Yelas, one of the top-performing anglers in BASS history, who has won more than $1.3 million in BASS events and who is fishing in his sixteenth consecutive Bassmaster Classic, was more blunt.

> The reason that I'm not going to fish BASS tournaments any more is because their tournaments have changed so much over the years, and I don't enjoy the changes. I don't enjoy competing in their events. I don't enjoy the direction that a media-driven company like ESPN has taken the sport of bass fishing.
>
> I compete for a living against other people. I'm a professional athlete. I'm not a showman. And what ESPN seems to be requiring, because bass fishing tournaments in themselves are not entertaining enough for them to earn good advertising revenues from the TV show, they want the fishermen to be not only professional athletes but also showmen. I really envy athletes in other sports, where all they have to do is show up, play the game, talk to the media after the game, and then go home. They don't have to be miked up during the game, they don't have to be talking to the camera during the game, dancing, screaming, shouting, entertaining, and all that during the game. There is a fine line between being miked up and explaining to a TV audience your strategies and how you're catching fish, and putting on a big phoney act to entertain people. I'm just not going to be a showman.
>
> FLW's business model is not media driven. It's about selling boats. It's more of a fisherman-friendly atmosphere. What really makes their business tick is selling boats. You don't have that Hollywood atmosphere like you do in BASS tournaments. That fits my personality better. I'm a professional bass fisherman. I enjoy teaching people how to fish. I enjoy shar-

ing the love of fishing with people all over the country. But I'm not a loud showman.

The winner of the 2002 Citgo Bassmaster Classic, and the 2003 BASS Angler of the Year, Yelas has not received any calls from officials at BASS about his feelings. "But that doesn't surprise me," says Yelas, "because I've been vocal."

Yelas is also upset with ESPN's TV favoritism. "I would expect the media to give unbiased coverage to the people who perform the best," he says. "But they don't. A perfect example is Mark Davis, who won four Bassmaster E-50s in 2004 and 2005. You hardly ever see him on their show. But you have other guys who haven't won anything in 2004 and 2005 and they have them on there all the time. They're their pets. That's biased. I hate media coverage that is biased, whether it's sports, politics, whatever. That rubs me the wrong way."

Davis isn't fishing BASS anymore, incidentally, and it seems to be a growing trend.

"ESPN has alienated many of their pros," says Yelas, "and at least half of the Bass Federation."

Actually, it's more like over 80 percent of the Federation.

Not surprisingly, so far at the 2006 Citgo Bassmaster Classic, Yelas, King, and Walker have been barely visible as far as ESPN's cameras and television coverage are concerned. Cochran and Nixon are just a few frames behind them. Despite his performance today, Shuffield wasn't even miked for the stage, and you have to suspect that they would avoid Clausen, too (he wasn't miked or included in yesterday's weigh-in show, even though they knew he was contending for the lead and had one of the day's best catches), if he wasn't leading now.

You also have to wonder how realistic it is for any astute observer outside of ESPN to expect professional bass fishing to be considered a serious sport if this is how ESPN is going to manipulate it.

Clausen tells bassfan.com that he hasn't felt any negativity from BASS and is quoted as saying, "BASS probably doesn't like the fact that I'm leading, but I don't know that. I guess it's not a real positive thing for them."

In a twist of irony, Clausen was affiliated with Triton when he won the FLW, so he's been down the sponsor-conflict road before, too.

NINETEEN

Another Dreamer Triumphs

*Never laugh at anyone's dream. People who don't
have dreams don't have much.*

—MOTIVATIONAL GURU ANTHONY ROBBINS

Sunday, February 26, 2006

It's raining lightly at six o'clock in Kissimmee, and there's lightning in
the distance. Twenty-five Toyotas towing boats on trailers are lined up
and waiting. The 6:40 launch has been delayed thirty minutes, as a
meteorologist here on the dock at Big Toho Marina says the lightning
will be over shortly. The forecast is showers and thunderstorms before
a cold front passes through and is followed by falling temperatures
and strong winds out of the north-northeast.

There's a sparse crowd of bassheads—mostly friends and family, I
suspect—at the marina, many in raingear and most huddled under
umbrellas. Over by the yacht club, large blue tarps are draped around
the *BassCenter* set. Tied to a pylon nearby is the Yamaha guerrilla-
marketing boat, a thirty-six-foot Contender with three Yamaha 225s
on the extended transom. This is a muscle boat for saltwater anglers
who chase big, hard-fighting pelagic species miles from shore, fish
that can't be derricked into the boat in three or four seconds.

The pros begin to arrive at the dock at 6:32, and I head over to the
launch ramp to catch my media boat, which is being driven by David

Smith, a retired law enforcement officer and Federation volunteer from Okeechobee. He's dressed for weather, as am I, and as we boat over to the marina, he says, "The south end of the lake will get very nasty today."

We decide to stay on the upper part of Toho, since we have to be back by nine thirty. I just want to watch a couple of the anglers anyway, Preston Clark in particular, because I know he's in this vicinity.

The anglers take off at 7:09, roaring past us headed south. Many of them look like bandits in their goggles and hooded jackets or like race drivers with their helmets on. Driving 70-plus mph into the wind or rain is punishing on exposed flesh and especially tough on unprotected eyes. A few fan boats take off in pursuit, and Smith says the fan-boat contingent is very light compared to yesterday.

Clark didn't start fishing where Smith and I thought he would, and we can't find him. We do watch Mark Tucker for a while and Jay Yelas, who politely waves.

We're still searching for Clark at 8:15 when a squall pelts us with driving rain. Visibility is reduced to a few yards, and the accompanying wind, which must be fifty or more miles per hour, pushes the rain horizontally across the lake the way it looks when the Weather Channel is showing a hurricane. We're moving to the east shore, where we've been told that Clark is, and the wind is pounding the rain into my face so that it feels like a hundred needle points. I turn my back to it and hunker down.

It's over in ten minutes, and the temperature change is dramatic, like walking into a refrigerated room. In a short while, the situation is made worse by an increasing wind out of the north. "This will shut the fish right down," offers Smith, a veteran of the Kissimmee Chain and Lake Okeechobee. "If you didn't get 'em by now, you're out of luck."

We had no luck finding Clark, who had vacated every place that we'd been told to find him. And it's downright unpleasant on Toho. By nine thirty, we're back at the dock and find that almost everyone else scheduled to be on a media boat canceled or didn't show.

Over at the yacht club, Kernan and Velvick have been chased off the wet and windy *BassCenter* set into an adjacent trailer. At the convention center, Sanders and Brauer are doing their live gig in raingear under a canopy.

Driving back to Orlando, I'm thinking that it's somehow fitting that fickle and stormy weather should be the biggest story of the Classic.

Sight-fishing has been on and off, hampered for most anglers by predominantly cloudy conditions and changing wind directions. A falling barometer, an advancing storm, and then severe postfrontal cold and wind have had an impact on where and how the anglers can fish. Most of them have had to constantly make adjustments, and the impact of the most severe changes today are yet to be realized.

It's a metaphor for the changing times and the turbulent conditions that face professional bass fishing, the bass pros, BASS, and ESPN.

The weigh-in show at the Orange County Convention Center begins at two thirty, and the arena, which seats about ten thousand, is full. To the left of the stage, several hundred people wearing identical Toyota or Purolator hats fill a large reserved-seating area. Many have pro-angler-support signs that appear to have been made by sponsors. To the far right side of the stage is a live funk-rock band, Spookie Daly Pride, which has been providing sporadic entertainment for three days.

During the first hour, after various activities to rev up the crowd, tournament sponsor Mercury has the spotlight to present its most enthusiastic fan award. Former Classic winner and TV fishing show host Hank Parker is escorted to the infield pit in front of the stage, where he's mobbed by people jumping up and down and banging noisemakers. He doesn't have to go far to find New Yorker David Hough, a potbellied man wearing a homemade, black, fabric-over-foam Mercury-motor-imitating headpiece. It's a larger and darker cheesehead sort of hat, complete with skeg and lettering. Parker selects him as the winner of a 9.9 hp outboard. Hough and his wife, who made the "hat" for him after he noticed that the prize last year went to someone with strange headgear (that would be hard-hatted Ed Matuizek), get a moment onstage.

Then Ray Scott is brought on to present the BASS Outstanding Achievement Award to Bob Cobb. In the introduction accompanying a big-screen video biography, it is stated that BASS was helped in the early days by writers who were cloning Cobb's writing skills under their own byline. It was certainly true that writers for some small papers simply put their names on the media releases that Cobb, and others, wrote. Some may still be putting their names on BASS releases, regurgitating the party line. Cobb is not provided with a new boat or other goodies as Pooley was in Pittsburgh.

The anglers begin weighing in about three thirty, with the top six held for the grand finale. Larry Nixon, who finishes in tenth place, comments that fishing in the Kissimmee Chain is 100 percent better now than when he was here in the 1977 Classic.

Keith Alan, who has done a much better job as emcee this year, compliments Nixon on his great career and sends him off saying, "We're gonna miss you, man." It's a nice gesture but one that doesn't explain to the fans what he means. The crowd gives Nixon a very nice ovation.

Scott Rook, who follows Nixon, is one of the few anglers to compliment the locals, saying, "I want to thank everybody in Orlando for being such a great host." He gets a good hand, and it occurs to me that very few of the pros have complimented the local hosts and weigh-in attendees. In Pittsburgh, most of them did.

When Aaron Martens weighs in with just over 8 pounds, finishing in seventeenth place, Alan exclaims, "Ladies and gentlemen, he's not in second place!"

To which a good-natured, broad-smiling Martens retorts, "That would be better than where I am."

Jimmy Johnson, the only Federation angler to have made the cut, improves his standing today with 13 pounds 14 ounces, the second-best catch of the day. Johnson, a laboratory research technician who hails from Wisconsin, finishes ninth and gets better applause than many of the pros, perhaps proving that there is indeed significant appreciation for amateurs from the Federation ranks who are fulfilling their dream of fishing in the Citgo Bassmaster Classic.

Kevin VanDam's limit of 15 pounds 7 ounces is the largest catch of the day and also draws a lot of applause. He temporarily moves into first place, but then the Super Six, the top finishers from day 2, are brought onstage amid fanfare and spotlight-flaring similar to the introductions of professional basketball players at the NBA All-Star Game.

From the left, Preston Clark, Terry Scroggins, Ron Shuffield, and Luke Clausen await the weigh-in of Rick Morris, not shown.

Kevin Wirth is first to weigh in. With five small fish, he drops from sixth to eighth place, noting that the wind today almost blew him out of the boat.

Then Rick Morris registers five bass that weigh 13 pounds 11 ounces, putting him in first place. Morris ran farther than anyone else, wasn't sight-fishing, and had an area in the Kissimmee River (which is below Lake Kissimmee and more like a canal than a river) to himself each day. He was the only angler to go through two locks daily, and he spent only five hours per day fishing. But his area was relatively protected even when the wind blew and changed direction.

Alan escorts Morris to the leader's "hot seat" and brings Preston Clark to the weigh-in podium. But Clark has only one bass to show and drops to sixth. His former team-tournament partner, the overconfident Terry Scroggins, follows with five fish that weigh just 7 pounds 11 ounces, putting him temporarily in second place.

Then Alan introduces Ron Shuffield, whom he calls, "a living legend in the sport, one of the all-time money winners in BASS history." Shuffield comes up with just three bass weighing 7-15, putting him temporarily in third place. So much for his guarantee.

"The wind trashed everything," says Shuffield. "I had thirteen bites today, which is the most I've had any day. And I only landed three of 'em. I had a six- or seven-pound fish right beside the boat, and it just pulled off."

"Thank you, Ron. We're gonna miss you, and we wish you the very best," says Alan without further explanation, making it mysteriously sound like Shuffield is sick, retiring, or going to another planet.

So it's down to anglers from opposite ends of the continent: twenty-seven-year-old Clausen of Spokane Valley, Washington, and forty-four-year-old Morris of Lanexa, Virginia.

Clausen is calm and looks relaxed. Of the Super Six, he's the only angler in shorts and sandals. The only one not wearing a piece of clothing that says Mercury. The only one not currently sponsored by Triton. The only one under thirty. The only one who is single. The only one from the West Coast. The only one who has known no other adult job besides being a professional bass fisherman. The only one who has already won a bass fishing tournament with a $500,000 first-place prize.

"Mother Nature served up everything she had today," says Alan, dragging out the suspense. "How did you deal with it?"

"First of all," answers Clausen, "I lost my cameraman. He fell in the lake this morning and lost a camera."

"Those are only worth about $80,000," quips Alan, noting that the cameraman is okay and that the gators didn't get him.

Alan reminds everyone that Clausen could set a new five-bass-limit record for the heaviest total weight in the Classic.

Clausen opens both of his livewells and stands up with a nice bass in one hand and a full bag in the other. The crowd begins clapping.

Morris is clapping.

Weldon puts five flopping fish in the weigh-in tub, and some people in the crowd start to yell.

Clausen needs 6 pounds 12 ounces to win, and when the scale settles, Weldon smiles and gives a dual thumbs-up.

"Eleven pounds thirteen ounces!" shouts Alan as Clausen raises both arms in triumph.

"Luke Clausen takes the title of Citgo Bassmaster Classic champion. Wow!"

Luke Clausen lifts his 2006 Citgo Bassmaster Classic Champion trophy.

Seconds later, standing on his mark as he'd been instructed to do, Clausen lifts the 2006 Citgo Bassmaster Classic trophy above his head. An arena full of bassheads erupts. Music blares. Pyrotechnics fire behind Clausen. Confetti streamers fall in a deluge, wrapping over his arms and the trophy. Strobelike spotlights bounce all over the arena. Camera flashes pop from everywhere. Ticker-tape confetti flutters nonstop above the stage.

Clausen has a huge smile on his face.

His total of 56 pounds 2 ounces is a new Classic record, it's netted bass fishing's Super Bowl championship, and it's worth $8,929 a pound.

Later, when asked how he felt about standing on the stage and holding the trophy, he said, "It was like being in the middle of a dream."

Epilogue

Not only was Luke Clausen the champion of the 2006 Citgo Bassmaster Classic, but he also set two five-fish limit records for this event: largest single-day catch and largest three-day catch. In addition, he had the largest bass on the final day, which weighed 5 pounds 13 ounces and earned a $1,000 bonus, bringing his total winnings to $501,000.

The top five anglers in the 2006 Classic, in order, were Clausen, Morris, Shuffield, Scroggins, and VanDam. The payouts for first through fifth place, respectively, were $500,000; $45,000; $40,000; $30,000; and $25,000. The sixth- through tenth-place anglers, in order, were Clark, Cochran, Wirth, Johnson, and Nixon. Former Classic champs Hite, Clunn, and Yelas finished sixteenth, twenty-first, and twenty-second, respectively.

The media conference after the Classic was attended by thirty-five to forty people, which included a number of BASS and bass master.com staffers.

Terry Scroggins stated that he lost the tournament on the first day. He and Clark, who were heavy pretournament favorites, upheld a

continuous streak of Classics in which no angler from the state hosting the Classic has won.

Rick Morris was upbeat and analytical. Kevin VanDam was disappointed. Ron Shuffield was disappointed, too, but he was frank,
gracious, and tearful when asked about the end of his BASS tournament career.

"This is probably my last Bassmaster Classic," said Shuffield, who
fished his first BASS event in 1985. "I wish BASS the best. It's been
real exciting. I'll be fishing FLW. . . . This is the last time you'll see me
in a Triton shirt. Tomorrow I'll be with Ranger, Yamaha, Minn-Kota,
Berkley, and Abu-Garcia."

None of the top three anglers was deliberately sight-fishing
for bedded bass during the tournament. Shuffield made a point of saying
that he doesn't sight-fish, but he didn't elaborate and no one asked why.

Back in Pittsburgh, Rick Clunn had opined that someone might
get lucky at Toho and catch a monster that could cause him to win the
Classic. While that certainly could have happened in this event, it
didn't. Luke Clausen did not have a monster bass any of the three
days. He did not get lucky. He showed exceptional patience and lots
of confidence. As he said at the media conference, he didn't get nervous until the final weigh-in began.

Clausen caught almost all of his fish over three days on a Mann's
HardNose plastic worm, which is part of a new lure series introduced the
previous summer by Mann's Bait Company. Celebrating its fiftieth
anniversary in 2006, the Eufaula, Alabama–based lure manufacturer was
founded in 1956 by Tom Mann, a former game warden turned professional bass angler and lure inventor. Mann, who sold the lure manufacturing company in 1977 and died in February 2005, placed second in the
first Bassmaster Classic at Lake Mead, using his own company's worms.

When asked whether he was fishing BASS tournaments next year,
Clausen declined to discuss that subject.

When asked what his parents thought about his career choice, he
answered, "They had their doubts. I graduated from college and told
them I was packing my bags and moving to California. I told them I
was going to fish professionally and then get a job. They definitely had
their doubts, but I've had some success, and they've been very sup-
portive." That success has rewarded him with more than $1 million
cash in just over the past year and a half.

There was confusion after the media conference about whether Clausen could or would defend his victory at the next Classic. Nearly two weeks later, after bassfan.com questioned both Trip Weldon and George McNeilly, it was determined that Clausen was not barred from being in the Classic in 2007 or for four more years afterward, but that he could not exercise his exemption for the 2007 Classic because he is not fishing in the 2006 Elite events, the first of which was set to begin in Texas two weeks after the Bassmaster Classic concluded. BASS said that Clausen could, however, qualify to be in the next Classic by competing with twenty thousand other anglers through the "amateur" Federation events or through BASS's regional events or tournaments for "weekend anglers."

Bassfan.com covered this in detail and spoke with Clausen, who said he was disappointed not to be in the next Classic. "I feel like with BASS, I'm up against a rule battle I'm not going to win," Clausen was quoted as saying by bassfan.com. "It's so convoluted, I don't know what the true rules were."

In a later interview published on the Web site of the Professional Anglers Association (PAA), Clausen was asked about ESPN's television coverage of him. "I felt the coverage was totally unfair but not unexpected," said Clausen. "If you're not one of Jerry's [McKinnis] kids, you don't get the air time. It also may have been since I didn't wear their sponsor clothing. Ever since ESPN has taken over, it's been that way."

When asked about whether he made a lot of additional money from his Classic win, Clausen said, "All of the talk about the Classic getting you an extra million dollars in sponsor money is a farce. I've had some opportunity from the win but nothing hugely substantial. The extra money I've made so far is from sponsor-driven agreements. I received more exposure and opportunity after I won the FLW Championship."

In the May 2006 issue of *Bassmaster*, editor James Hall devoted his editorial to a snippy critique of Clausen for not defending his title, questioning whether the FLW twisted Clausen's arm and noting that Clausen had made statements about "being mistreated by BASS." Hall closed with the comment, "From here on out, Clausen will be watching the Classic . . . from a much lower perch."

TV Coverage, Ratings, and Attendance

ESPN's television coverage improved in most respects on the last day of the Classic.

BassCenter and the following live in-game show were hampered by the weather, and Tommy Sanders and company had to scramble to provide substitute content, since there was little to show about ongoing events due to weather conditions.

On *BassCenter*, Mark Zona gave the most detailed blow-by-blow description of how sight-fishing for bedded bass is accomplished. He did not discuss the propriety of this method. Not once that I saw did that subject get raised in any of ESPN's programming.

Not once in thirteen-plus hours of coverage was a Florida fisheries biologist brought in to discuss the Kissimmee Chain, the state's habitat restoration programs for these lakes, the status of the bass fishery here and throughout central Florida, or the effects of catching and hauling around bass that are spawning.

Zona and Trey Reid did a good job of analyzing how the weather might impact anglers and the importance of early success. Anchor John Kernan, who has the least fishing knowledge of all of ESPN's on-camera talent, was the only one to correctly predict the winner. The producers of the in-game live show provided some very appealing scenes of the Kissimmee lakes and a lot of identical-looking hook-setting shots.

Denny Brauer's analysis improved, and he provided more insight, perhaps because to fill time he had more opportunity for expression. But he still inappropriately dropped in the occasional *them* word.

The concluding weigh-in show was fairly compelling, and the producers scored a home run with their introduction, as well as with an interesting short segment on how much weightlifting the slender tournament director has had to do over the course of the weigh-ins.

Still, they wasted time showing the weigh-in of Skeet Reese, who caught nothing and fell to twenty-fourth place, perhaps because he's one of their pets and they failed to get him in the day before. And they overlooked Jimmy Johnson, the steady Federation angler who had the second-best catch of the day and moved up to ninth place. And Byron Velvick continued to be a West Coast cheerleader.

On March 2, BASS issued a media release stating that the television coverage on ESPN and ESPN2 "reached more viewers than ever, averaged a 21 percent larger audience than last year, and was the highest-rated Classic in ESPN2's history of airing the tournament."

According to Todd Myers, ESPN's manager of strategic program planning, the average household viewership for the five telecasts of the 2006 Citgo Bassmaster Classic was 367,690 households, which was up 21 percent from 2005 and 15 percent from 2004. "This was due in part," he said, "to an improved television schedule on ESPN." The Saturday day 2 weigh-in, he said, "was the highest-rated Saturday *Bassmasters* telecast ever, with a 0.62 household rating." That was seen in 555,000 households.

While Saturday viewership was good, especially since that evening was the end of the Winter Olympics competition, Saturday was the second day of the event. The final weigh-in, on Sunday, is when the winner is crowned and when all of the world's bassheads are supposed to be eagerly watching to see who wins. That should be the major yardstick for viewer interest.

Alas, the Sunday final weigh-in had a household rating of 0.4, which translates into 380,000 households. BASS chose not to mention this in its media release. What is significant about this rating is that the final weigh-in telecast in Pittsburgh drew 526,000. Comparing apples to apples, that's a 28 percent decrease in viewers tuning in to see the 2006 grand finale, at a time in which ESPN was competing with almost no other sporting event.

Somebody must be worried about that. Somebody at ESPN must be asking how come they didn't grow the final weigh-in audience. Maybe the final weigh-in shouldn't be held on a Sunday. Maybe it shouldn't be in February. Maybe no one has the answer.

As a side note, on February 21, 2006, NASCAR said that based on data from Nielsen Media Research, NBC Sports coverage of the 2006 Daytona 500 (on Sunday) attracted 37.2 million viewers and drew a record 11.3 household rating/23 share, which made the race the most-watched Daytona 500, as well as the highest rated NASCAR event, in history.

Five days earlier, prior to the broadcast of the Daytona 500, the *Wall Street Journal* reported on the new ad campaigns that were being unveiled during the event, noting that the collection of national advertisers during the broadcast indicated how big, and mainstream, stock car racing has become.

"Nielsen Media Research says the sport's TV audience has grown nearly 80 percent over the past 15 years," the *Journal* reported. "The race is also good for marketers because its audience is a known quantity: about 64 percent of last year's viewers over 18 were men."

If professional bass fishing's biggest event is ever to compare to NASCAR, it obviously has a long way to go.

BASS also reported that 62,044 people attended the entire Classic, which included 21,742 in total for the three weigh-ins, of which 10,019 were at the Sunday weigh-in. Since there were no visible counting devices, no paid admissions to the show or the weigh-ins, and no mechanism for accounting for duplication and separation of attendees from media, show exhibitor staff, event production staff, families of the anglers, and so on, it is not even remotely clear what the actual numbers were.

Iaconelli Takes More Heat

On February 28, two days after the conclusion of the 2006 Citgo Bassmaster Classic, Ranger Boats dropped Mike Iaconelli from its pro team. Ranger president Randy Hopper, the son-in-law of Forrest Wood, said in a statement, "Based on a series of events that occurred during the recent Classic competition, Ranger Boats is withdrawing its sponsorship and affiliation with Mike Iaconelli. We do not believe that Mike's conduct during the tournament appropriately represents the deep-seated values on which our company was built and continues to operate.

"Ranger further acknowledges Iaconelli's impressive angling achievements as well as his commitment to promoting the sport of fishing. His efforts to encourage others through the platform of fishing are a credit to his many accomplishments. While we regret his actions leading to this decision, we wish Mike well in future ventures."

Iaconelli—who had called Ranger an "amazing" boat onstage during the 2005 Classic—was contrite and apologetic in an interview that aired the following weekend on *BassCenter*, and he told bassfan.com on March 1 that he had made a mistake and handled his frustration and anger the wrong way.

Bassfan.com received "hundreds of letters from fans" deploring Iaconelli's treatment of the American flag, and Iaconelli stated that in his outburst, the presence of the flag didn't even register in his mind.

Black Angler Wins by Sight-Fishing

The first BASS Elite Series event in which Iaconelli fished was held March 9–12 at Lake Amistad on the Texas-Mexico border. Bass were on their spawning beds for that event, and huge limits were caught by many anglers. The tournament was televised by ESPN2 on March 18. During the one-hour telecast, many anglers were shown sitting a few feet from bedding bass, spotting big females, pitching to them, and catching them.

One of those anglers, Ishama Monroe of California, won with the second-highest four-day total of bass ever caught in a BASS event. Fresh from a fifteenth-place finish in the Bassmaster Classic, Monroe's winning weight of 104 pounds 8 pounces was just 4 pounds 4 ounces behind Dean Rojas's spawning-bed record set in 2001 on Lake Toho. The huge total weights and numerous giant female bass caught by the contestants caused BASS and ESPN to call Amistad the best bass lake in the world and to later incessantly show clips of the excitement of anglers catching these big females.

The telecast also showed Monroe, after failing to hook a bedded bass, throwing a fit by dropping his rod, running to the back of his boat, and whacking his motor. He evidently said some choice things, although that was not audible. Likewise, Greg Hackney was shown getting angry, too, and evidently cursed when he missed a big fish on a bed. Neither man was disciplined by BASS.

On its March 18 broadcast, *BassCenter* reported that Ish Monroe was the first African American angler to win a BASS Tour–level fishing tournament. He is the only black angler among the 106 fishing in the 2006 Elite Series.

"The only color I care about is the green," said Monroe on *Bass-Center*, coincidentally the day after St. Patrick's Day, "and that's the green bass and the green money. . . . I do hope that any minority kid can relate to me."

World Record Bass Foul-Hooked by Sight Fisherman

While not one person questioned the propriety of fishing for bass on spawning beds during the 2006 Citgo Bassmaster Classic (although several pros expressed misgivings about it), the fact that this has become so ingrained in fishing was made clearer with the results of Monroe's victory in Texas and by several other unrelated events.

Early in the morning on March 20, California angler Mac Wheatley caught a bass off a spawning bed that weighed 25 pounds 1 ounce on an uncertified handheld scale. That is nearly 3 pounds more than the current world record, set in 1932. Wheatley snagged the fish—accidentally, he said—in the dorsal fin with the lure he was using. He and his companions were on Dixon Lake and had spotted the big female on a spawning bed the day before when another angler had been fishing for her. Wheatley had offered the other angler $1,000 to let him fish for the bass but was turned down.

Several observers saw Wheatley snag the big bass early the next morning. The fish was brought to the dock and photographed but was released after Wheatley called his attorney and after learning that the International Game Fish Association would not recognize an intentionally foul-hooked fish as a record. California law also prohibits keeping a foul-hooked fish. Wheatley did not take measurements of the fish, which is also a requirement for record approval.

The catch caused a sensation among bassheads and was the subject of Web site attention—including the Drudge Report—for weeks. Web traffic spiked on the site of the *San Diego Union-Tribune*, which broke the original story and did many follow-ups.

That same week, two magazines arrived that made reference to spawning bass. One was the April issue of *Field & Stream*, which contained an article written by Mark Hicks, a writer who fishes bass tournaments, titled "How to Fish a Bed." It described how to determine whether bass on beds were catchable and what approaches to take. There was no mention of the propriety of this activity. In earlier times, that magazine would never have run such an article without explaining whether such an activity was appropriate and would have included a sidebar about the proper handling of egg-laden fish for release or otherwise addressing sportsmanship or conservation concerns.

The other magazine was the April issue of *In Fisherman*, which contained an article by Don Wirth interviewing inventor and well-known big-bass specialist Doug Hannon about catching "monster" bass. Hannon, a longtime Floridian, stated that he could catch more big bass by sight-fishing on their beds, which he doesn't do. "Blame Florida's big bass decline on decades of over-zealous bed-fishing by trophy hogs," Hannon was quoted as saying, "and severe loss of prime bass habitat due to incessant overdevelopment."

A week later, on March 31, California angler George Coniglio caught a 19-pound 11-ounce largemouth off a spawning bed on Mission Viejo Lake. According to a later article in *Bassmaster*, Coniglio spotted the bass on a bed in fifteen feet of water and repeatedly cast different lures until the bass finally struck a green jig. The fish was weighed on certified scales at the lake by a biologist and released where it was caught. It is the twelfth-biggest largemouth bass formally recorded.

VanDam and Jones Disqualified while Sight-Fishing

On March 27, 2006, after the first day of practice for the third BASS Elite tournament, two-time Citgo Bassmaster Classic champion Kevin VanDam was disqualified for allowing his partner to run his boat. VanDam was on the front deck of the boat looking for largemouth bass beds while his partner was behind the console, driving. The incident took place at Santee-Cooper in South Carolina. BASS rules stipulate that only the professional angler can drive the boat, except in an emergency or when loading or unloading the boat.

VanDam was disqualified from the entire event, and he issued a statement through BASS saying that he took full responsibility for violating a BASS rule, did not do it purposely, and did not realize he was breaking any rules. After completion of the first day of that tournament, then second-place angler Alton Jones was disqualified for the same reason. In his case, his son had driven the boat during practice while Jones looked for fish on beds.

On June 18, after a third-place finish at an Elite tournament on Kentucky Lake, VanDam became the first person to surpass $2 million in career BASS winnings. In a BASS press release, VanDam said about his accomplishment: "I never really dreamed it."

Clark Sets Record by Sight-Fishing

That same Santee-Cooper tournament was won on April 2 by Preston Clark, whose four-day weight total was 115 pounds 15 ounces, which exceeded the previous record set by Dean Rojas on Lake Tohopekaliga by more than 7 pounds. Six anglers caught more than 100 pounds apiece, and nearly all of the top-placing pros were catching bass on or near beds. According to a BASS news release, "Clark used a push-pole to locate bedding fish."

Pros Plan Major Tournament

In what may be the start of a professional bass anglers tournament trail, similar to the PGA in golf, the Professional Anglers Association agreed to host a tournament at Lake Fork, Texas, in conjunction with Toyota and the Texas Parks and Wildlife Department (TPWD). The event, a charity tournament with an anticipated $1 million purse, was slated for April 2007. Media reports stated that the tournament was intended to raise $250,000 for TPWD freshwater fisheries management programs and children's fishing events and activities and would be televised on Versus (formerly OLN).

Lake Fork has long been one of the best big-bass lakes in the United States, and a model for fisheries management programs. The PAA, a group that has had its ups and downs over the years and is composed of professional bass anglers, has been at odds with the two major bass tournament organizations, BASS in particular, over many issues, including tournament payouts, and some of its members have expressed interest in having the PAA form its own tournament trail. The Lake Fork tournament was announced as a stand-alone event, with no entry fees for the anglers and a team-style tournament that would include perhaps 150 PAA members.

Among those active as officers or directors of the PAA were Mike Auten, Brent Chapman, Mark Davis, Edwin Evers, Shaw Grigsby, Tim Horton, Alton Jones, Gary Klein, Stacey King, Kevin VanDam, and Jay Yelas.

Iaconelli Steady

On April 23, Mike Iaconelli won the BASS Elite tournament on Lake Guntersville (and the $100,000 top prize) by 2 ounces over Alton Jones. He placed second in another tournament in May. By late July, after nine of the series' eleven events had concluded, Iaconelli had finished in the top twenty seven times and was the leading points earner in the race for Angler of the Year (and a $125,000 reward).

According to a statement he made to BASS, Iaconelli claimed that his life had spiraled out of control at the time of the February Classic. "Maybe I've matured a little bit in the last couple of months," he said. As of mid-May, he was still using his Toyota-wrapped Ranger, a boat that he was forced to buy, despite no longer being associated with Ranger Boats.

On May 24, Iaconelli appeared on ABC's late-night show *Jimmy Kimmel Live*.

Oil and Military Sponsors

As gasoline reached new record highs at the pump, Middle East strife deepened, and the United States braced for a new hurricane season, speculation had it that Venezuelan-owned Citgo might not remain the title sponsor of the Bassmaster Classic through its contracted period of 2009.

Perhaps fueling this was the July 12 announcement by Citgo that it would stop selling gas at eighteen stations in the United States. *BusinessWeek* reported that this followed calls by Venezuelan president Hugo Chavez "to nix contracts that benefit U.S. consumers more than Venezuelans" since Chavez had long claimed that "part of Citgo's business produce losses for Venezuela and constitute a subsidy for the U.S. economy."

On July 20, FLW Outdoors announced that BP would be a platinum-level sponsor of its fishing tournaments for 2007 and beyond. Described by Reuters as "the world's second-largest fully quoted oil company by market value," BP will sponsor all twelve of the FLW Outdoors tournament trails and will be the title sponsor of one of the two divisions in the revamped 2007 Wal-Mart FLW Series. BP will also be the presenting sponsor for several of FLW's tournament series and will field teams of professional anglers who will compete in FLW Outdoor–administered events.

Headquartered in London, BP annually sells more than 15 billion gallons of gasoline in the United States. On July 25, BP posted a record $7.27 billion profit in its second quarter, 30 perecent more than a year earlier, and had a net profit of $12.9 billion in the first half of 2006.

Announced at the same time by FLW Outdoors was that the other new division will be sponsored by the National Guard, which had previously allied with FLW by supporting programs of the Bass Federation. The National Guard, which has a team of four professional bass anglers, will also be the title sponsor of one of FLW's major bass tournaments in 2007.

See You Next Year

On May 23, BASS announced that the 2007 Citgo Bassmaster Classic will be held February 23–25 at Lay Lake in Alabama and hosted by the city of Birmingham. The Classic was previously held at this location in 2002, when it was won by Jay Yelas, and in 1996, when it was won by George Cochran. Both anglers will not be eligible to participate, since they no longer fish BASS-qualifying events.

The news release announcing the date and location of the 2007 Classic stated that BASS had "nearly 550,000 members," and that "nearly 210,000" of those members live within a five-hundred-mile radius of Birmingham.

This will be the tenth time in thirty-seven years that the Classic has been held in Alabama but the first time that it will take place there in what is technically "winter." Cold weather and slow fishing are distinct possibilities.

Also on May 23, BASS announced that the Mercury Marine Women's Bassmaster Tour Championship presented by Triton Boats will take place February 22–25, 2007, on Lake Mitchell near Birmingham. The women will weigh in on the same stage as the participants in the Citgo Bassmaster Classic.

INDEX

Page numbers in italics indicate photos.

10/06

10/27